Safeguarding in Social Work Practice

SAGE was founded in 1965 by Sara Miller McCune to support the dissemination of usable knowledge by publishing innovative and high-quality research and teaching content. Today, we publish over 900 journals, including those of more than 400 learned societies, more than 800 new books per year, and a growing range of library products including archives, data, case studies, reports, and video. SAGE remains majority-owned by our founder, and after Sara's lifetime will become owned by a charitable trust that secures our continued independence.

Los Angeles | London | New Delhi | Singapore | Washington DC | Melbourne

Safeguarding in Social Work Practice

A Lifespan Approach

Charlotte Chisnell and Caroline Kelly

Los Angeles | London | New Delhi
Singapore | Washington DC | Melbourne

Series Editors:
Jonathan Parker and Greta Bradley

Learning Matters
An imprint of SAGE Publications Ltd
1 Oliver's Yard
55 City Road
London EC1Y 1SP

SAGE Publications Inc.
2455 Teller Road
Thousand Oaks, California 91320

SAGE Publications India Pvt Ltd
B 1/I 1 Mohan Cooperative Industrial Area
Mathura Road
New Delhi 110 044

SAGE Publications Asia-Pacific Pte Ltd
3 Church Street
#10–04 Samsung Hub
Singapore 049483

Editor: Kate Wharton
Production editor: Chris Marke
Marketing manager: Tamara Navaratnam
Cover design: Wendy Scott
Typeset by: C&M Digitals (P) Ltd, Chennai, India
Printed and bound by CPI Group (UK) Ltd, Croydon, CR0 4YY

Library of Congress Control Number: 2015955832

British Library Cataloguing in Publication Data

A catalogue record for this book is available from the British Library

ISBN 978-1-47391-954-9 (pbk)
ISBN 978-1-47391-953-2

At SAGE we take sustainability seriously. Most of our products are printed in the UK using FSC papers and boards. When we print overseas we ensure sustainable papers are used as measured by the PREPS grading system. We undertake an annual audit to monitor our sustainability.

Contents

About the authors

Charlotte Chisnell is a Senior Lecturer in Social Work at Teesside University. She has been involved in social work education for the past 11 years. Before commencing her academic career, Charlotte was a social worker working in the practice area of children and families and youth justice. Her research interests include children's rights and social justice.

Caroline Kelly is a Senior Lecturer in Social Work at Teesside University. Her social work background spans across adults and children, but particularly with people with learning disabilities, people with mental health problems and older people. Interests include achieving service improvements in safeguarding adults and inclusion.

Phil Watson qualified as a social worker in 1988 and has worked in both the statutory and voluntary sectors with a range of service user groups, including children, families and adults. For the last 14 years he has worked in education, teaching topics relating to social work, social policy and social care. He is especially interested in the promotion of community work.

Jane Maffey is a Senior Lecturer in Social Work at Teesside University and is currently the Programme Lead for the CPD programme for Social Workers. Prior to commencing her academic career in 2005, Jane has worked for local authorities since 1990 covering posts in both adult and children's services, in strategic roles and in front line practice.

Dedication

Dedicated to our families. Thank you for your support and motivation.

Introduction: Safeguarding across the lifespan

There has been a separatist approach to work with people at risk over many years which does not reflect the need for practitioners to develop universal knowledge and skills with regard to safeguarding. Most social workers and other practitioners involved in safeguarding will work in a wide variety of different contexts and with a range of service users, families and carers over the course of their careers. Developing an understanding of common themes from the outset provides core knowledge and skills which are transferable into the full range of potential future contexts. While policy and systems artificially categorise individuals, in reality, service users and carers do not exist in a vacuum. The needs and risks of individuals are inextricably linked with people around them and approaches such as *Think Family* have developed which aim to equip social workers with the skills in assessment and intervention that are required to respond effectively to multiple adult and child needs within families.

This book aims to reflect a more holistic agenda in social work and safeguarding. Many local authorities are developing life stages services because the separation of services into those for adults and those for children does not reflect the needs of service users but more reflects organisational needs. For instance, a 22 year old person with learning disabilities is more likely to have similar needs to an 18 year old than a 60 year old. People do not experience their lives in the segregated way that services are traditionally provided, as simply an adult or a child. A separatist approach to social work can cause a narrowness of thinking in relation to remit that fails to support people effectively in their family or community context. It also creates a barrier to developing good practice in working with people at risk across the lifespan.

Safeguarding is a central theme within social work practice and all practitioners should be facilitated to identify and respond effectively to people of any age who are at risk. A large proportion of the knowledge and skills required to do this is relevant to both children and adults. Many social work safeguarding texts have focused on the differences between safeguarding adults and children but this book recognises the commonality of many important aspects. It provides a base knowledge in safeguarding themes for social workers and practitioners in other related fields which is relevant to a wide range of practice contexts. This book aims to provide a contemporary overview of the principal theories on the causation and effects of abuse and approaches to practice in safeguarding across the lifespan. It offers an introduction to key areas of safeguarding policy together with an overview of professional practice and assessment. We encourage you as readers to develop the knowledge, competency and skills to enable you to understand how informed and evidence-based professional judgements are made. Activities for reflection are included throughout the chapters to aid learning. The chapters will also support you in identifying themes in safeguarding which are applicable to social work with both adults and children. Such themes are at the heart of social work and central to collaborative work with other agencies and will be explored throughout the book.

How the book is organised

In **Chapter 1** we introduce an overview of the development of safeguarding and protection across the lifespan. Comparisons are made in relation to adults' and children's safeguarding to help provide an understanding of the historical and political context of the different safeguarding systems. Several consistent themes begin to emerge particularly in relation to the failings within safeguarding systems.

Chapter 2 explores the ways in which abuse is categorised in our society and looks at statistics in relation to recorded abuse. Although differences occur in relation to safeguarding across the lifespan there are also areas where clear parallels can be drawn in relation to exploitation, grooming and abuse of power. Theories for understanding abuse are reviewed and the indicators of abuse across the lifespan are also considered.

Chapter 3 introduces you to an overview of the current legal and policy context. There is a comparison between the differing legislative frameworks and discussion in relation to how this difference can impact on safeguarding practice across the lifespan. The chapter also compares the safeguarding processes within different parts of the UK.

Chapter 4 provides an overview of factors that can increase the likelihood of abuse of children and adults in domestic settings. The chapter explores the impact that specific behaviours can have on individuals and families, such as domestic abuse, mental health issues and substance use. The factors underlying abuse across the lifespan within families are considered along with different models of intervention and support, such as family group conferencing and Signs of Safety®.

Chapter 5 provides an overview of factors that can increase the likelihood of abuse of children and adults in community settings. The possible impact that specific behaviours can have on individuals, such as child sexual exploitation and hate crime, is considered. There is also an exploration of the different models of intervention and support to promote safeguarding in communities, such as effective multi-agency initiatives.

Chapter 6 provides an overview of adult and children's residential care systems and will help you to gain an understanding of how both practice and systems have failed children and adults through examples such as Rochdale, Winterbourne and the inappropriate use of Deprivation of Liberty Safeguards. Changes in law and policy that have been developed to challenge institutional abuse and promote improved outcomes will be critically reviewed

Chapter 7 examines the skills that are required for effective assessment and intervention within safeguarding practice. Key themes are considered such as the importance of effective collaborative working in safeguarding, the implications of key failings in previous practice with reference to serious case reviews, and how thinking around risk impacts on safeguarding.

Chapter 8 identifies priorities and some of the key challenges to effective safeguarding such as the impact of austerity on social work practice. There is also an overview of wider approaches to planning for safety, such as initiatives which focus on prevention and community support.

Finally, in the **Conclusion**, key themes across the areas of working with people at risk considered in earlier chapters are discussed and consolidated.

This book has been carefully mapped to the Professional Capabilities Framework (PCF) for Social Workers in England and will help you to develop the appropriate standards at the right level. These standards are:

- **Professionalism**

  Identify and behave as a professional social worker committed to professional development.

- **Values and ethics**

  Apply social work ethical principles and values to guide professional practice.

- **Diversity**

  Recognise diversity and apply anti-discriminatory and anti-oppressive principles in practice.

- **Rights, justice and economic wellbeing**

  Advance human rights and promote social justice and economic wellbeing.

- **Knowledge**

  Apply knowledge of social sciences, law and social work practice theory.

- **Critical reflection and analysis**

  Apply critical reflection and analysis to inform and provide a rationale for professional decision-making.

- **Intervention and skills**

  Use judgement and authority to intervene with individuals, families and communities to promote independence, provide support and prevent harm, neglect and abuse.

- **Contexts and organisations**

  Engage with, inform, and adapt to changing contexts that shape practice. Operate effectively within your own organisational frameworks and contribute to the development of services and organisations. Operate effectively within multi-agency and inter-professional settings.

- **Professional leadership**

  Take responsibility for the professional learning and development of others through supervision, mentoring, assessing, research, teaching, leadership and management.

  References to these standards will be made throughout the text and you will find a diagram of the Professional Capability Framework in an Appendix on page 185.

Chapter 1

The historical development of safeguarding and protection across the lifespan

ACHIEVING A SOCIAL WORK DEGREE

This chapter will help you to develop the following capabilities from the Professional Capabilities Framework:

- **Professionalism:** Identify and behave as a professional social worker committed to professional development.
- **Values and ethics:** Apply social work ethical principles and values to guide professional practice.
- **Diversity:** Recognise diversity and apply anti-discriminatory and anti-oppressive principles in practice.
- **Rights, justice and economic wellbeing:** Advance human rights and promote social justice and economic wellbeing.
- **Knowledge:** Apply knowledge of social sciences, law and social work practice theory.
- **Critical reflection and analysis:** Apply critical reflection and analysis to inform and provide a rationale for professional decision-making.
- **Intervention and skills:** Use judgement and authority to intervene with individuals, families and communities to promote independence, provide support and prevent harm, neglect and abuse.
- **Contexts and organisations:** Engage with, inform, and adapt to changing contexts that shape practice. Operate effectively within your own organisational frameworks and contribute to the development of services and organisations. Operate effectively within multi-agency and inter-professional settings.

It will also introduce you to the following standards as set out in the 2008 social work subject benchmark statement:

5.1.1 Social work services, service users and carers
5.1.3 Values and ethics
5.1.4 Social work theory
5.1.5 The nature of social work practice

Introduction

Developments in safeguarding policy and reforms to social work practice have been influenced by high profile cases which have invariably drawn attention to failings in protection systems. Developing an understanding of the historical and political context of safeguarding enables you as a practitioner to analyse and learn from the lessons of the past. The history of responses to abuse is also important in terms of how this has impacted on current attitudes and norms within society and practice with people at risk. Identifying key developments in safeguarding children and adults also highlights how legal, policy and practice approaches have developed in completely separate ways and along different time frames. This knowledge is central in terms of starting to ask what has been different about the approaches but also why such differences have occurred. Analysis of the differences also gives the opportunity to begin to question what the common features are and how these impact on work with people at risk across the lifespan. This chapter will look at the historical construction of child protection and how responses to child deaths and policy developments have led to the current system for safeguarding children. Historical responses to adults at risk in the UK will then be considered in the context of prevailing societal attitudes to marginalised groups. Themes emerging which are applicable to people at risk will then be reviewed.

ACTIVITY **1.1**

As you read the chapter consider how the people in the case studies below are affected by the historical time that they live in and the prevailing responses to people at risk.

John

In 1971 John, a 7 year old boy, was changing for a PE lesson at school when his teacher noticed that he had lots of different coloured bruising on his abdomen and back. When his teacher asked him what had happened, John didn't want to talk about it as the other children started laughing at him. His teacher persisted and he eventually said that he had fallen down the stairs at home. John's teacher told him he would need to be more careful. He also wrote a note for John to give to his parents suggesting that he might need his sight checked.

Zena

In 1989 Zena, a 21 year old woman with learning disabilities, was very upset at her day centre. When her keyworker spoke to her she said that Bob, another person attending the day centre, had followed her into the toilet and forced her to do things that hurt. Zena's keyworker told the centre manager and when they spoke to Zena together, the details she gave them suggested that Bob had forced her to have sex. The centre manager met with a staff member from the residential home where Zena lived and they agreed that it was difficult to know exactly what happened but Zena should move to another day centre as she was quite distressed now whenever she saw Bob. They talked to Zena after the meeting

(Continued)

---

to tell her what was going to happen and asked her not to talk to other people about the incident as it was private.

Mary

In 2013 Mary, an 83 year old woman with severe osteoarthritis, had a visit at home from her occupational therapist (OT). Mary became upset while they were talking and said that she was worried about money. Her son Alan sorted out household bills and shopping for her but she was getting letters threatening to take her to court for unpaid bills. Mary looked extremely thin and there was no evidence of any food in the house but she said Alan was her only relative and she would be distraught if she couldn't see him. After discussing the situation, Mary agreed that her OT could make a safeguarding referral. Mary was reassured to hear that arrangements could be made for her bills to be paid without involving her son and that she could get help with her shopping.

The historical construction of child protection

Protection, prevention and safeguarding

The historical and social construction of child protection has undoubtedly been influenced by cultural and political factors, with policies often being driven as a reactive response to tragedy. Another factor which continues to influence social work practice is the complex interplay between parental rights and responsibilities and the state's duty to protect.

In a landmark case in 1860 (*R v Hopley*), the defendant was a schoolmaster who had asked a pupil's father for permission to punish a pupil for 'obstinacy'. The father agreed, and Hopley subsequently beat the boy repeatedly for over two hours – the boy died. The judge, Lord Cockburn, held that:

> *By the law of England, a parent... may for the purpose of correcting what is evil in the child, [to] inflict moderate and reasonable corporal punishment.*

This debate around parental rights to reasonable chastisement continues to be a contentious issue within contemporary practice (Barrett, 2015). Following Cockburn's judgment, social and political awareness of child maltreatment grew and in the 1880s the concept of child cruelty began to be viewed as a significant social disease. In 1884, Rev. Benjamin Waugh founded the London Society for the Prevention of Cruelty to Children, which then became the NSPCC in 1889 following the enactment of the English Prevention of Cruelty to Children Act. The Act provided the legal mandate which enabled the prosecution of perpetrators of abuse, thereby allowing the state to assume some responsibility for the protection of children (Corby et al., 2012).

The Prevention of Cruelty to Children Act 1904 allowed removal of a child from home on the authority of a Justice of the Peace. This piece of legislation laid the foundations of the state's ability to remove a child at risk to a place of safety. The Punishment of

Incest Act 1908 made intra-familial sexual abuse (incest) an offence (Hendrick, 2003). Prior to 1857 sexual activity within the family was regarded as sinful but not actually illegal, and had been dealt with by the clergy. From 1857 it was removed from ecclesiastical jurisdiction. In contrast, incest in Scotland was illegal from 1567 and punishable by death from to 1887 (Corby et al., 2012).

The welfare state, social democracy and children's services

Following the Beveridge Report in 1942, the state assumed a more collective responsibility for the provision of welfare services. In 1945 the first public enquiry into the death of a child was held following the death of Dennis O'Neill, who was killed by his foster carers. The issue of child maltreatment and protection achieved political and media attention and the inquiry was instrumental in the creation of children's departments in 1948 (Corby et al., 2012).

In 1961 at a Symposium at the American Academy of Paediatrics, Henry Kempe was the first practitioner to identify the previously 'unthinkable' notion that there are parents who deliberately harm their young children (Kempe et al., 1962) in the *Journal of the American Medical Association*. Parton (2014) suggests that the child protection discourse developed from this medical discovery of 'Battered Child Syndrome'. However, this medicalised view that child abuse could be accounted for on the basis of individual pathology diverted attention away from other structural factors which could impact on abuse, such as poverty.

During the 1970s and 1980s this tendency to blame was reinforced by the intense public and media interest in the public inquiries into a number of child deaths. In 1973 Maria Colwell died after being starved and beaten by her stepfather, despite the fact that there had been 50 visits made to the family by social services. The inquiry into her death found that the greatest failure was the lack of communication and liaison between the agencies involved.

In 1984 Jasmine Beckford was starved and battered to death by her stepfather. She had been in the care of Brent social services for two and a half years before she died. By 1985 a further 29 inquiries had been held into child deaths that had resulted from abuse. Parton suggests that the findings from the inquiry reports revealed similar themes, including an excessive focus on adults rather than on the child.

As a consequence of these cases a new political driver emerged in which resources were to be diverted to investigating abuse as opposed to prevention. This over-preoccupation with investigation and the view that social workers had too much power to intervene in the private lives of families was reinforced by the Cleveland Inquiry in 1987, which investigated the fact that within a five-month period 121 children had been removed to places of safety. An over-reliance on invasive medical tests to diagnose suspected sexual abuse was heavily criticised. The public inquiry into the Cleveland cases led to queries being raised about the appropriate balance between a family's right to privacy and autonomy and the state's right to intervene when child abuse is suspected

(Corby et al., 2012). This public inquiry became pivotal to the structural changes in child protection which were introduced by the Children Act 1989.

Children Act 1989 and the new right

The legislative changes brought in by the Children Act 1989 were introduced by a new right Conservative government – at that time, the direction of the child protection agenda was being driven by themes such as individual responsibility, choice, freedom and a move away from state interference. Culpitt argues that this rhetoric of neoliberalism has placed the *'lessening of risk, not the meeting of need'* at the heart of social policy (Culpitt, 1999). The Act brought together the domains of private and public law. One of its main aims was to balance the protection of children whilst respecting the privacy of family life, thus emphasising the concept of parental responsibility as opposed to parental rights. Core principles were introduced to safeguard a child's welfare but intervention by the state should only take place as a last resort. The concept of significant harm was also introduced and the threshold criteria which, if met, provide the legal mandate for compulsory state intervention to protect a child at risk.

In 2001 research was undertaken into the operation of the Children Act 1989, which suggested that resources were being disproportionately directed to children at risk as opposed to the preventative services which could be provided via children in need; priority being given to risk as opposed to need. The research further highlighted that resources for early intervention were not being used effectively to avoid an escalation into the child protection system (Aldgate and Stratham, 2001); a clear indication that the differential between risk and need was again being firmly reinforced.

The death of Victoria Climbié: New Labour, the refocusing debate and safeguarding

The food would be cold and would be given to her on a piece of plastic while she was tied up in the bath. She would eat it like a dog, pushing her face to the plate. Except, of course that a dog is not usually tied up in a plastic bag full of its excrement.

(House of Commons Health Committee, 2003)

On 25 February 2000 Victoria Climbié died after being systematically tortured by her great-aunt and her great-aunt's partner. She had 128 injuries from beatings with coat hangers, wooden spoons, shoes, a bicycle chain and fists. Her body had scars, ulcers and cigarette burns. She had been left naked, in a bin-liner, tied hand and foot for several days. Her temperature was so low it could not be recorded on the hospital's thermometer. Victoria was known to social workers at two social services departments, paediatricians at two hospitals, police officers, the church and other organisations. A public inquiry headed by Lord Laming identified comprehensive failings of the protection system, including widespread organisational malaise. The inquiry highlighted 12 different occasions when different services could have intervened to save Victoria's life (Laming, 2003).

As a direct response to the death of Victoria Climbié the new Labour government introduced policy and legislative changes which led to a shift away from the concept of child protection towards safeguarding. The safeguarding agenda placed a responsibility on social workers to work in partnership with other professionals to prevent impairment to children's health and development alongside the promotion of their welfare. Work was to become proactive as opposed to reactive; the focus was on early intervention as a means of avoiding an escalation into the safeguarding system. The essence of the approach was that safeguarding should involve being able to enhance the protective factors in a child's life whilst also dealing with risk.

The government introduced the *Every Child Matters* programme in 2003 to support the safeguarding agenda. ECM aimed to provide universal services for children and set out five outcomes for children, one of which was to stay safe (DCSF, 2003). This approach introduced the provision of universal services for children and families and more specialised services for children who had more complex needs. To achieve these aims the Labour government introduced a number of indicatives including the common assessment framework (CAF) and Sure Start. Statutory changes to the structure of the child protection system were made via the Children Act 2004, which placed a specific duty on different agencies to cooperate and work together to safeguard children and young people. This emphasis on multi-agency cooperation was highlighted by the introduction of the guidance *Working Together to Safeguard Children* in 2006 (HM Government, 2006).

The Child Protection Register was abolished in 2008. Children are now subject to a protection plan with information to be held on centralised databases. Davies and Duckett (2008) suggest that this policy shift has introduced a new set of professional terms, in a move from investigation, abuse and protection to assessment, need and safeguarding. Despite the introduction of these new safeguarding policies and procedures the incidences of child deaths have continued, with public inquiries continuing to reiterate multi-agency and system failures.

The tragic death of baby Peter Connelly in 2007 dominated both politics and the media, causing a highly critical public outcry. Corby (2006) argued that this political and public outcry effectively led to the shift in policy away from safeguarding towards a rediscovery of child protection.

RESEARCH SUMMARY

The government called for an urgent review into the safeguarding system which led to The Protection of Children in England: A Progress Report (Laming, 2009) and the Munro Report (2011) into the child protection system.

Once again failings in the system were identified, including:

- *failure to challenge;*
- *failure to appreciate risk;*
- *failure to investigate;*

(Continued)

- *failure to trust instinct;*

- *low quality of CP training;*

- *inspection processes not effective;*

- *failure by professionals to communicate directly with, or observe the child.*

Austerity and the 'big society'

Following the general election, in 2010, the government has introduced a political mandate which supports austerity and comprehensive cuts to the welfare system. The impact of these welfare cuts and reforms has contributed to a widening gap in incomes and a rise in child poverty.

RESEARCH SUMMARY

The Joseph Rowntree Foundation commissioned research which examined changes in the adequacy of household incomes between 2008/9 and 2012/13. It found that the links between poverty and a child's chances of becoming subject to child protection processes or being looked after are becoming more evident.

Using the latest available data on household incomes, the report highlights that the percentage of families who live below the minimum income standard is increasing; 39 per cent of people in households with children (8.1 million individuals) live below the minimum income standard. Of these families, those headed by lone parents face particular pressure: 71 per cent live on inadequate incomes (2.3 million individuals), up from 65 per cent (2.2 million).

Recent statistics from the Department for Education (2015a) highlight that the numbers of children in care rose from 64,470 in March 2010 to 69,707 in March 2015, a rise of 8.1 per cent. Meanwhile, the number of vulnerable children placed on child protection plans increased by 32.6 per cent.

The number of Section 47 enquiries – which are conducted by social work teams to decide whether children are at risk of abuse or neglect – increased by 42.5 per cent in 2014/15 and the number of children placed on child protection plans rose by 33 per cent (Puffett, 2015).

Although the coalition government reiterated its commitment to early intervention, the austerity measures that were introduced following the election of the coalition government in 2010 led to cuts in public welfare spending. Restricted budgets have led to a refocusing of funds away from prevention and early intervention towards risk management.

Davies and Ward (2012) suggest that new policy initiatives have been introduced which call for the use of greater innovation and autonomy in the delivery of services, with the role of central government being reduced in favour of local partnerships. However, caseloads and organisational demands remain high, contradicting many of the Munro Report's recommendations, which call for a return to relationship-based social work and less bureaucracy. There have also been calls to restructure, privatise and specialise frontline protection services. The future of children's safeguarding and protection appears to be in a further state of flux with scrutiny from both the public and politicians.

ACTIVITY **1.2**

Examine the changes that have taken place in relation to the protection of children and think about what knowledge you might need to cope with the changing demands of work in this field. In 2013, Children's Minister Edward Timpson called for a 'fundamental rethink' *in how children are protected.* 'I want to support and liberate you to improve faster, get better value for money, do the job you came into the profession to do. But to do this, I need you to demonstrate to me what you have to offer' *(Pemberton, 2013).*

The development of adult safeguarding

The abuse and neglect of adults with care and support needs have been present throughout history but, like child abuse, it is only relatively recently that awareness has been raised of their prevalence in our society (Pritchard, 2007). Pritchard suggests that a focus on adult abuse has been slower than for children due to the emotive nature of babies and children and the assumption that adults should be able to look after themselves. In a UK context, the early roots of our current system of responding to needs lie in the Act for the Relief of the Poor Law, which came into force in 1601. New formats of the Poor Law were developed in the 1800s which required recipients to undergo degrading treatment to prove their need for help, as a deterrent to discourage people from accessing support (Blakemore and Warwick-Booth, 2013). The system provided for the most basic human needs in terms of food and shelter and was the last resort for those with no other avenues of support.

The link between support needs and stigmatisation was engrained in these early policy responses to need. Marginalisation and segregation of people with support needs continued to characterise provision into the 1900s. The eugenics movement espoused now widely discredited ideas around the notion of genetic improvement of the human race. In the UK, the government set up a royal commission in 1904 to research the extent of 'mental deficiency'. The commission accepted the hereditary notion of learning disability and suggested 'treatments' such as sterilisation and segregation (O'Driscoll, 2013). Under the Mental Deficiency Act 1913, local councils were required to provide local services for people with learning disabilities. Segregation from the general population, and sexual segregation to prevent reproduction, were key elements of interventions under the Act. People were categorised under a range of what are now seen as highly derogatory labels such as 'feeble minded'. This also included the category of 'moral imbecile' which O' Driscoll notes was a catch all category which was applied to a wide range of people including sexually active young women and people committing minor criminal offences. The post-Second World War development of the welfare state enshrined the notion of state responsibility for providing support to those in need in UK society; however, the marginalisation of many adults with additional needs continued. Large long-stay institutions prevailed until the later decades of the twentieth century as the overriding policy response to a range of adults with care and support needs (Goble, 2011).

Institutional abuse

Institutional abuse and its impact was increasingly documented through the mid-twentieth century (Goffman, 1961; Townsend, 1962). People with a wide range of care needs were subject to a medicalisation of their support, often living in large ward environments. The harsh and depersonalising regimes alone of large long-stay institutions constituted an abuse of the adults who experienced them. The removal of people with support needs from their local environments to isolated facilities lacking privacy and dignity provided a breeding ground for, and was often accompanied by, further forms of physical, sexual and emotional abuse and neglect. Individual resistance to inhumane forms of treatment was pathologised and responded to with powerful medication and behaviour modification programmes (Goble, 2011). Growing awareness of the inadequacies and inhuman treatment under such regimes, alongside political concern to reduce expenditure and state responsibility for care, led to the growth and implementation of community care policies in the latter decades of the twentieth century, culminating in the NHS and Community Care Act 1990 (Blakemore and Warwick-Booth, 2013).

ACTIVITY **1.3**

Recent studies have demonstrated that people with learning disabilities and mental health problems continue to face social exclusion and marginalisation. How do you think current attitudes in society been affected by previous policy responses?

Abuse in a community context

Older people were one of the earliest groups to be highlighted in relation to abuse within a community setting in the UK. Elder abuse was described for the first time in a British scientific publication in the year 1975 using the term *'granny bashing or granny battering'* (De Donder et al., 2011).The use of such terms was not only stigmatising but also obscured the broader context of the abuse of adults (Stewart and Atkinson, 2012).

As discussed earlier, under the new right Conservative government, the direction of the child protection agenda was driven by themes such as individual responsibility, choice and reduced state control. The community care reforms of the 1990s were also built around economic priorities and ideological assumptions about the role of a free market economy in the provision of welfare. Inherent within this was the idea that individuals, families and communities should do more to support themselves. The NHS and Community Care Act 1990 introduced the first formal complaints systems for reporting abuse in care services. The formation of Action on Elder Abuse in 1993 increased awareness of the abuse of older people and moved adult protection onto the policy agenda. The Department of Health published guidelines, *No Longer Afraid* (1993), and local authorities were encouraged to consider their own policies and procedures. The guidelines included the first British definition of adult abuse within policy:

> *Abuse may be described as physical, sexual, psychological, or financial. It may be intentional or the result of neglect. It causes harm to the older person, either temporarily or over a period of time.*

> (Department of Health, 1993: 3)

The initial focus around elder abuse was with intergenerational violence linked to the stress of caring roles (Brown et al., 1999). Connecting abuse to the stress of caring can be linked to wider societal perceptions of older people as a burden, and can emphasise their dependency. More recent research has highlighted the significance of themes such as longer-term relationship patterns and environmental factors (Samsi et al., 2014). Early accounts of elder abuse also focused on abuse within the home, effectively masking abuse in residential settings. This has been seen as a purposeful attempt to draw attention away from institutional abuse at a time when UK government policy was facilitating growth of the private sector in care home provision (Biggs, 1996). Subsequent research highlighted the prevalence of abuse in spousal relationships, financial exploitation of older people and also abuse in care settings (Brown et al., 1999).

Initial moves towards a community context for adults with learning disabilities were often still large-scale group homes and day care facilities. While these were usually located in community settings, this tended to be a physical shift rather than a change in philosophy. Provision often continued to be characterised by lack of choice, control and dignity for the people who used the services and, as such, an environment where the potential for abuse was high (Bigby and Frawley, 2010). Sexual abuse was the first area to be highlighted within community-based services for people with learning disabilities and initial policies focused on themes around consent and exploitation (Brown et al., 1999). Despite this, evidence suggests that physical abuse has been the most common form of abuse of people with learning disabilities (Emerson et al., 2012).

People with mental health problems have experienced a similar history of institutionalisation and marginalisation which has focused on control and restriction. Links between dangerousness and mental health have also been conflated in the media, as opposed to the risk of abuse faced by people with mental health problems (Golightly, 2014). The mistreatment of people with mental health problems was highlighted in relation to physical assault, intimidation and illegal restraint at Beech Ward in London's St Pancras Hospital. The abuse only came to light after a healthcare assistant informed on five colleagues in 1996. The internal inquiry held by Camden and Islington Community Services Trust highlighted ignorance, low morale, poor management and inadequate training as key issues which have been repeatedly reflected in subsequent inquiries (Gisby and Butler, 2012). Over 60 recommendations were made, including the proposal that people working with vulnerable adults should undergo the same police checks as staff working with children (BBC News, 1999). Moves towards community provision for a range of adults with care and support needs have clearly not always signified improved care and treatment. Chapter 6 explores the way that negative cultures of care and abusive practices can pervade service provision whatever the setting.

Physically disabled people have been at the forefront of their own political campaigns to tackle exclusion and discrimination in society. Again, a history of institutionalised provision has been accompanied by a range of widespread abuse of disabled people. There is considerable evidence that despite the move to community-based support for disabled people, abuse rates remain high, including hate crime and discrimination (Emerson et al., 2012).

The twenty-first century and *No Secrets*

Despite ongoing discussion from the mid-1990s onwards about the need for a legislative framework, this was not implemented and instead the government issued a policy framework. The *No Secrets* guidance (Department of Health, 2000) built on the rights-based approach signified by the Human Rights Act 1998. It provided the central framework for adult protection for councils with social services responsibilities, local NHS bodies, police forces and other partners to develop multi-agency codes of practice to prevent and investigate abuse.

The guidance states that:

> *The aim should be to create a framework for action within which all responsible agencies work together to ensure a coherent policy for the protection of vulnerable adults at risk of abuse and a consistent and effective response to any circumstances giving ground for concern or formal complaints or expressions of anxiety. The agencies' primary aim should be to prevent abuse where possible but, if the preventive strategy fails, agencies should ensure that robust procedures are in place for dealing with incidents of abuse. The circumstances in which harm and exploitation occur are known to be extremely diverse, as is the membership of the at-risk group. The challenge has been to identify the next step forward in responding to this diversity.*

(Department of Health, 2000: 6)

No Secrets set out central principles of empowerment, confidentiality, information, advocacy and rights. It also stated that outcomes should be audited routinely so that problems can be learned from and practice improved. The potential conflict between risk and freedom of choice, and also between openness and confidentiality, is apparent throughout the *No Secrets* guidance (www.scie.org.uk). *No Secrets* also makes reference to the importance of involving people who use services, families and carers. The use of advocates and the importance of providing appropriate information around safeguarding are also introduced within the policy document.

The Care Standards Act 2000 legislated for overarching regulation and inspection of all care services, including private providers. It required providers to have adult protection procedures and to check the Protection of Vulnerable Adults (PoVA) list when employing new staff (Gisby and Butler, 2012). While these developments have been important, the history of social exclusion and marginalisation that has been experienced by adults with care and support needs has often worked against them having the personal power to use such systems for complaints. The difficulties around being listened to for service users, families and whistleblowers are highlighted through events such as those at Winterbourne View and will be examined further in Chapter 6. The developments in advocacy and self-advocacy in the twenty-first century have provided support to people in speaking out about their needs and raising the profile of adult abuse.

The impact of inquiries into adult abuse

While adult abuse has not gained the same level of public exposure as child abuse there have been a significant number of inquiries which have raised awareness of themes around safeguarding adults. One case which did achieve a high media profile was that of Harold Shipman, a doctor who was convicted of the murder of 15 older people with lethal injections of morphine in 2000. In 2001 a public inquiry was established to investigate the magnitude of his crimes and the lessons that could be learned. A total of 250 murders of patients were attributed to Shipman over 23 years. The inquiry found that some victims could have been saved if the police had investigated other patients' deaths more fully. The General Medical Council was also criticised for prioritising the protection of doctors over that of the central task to look after and protect patients (Smith, 2002).

In 2004 the Parliamentary Select Committee on Health looked at the prevalence of elder abuse and noted the comments of Gary Fitzgerald from the charity Action on Elder Abuse that while most people would be familiar with the murder of Victoria Climbié they would be much less likely to be familiar with comparable cases involving older people (House of Commons Health Committee, 2004). He referred to the death of Margaret Panting, a 78 year old woman who died in 2001 after suffering multiple injuries including cuts, probably made by a razor blade, and cigarette burns. She had moved from sheltered accommodation to her son-in-law's home and died five weeks later. As the cause of Margaret Panting's death could not be established, no one was ever charged and an inquest in 2002 recorded an open verdict (House of Commons Health Committee, 2004). Margaret's death was instrumental in the development of the Domestic Violence, Crime and Victims Bill in 2002 in England, which ultimately introduced the Section 4 offence in the Domestic Violence, Crime and Victims Act 2004 of *'causing or allowing the death of a child or vulnerable adult'* (Hampshire Safeguarding Adults Board, 2015).

There has been wider coverage of adult abuse and neglect in the media in recent decades and growing awareness of the role of serious case reviews (SCRs) in examining specific incidents. Tragedies, such as the death of Steven Hoskin, a 38 year old man with learning disabilities who was tortured, forced to hang from a viaduct and ultimately murdered by a gang, have highlighted significant failings in adult safeguarding systems. The serious case review found more than 40 warnings and chances for intervention were missed by the agencies involved (Flynn, 2007). Key themes were inadequate inter-agency working and a lack of appropriate responses to people who are marginalised within their communities and on the fringes of service involvement. Such cases have raised awareness of the need for accountability among all agencies who come into contact with adults at risk and the importance of effective information sharing.

RESEARCH SUMMARY

The UK Study of Abuse and Neglect of Older People (2007) was commissioned by Comic Relief and the Department of Health and carried out by the National Centre for Social Research and King's College London. Over 2,100 people in England, Scotland, Wales and Northern Ireland took part in the survey between March and September 2006. The survey included people aged 66 and over living in private households (including sheltered accommodation) (Comic Relief, 2007).

Overall, 2.6 per cent of people aged 66 and over living in private households reported that they had experienced mistreatment involving a family member, close friend or care worker during the past year. This equates to about 227,000 people aged 66 and over in the UK who were neglected or abused in the past year. When prevalence was broadened to include incidents involving neighbours and acquaintances, the overall prevalence increased from 2.6 per cent to 4 per cent. This would give a figure of approximately 342,400 older people subject to some form of mistreatment.

Women were more likely than men to be the victims of harm/abuse (3.8 per cent of women and 1.1 per cent of men) and people over 85 years old were particularly at risk. Those who lived alone experienced higher levels of neglect while those who had poor health or a poor quality of life were found to be more likely to experience abuse of other types. Those from lower socio-economic backgrounds and living in social or private rented housing also had higher prevalence rates of abuse. Partners, family members and neighbours were the most likely abusers, followed by care workers and friends. The study did not cover stranger abuse, abuse of people with severe dementia or abuse in care settings, which suggests that actual rates of abuse would be far higher. The types of abuse perpetrated included: neglect, financial, psychological, physical and sexual.

Cooper et al. (2008) carried out a review of 49 studies of elder abuse and neglect from across the world. They found that 6 per cent of older people reported significant abuse in the last month and 5 per cent of couples reported physical violence in their relationships. Nearly 25 per cent reported significant levels of psychological abuse. Sixteen per cent of care home staff admitted significant psychological abuse. However, rates of reported or recorded abuse were low (1–2 per cent). The study concludes that a quarter of vulnerable adults are at risk of abuse and that only a small proportion of abuse is currently detected. Both types and rates of abuse were at a similar level to those found in the UK study.

Personalisation and beyond

Initial moves towards community care have subsequently been developed within the personalisation agenda, which emphasises the importance of individual choice, control and self-directed support. Smethurst suggests that through the concept of personalisation *'New Labour was able to square the circle of using individualised, market solutions to address collective principles of social wellbeing'* (2012: 44). Ensuring that people have greater choice and control over their own care has been one of the central aims of the personalisation of services in recent decades. While personalisation has been highly welcomed in terms of providing people with care and support needs with more control and choice in terms of how and by whom their needs are met, there have been ongoing concerns around safeguarding and managing risk. While personalisation and safeguarding have been two of the most central priorities in adult social care for successive governments in the UK, they have often been addressed in parallel and Manthorpe et al. (2015) suggest that a more coherent approach to the two agendas is still required.

In 2005 the then Association of Directors of Social Services (ADSS) produced a framework of standards for good practice and outcomes in adult protection work which has provided a structure for adult safeguarding procedures. Alongside *No Secrets* this has been a significant document in supporting local authorities to provide more coherent responses to safeguarding adults (ADSS, 2005). The Mental Capacity Act 2005 (MCA) has also been a key development in the legal and policy framework applicable to safeguarding. The Act enshrines the presumption of capacity to make decisions and the right of adults to make unwise decisions. It also provides a best interest framework when someone lacks capacity to make a decision for themselves.

The Review of No Secrets (Department of Health, 2009) was published after widespread consultation with service users, families and other stakeholders. The document reflected the priorities of personalisation particularly in relation to the importance of individual choice and control and the need to consider adult protection in the wider context of people's lives. The document suggests that:

> *Safeguarding must be built on empowerment – or listening to the victim's voice. Without this, safeguarding is experienced as safety at the expense of other qualities of life, such as self-determination and the right to family life . . . Everyone must help to empower individuals but safeguarding decisions should be taken by the individual concerned. People wanted help with options, information and support. However, they wanted to retain control and make their own choices.*

> (Department of Health, 2009: 5)

Significant changes in terminology have occurred in the UK with a move from the term 'vulnerable adult' to terms such as 'adult at risk' to shift the framing of the cause of abuse away from the abused person towards the perpetrator. The concept of 'safeguarding' also encompasses a wider approach including prevention and partnership working as opposed to 'adult protection' with a focus on 'enforcing' safety measures on individuals. The move towards individual decision making signifies a rhetorical transfer of responsibility for managing risk onto the individuals themselves. While acknowledging the central notion of increased autonomy, it is a significant shift in relation to the original values and state responsibilities enshrined in the development of the welfare state.

The coalition government of 2010 outlined its approach to addressing the abuse of older people in *A Vision for Adult Social Care: Capable Communities and Active Citizens* (Department of Health, 2010). This document suggested a shift in responsibility for preventing abuse and protecting people at risk of harm. The government stated that:

> *people and communities have a part to play in preventing, recognizing and reporting neglect and abuse. It is everyone's responsibility to be vigilant while Government provides direction and leadership, ensuring the law is clear but not over intrusive.*

> (Department of Health, 2010: 25)

Galpin (2014) notes that subsequently the world economic crisis arising from the global financial sector was reframed in the UK as an attack on public sector spending. The concept of the 'big society' espoused by David Cameron suggests that informal networks of support provide the central backdrop to support individuals with a smaller role for government. The ability and motivation for families and wider communities to provide such a role has been called into question and appears at best overly optimistic in the context of many past and present examples of abuse and neglect (Galpin, 2014).

The Care Act 2014 is the first piece of legislation to place a statutory duty on local authorities to make enquiries when adults with care and support needs may be at risk. The Act also places Safeguarding Adults Boards (SABs) on a statutory footing and requires local authorities to arrange a safeguarding adults review (SAR) in some circumstances (Department of Health, 2015). Previous safeguarding adults policy such as *No Secrets* is repealed by the Act and it enshrines in legislation notions of personalised responses to adults at risk and a move away from process-driven safeguarding activity. The potential of the Act will be considered in more depth in Chapter 3.

The impact of discrimination and marginalisation

Adult abuse has not as yet achieved the level of awareness within society comparable with child abuse and developments in policy continue to be significantly behind those for children. Responses to safeguarding adults have often been reactive and there have been significant differences across different parts of the UK (Stewart and Atkinson, 2012). Throughout the history of responses to the abuse of adults, it is clear that there are close links with the marginalisation and treatment of people with care and support needs in society as a whole. From the Poor Law onwards, those in our society who were seen as not able to contribute to the political economy have been stigmatised. Historically, 'difference' has been characterised as shameful and something to be hidden and the care and support needs of adults have been seen as a burden to the state and to families. The disempowerment of people at risk has influenced their treatment within institutions, families and communities throughout history and has maintained the relatively low profile of adult abuse and neglect in our society. While incidents such as the abuse of individuals in Broadmoor by Jimmy Savile have been framed as a 'this wouldn't happen now' situation, it is clear from the abuse that took place, for example, at Winterbourne View, that mistreatment of those most at risk in our society continues (Flynn and Citarella, 2012; Green, 2013).

While significant progress has been made towards developing more inclusive responses to need, awareness of safeguarding adults is comparatively in its infancy. Safeguarding adults is a highly complex activity which can often involve significant impasses between self-determination and protection from harm. Historical developments highlight the potential for vast differences in perspectives about what constitutes adult abuse and how society should respond. Recent developments have emphasised the rights of individuals to full citizenship and the need for effective community supports. Yet statistics on hate crime (Emerson et al., 2012) and adult serious case reviews clearly indicate that 'communities' continue to be places where many adults with care and support needs suffer abuse and are the target of criminal offences. There is a momentous challenge to services working with people at risk to achieve appropriate responses in safeguarding and this will be explored further throughout the book.

Safeguarding children and adults at risk

Safeguarding and protection are an integral part of social work practice; however, promoting the welfare of children and adults who may be at risk of harm is rarely straightforward and often complex. Over recent years policy and legislation have been increasingly driven by public inquiries which have highlighted failings within systems of support. Contemporary policy and practice reforms have been informed by debates about what constitutes effective and ethical practice. The failings that have been identified by numerous inquiries highlight themes that are common in both adult and children's services.

ACTIVITY *1.4*

Read the following statements which have been drawn from different SCRs.

1. *'Reports of abuse were ignored, warning signs were not picked up by the relevant authorities.'*

2. *'The key to protecting and safeguarding … is sharing information, so any professional – … . should be able to determine immediately if, and when, other agencies are involved and has a duty to share concerns.'*

3. *'The fundamental failing was that agencies did not work together. Despite the number of services involved there was never any inter-agency meeting.'*

4. *'The reports identify system-wide issues across the NHS and local agencies, which did not sufficiently protect or prevent sexual exploitation.'*

(Continued)

ACTIVITY **1.4** *continued*

5. *'If the principles and approaches described in this report had been applied by the four protecting professions, the situation would have been stopped in its tracks at the first serious incident.'*

6. *'Poor coordination (between different services); a failure to share information; the absence of anyone with a strong sense of accountability; and frontline workers trying to cope with staff vacancies, poor management and a lack of effective training'.*

What key themes are you able to identify? Can you determine whether the quotes relate to children or vulnerable adults?

The statements were obtained from the following SCRs.

1. *Winterbourne Inquiry. Available at: www.gov.uk/government/publications/winterbourne-view-hospital-department-of-health-review-and-response*

2. *Inquiry into the death of Steven Hoskin. Available at: www.cornwall.gov.uk/media/3630284/a_e_SCR_Executive_Summary1_Dec_2007_.pdf*

3. *Inquiry into the death of Child D. Available at: www.safeguardingchildren.co.uk/managed/File/executive-summary-Child-D.pdf*

4. *Rochdale Inquiry into Child Sexual Exploitation. Available at: file:///C:/Users/ichis_000/Downloads/Independent_inquiry_CSE_in_Rotherham.pdf*

5. *Inquiry into the death of Baby Peter Connelly. Available at: www.gov.uk/government/news/peter-connelly-serious-case-review-reports-published*

6. *Inquiry into the death of Victoria Climbié. Available at: www.publications.parliament.uk/pa/cm200203/cmselect/cmhealth/570/570.pdf*

COMMENT

Safeguarding children and adults at risk is complex and challenging and SCRs continue to identify similar themes within practice which demonstrate repeated issues. Galilee (2005) suggests that the recommendations of inquiries have generally remained consistent over the last 60 years, focusing on:

- *a lack of inter-agency working and information sharing;*

- *poor communication between agencies;*

- *a lack of understanding of other agencies and their role;*

- *poor recording and assessment skills;*

- *failure to recognise and respond to risk;*

- *inconsistent levels of staff support and supervision.*

(Continued)

Although there has been a separatist approach to work with people at risk over many years this does not reflect the need for practitioners to be equipped with core skills in relation to responding to abuse and planning for safety. The challenge lies in devising the most robust and reliable arrangements for anticipating and avoiding the flaws identified in previous practice. Developing and enhancing multi-agency practice lies at the heart of effective responses to abuse and to date this has not been fully achieved. Barriers which put people at risk are specifically related to different interpretations of appropriate information sharing and a failure to find common ground between different agency priorities. Assessing and responding effectively to risk are crucial in safeguarding across the lifespan and yet approaches are often inconsistent or absent. Recording information accurately and effectively is a further skill required in any safeguarding work and is essential to achieving robust responses which stand up to legal scrutiny. Providing staff with the high levels of support required to practise successfully in safeguarding contexts is also central to all work with people at risk.

CHAPTER SUMMARY

The historical development of protection systems has been diverse in terms of children and adults. Not only have separate policy and legislative frameworks emerged but they have also done so over significantly different timescales with responses to children at risk developing several decades ahead of those for adults. Despite this, many of the failings in safeguarding work have been found to be common across the lifespan. The commonality of issues suggests that a large proportion of the knowledge and skills required for safeguarding are relevant to both children and adults. This also implies that good practice and effective approaches in safeguarding are transferable to different contexts across the lifespan. Responses to people at risk have arisen in the context of wider prevailing social attitudes to specific groups and these continue to impact on safeguarding across the lifespan. All of these themes will be considered further in the different social contexts for safeguarding throughout the book. To further develop an understanding of differences and common themes, the nature and prevalence of abuse will be considered in Chapter 2.

FURTHER READING

Munro, E (2011b) *The Munro Review of Child Protection: Final Report: A Child-centred System.* London: Department for Education.

Ofsted (2011) *Ages of Concern: Learning Lessons from Serious Case Reviews: A Thematic Report of Ofsted's Evaluation of Serious Case Reviews from 1 April 2007 to 31 March 2011.* London: Ofsted.

SCIE (2015) *Adult Safeguarding: Sharing Information.* Available at: www.scie.org.uk/care-act-2014/safeguarding-adults/sharing-information/ (accessed 19 November 2015).

Chapter 2
The nature and prevalence of abuse across the lifespan

Introduction

The previous chapter has charted the historical development of both children's and adult's safeguarding. This discussion has highlighted the fact that abuse has been understood and responded to differently in child and adult contexts. This chapter will explore the ways in which abuse is categorised in our society and look at statistics that can inform us on the prevalence of recorded abuse. While some differences emerge in relation to the types of abuse that are linked to people at different stages of the lifespan there are also some significant areas such as physical abuse, sexual abuse or neglect, where clear parallels can be drawn. While the recognition of the abuse of adults has been much slower to develop than that of children, there are clear themes which emerge, such as exploitation and the abuse of power. A process of grooming can also be identified in a range of contexts across the lifespan. Likewise a context of social deprivation can be applicable to some abuse of both children and adults.

Categories of abuse at any life stage can be used in an oversimplistic way and in reality the boundaries between different types of abuse are often blurred. In fact the categorisation of types of abuse has itself changed over time as understanding and awareness has developed. A further common theme is that there is rarely one type of abuse occurring in isolation and that most forms of abuse have a psychological and emotional impact on the individual. High profile cases of abuse further suggest that addressing issues of abuse in a more coherent way across the lifespan is something which requires development. Also, grooming, exploitation and abuse that occur in childhood can continue into adulthood. This chapter will consider information around the nature and prevalence of child abuse along with an overview of indicators of abuse before moving on to consider these aspects in relation to adults. Emerging themes across the lifespan will then be considered.

Theories of abuse

Theory helps us to try to understand human relationships and the nature and complexity of family interactions. Theory can help inform our understanding but this knowledge and understanding should not be used to make assumptions or be judgemental. Understanding the aetiology of behaviour can help inform more effective interventions.

> *In everyday contexts, we seek and use knowledge in order to understand ourselves, others and the world around us. In professional circles, understanding others usually takes precedence but to do this well involves a degree of self-knowledge.*
>
> (Trevithick, 2003: 1214)

This section provides a broad overview of some of the main theories that have developed to try and understand the aetiology of abuse. First there are a number of *psychological theories* which posit that abuse occurs due to abnormalities and dysfunction within the perpetrator.

RESEARCH SUMMARY

Psychodynamic theory *originates from the work of Sigmund Freud (1856–1939). The focus of Freud's approach is upon the impact of the unconscious mind on the development of personality. His ideas develop a notion that human personality is influenced by an unconscious mind harbouring repressed memories and that this determines conscious thoughts and behaviour.*

(Continued)

Freud believed that humans are born with instinctual drives and that the personality is made of three parts: the 'id', which represents a person's basic biological drives; the 'ego', which tries to satisfy these drives whilst acknowledging the demands of the 'superego' and morality. Freud suggested that a person's experiences during childhood have a significant impact on the development of their personality. He proposed that personality develops through a number of psychosexual stages, and that a healthy personality will depend on how successfully the child progresses through these stages (Ingleby, 2010). Psychodynamic theory would suggest if a person has experienced abuse in their childhood they may be at an increased risk of becoming a perpetrator. This approach has been criticised because it focuses on individual pathology and does not take into account the social and environmental factors that could impact on abuse. (Corby et al., 2012).

***Learning theories** propose that aggression and abusive behaviour may develop as learned conditions as opposed to being a symptom of individual pathology. **Social learning theory** is most closely associated with Albert Bandura (Bandura et al., 1961), who proposed that behaviour is learned by the interaction between a person and their environment, learned from the environment through the process of observational learning. Bandura undertook the Bobo doll experiment with 72 children aged 3–6 years, where they were exposed to watching an adult acting aggressively towards a Bobo doll. The experiment suggested that the children modelled and shaped their behaviour on the basis of what they had observed; children tended to react violently towards the Bobo doll even when the aggressive role model was not present. Bandura suggested that learnt behaviour is then reinforced by a reoccurrence of such behaviours. This theory has been used to explain how violent behaviour can be learnt from observing aggressive role models, for example when children who have witnessed domestic violence later also engage in this behaviour. This approach has been criticised because it does not account for the victims of abuse who do not become perpetrators when they are adults.*

***Social ecological models:** Urie Bronfenbrenner developed the ecology of human development (1979), an ecological systems theory which was introduced to explain the dynamic interaction which exists between a person and a series of different environmental factors. He suggested that there are five complex and socially organised subsystems within society which impact on a person's development. He suggested that the first system is a microsystem, which denotes a person's immediate environment, such as family and school. The second subsystem is a mesosystem, which represents the relations that can exist between microsystems, e.g. the interaction between a parent and a teacher. Exosystems relate to the relations between a microsystem and a system in which the individual does not have an active role or direct contact such as a child's relationship with their parent's work. Macrosystems describes the cultural context in which a child lives. Chronosystem relates to the impact that different environment events and transitions over the life course can have on development. Thus a social ecological approach would suggest that poor environmental conditions can contribute to higher levels of stress and poorer psychological health, which can contribute to higher incidences of maltreatment. However, this theory does not*

(Continued)

take into account the significant number of families who experience deprivation who do not maltreat their children (Corby et al., 2012).

Integrated theories: During the past 30 years there has been a move away from single theory explanations of abuse to more holistic and integrated approaches. Finkelhor (1984) was critical of single-factor theories and proposed **a multifactor model** *which was developed to explain why perpetrators might develop a sexual interest in children. Finkelhor suggested that if abuse is likely to take place four preconditions would need to be present.*

The perpetrator:

1. *will be motivated to sexually abuse (want to);*
2. *is able to overcome internal inhibitors (guilt conscience);*
3. *is able to overcome external inhibitors (groom protectors/create opportunity);*
4. *is able to overcome child's resistance (groom child).*

Finkelhor's model has been criticised on the basis that this model illustrates more about how sexual abuse occurs rather than why it occurs. Ward et al. (2006) suggest that whilst the model provides a systematic approach to conceptualising the aetiology of sexual abuse, there needs to be more focus on the influence of developmental factors, more understanding in relation to the different offence styles which perpetrators can adopt and more clarification of the factors which can increase vulnerability.

It is important that social workers and other professionals develop an awareness of the different theoretical perspectives to enable violence and abuse to be recognised and addressed. There is no single theory which accounts for the existence of abusive behaviour, therefore practice should adopt a more integrated approach to understanding the aetiology of abuse. It is important to view both risk and abuse from a more holistic perspective to allow professionals to analyse the causes of abuse and enable more effective interventions to be implemented.

Consider how some of the theories might be useful in terms of being able to conceptualise the aetiology of abusive behaviour.

Consider how the theories could help inform your understanding of safeguarding within the family, e.g. the impact of domestic abuse or substance misuse.

What else do you think you need to know to extend your professional development and learning at this time?

Children and safeguarding

What do social workers need to know about child abuse?

Social workers need to know what child abuse is, the nature and prevalence of abuse, how to recognise abuse and how to respond effectively to abuse. Social workers have a duty to safeguard and promote the welfare of children and to protect children from maltreatment. However, not everyone is comfortable with the notion that they have a part to play in safeguarding children and there continues to be a reluctance to acknowledge that safeguarding is everyone's responsibility. Whilst Victoria Climbié lived in the UK she was known to a number of different agencies, including social healthcare, hospitals, housing departments and child protection teams. Lord Laming commented on the reluctance of all of the agencies who were involved with Victoria to take responsibility and be accountable for their failings towards her:

> *The single most important change in the future must be the clear line of account-ability from top to bottom, without doubt or ambiguity, about who is responsible at every level for the well-being of vulnerable children.*

> (Laming, 2003)

What is child maltreatment?

The World Health Organisation describes child maltreatment as child abuse and neglect which includes *'all forms of physical and emotional ill-treatment, sexual abuse, neglect, and exploitation that results in actual or potential harm to the child's health, development or dignity'* (WHO, 2015).

The NSPCC suggests that abuse and neglect are forms of maltreatment of a child:

> *Somebody may abuse or neglect a child either directly by inflicting harm, or indi-rectly, by failing to act to prevent harm. Children may be abused in a family or in an institutional or community setting; by those known to them; or, more rarely, by a stranger. They may be abused by an adult or adults, or another child or children.*

> (NSPCC, 2009a)

Prevalence of child maltreatment

On 31 March 2015, 49,690 children were recorded as being the subject of a child protection plan due to risk of significant harm (Department for Education, 2015c). Jütte et al. (2015) conducted research on behalf of the NSPCC which looked at 20 different indicators. Each indicator considered the question *'how safe are our chil-dren?'* These indicators included data on child deaths, serious injury, contact with social services, looked after young people, children who are subject to protection plans and public attitudes to abuse. The key messages from this extensive research suggested that more support is required for the victims of abuse, especially in terms of early therapeutic interventions. The authors also reinforced the importance of being able to recognise the impact that neglect can have on a child's health and development (Jütte et al., 2015).

Radford et al. (2011) interviewed 6,000 young people to research the nature and prevalence of child abuse and neglect in the UK. The research highlighted that one in five children had experienced severe maltreatment both at home and within their communities. Children who have been abused by parents or carers are almost three times more likely also to witness family violence. The research suggested that a third of children and young people who were sexually abused were reluctant to talk to anyone about their experiences. There was also evidence to suggest that sexual abuse and physical abuse had an impact on a child's emotional wellbeing and could be linked to self-harm.

Factors which increase the likelihood of abuse

There are a number of factors that are believed to increase the risk to children and make them more vulnerable to abuse, e.g. a child who has previously suffered abuse or trauma, or a child who has low self-esteem with limited opportunities to develop resilience.

RESEARCH SUMMARY

Research undertaken during the past 20 years has consistently highlighted that children and young people within the looked after system can lack resilience and self-esteem, which can significantly increase their vulnerability. Daniel et al. (2010) developed a resilience framework which enables a practitioner to assess both adverse and positive factors at all ecological levels of a child's socio-emotional environment.

Six domains of resilience have been identified which are believed to promote resilience:

- *secure base;*
- *education;*
- *positive values;*
- *friendships;*
- *social competencies;*
- *talents and interests.*

The researchers suggest that children in each of the domains require a secure base to develop security, self-esteem and self-efficacy. Gilligan (2009) suggests that a resilience led approach can enable looked after children to focus on their positives and strengths, and to develop resilience to adverse situations. This research is consistent with Stein (2012) who highlights that stable placements and good quality care can help improve the outcomes for looked after children and young people.

(Continued)

RESEARCH SUMMARY *continued*

Safeguarding and disability: *Unfortunately, there are particular groups of children and young people who are at an increased risk of experiencing abuse and neglect; research has highlighted that disabled children are three to four times more likely to be abused or mal-treated (Sullivan and Knutson, 2000). In their report for the NSPCC, Miller and Brown suggest that there is often a reluctance to believe that a child with a disability is being abused and there can be a tendency to attribute the indicators of abuse to the child's disability. It is further suggested that there is a lack of professional skills and confidence in identifying child protec-tion concerns and a lack of an effective response from agencies (Miller and Brown, 2014).*

Safeguarding and age: *Children under the age of 12 months are at a higher risk of being abused and on average, in England and Wales, one baby is killed every 20 days. Nearly two thirds of children killed at the hands of another person in England and Wales are aged under 5 years (NSPCC, 2014c).*

Toxic trio

Brandon et al. (2010) undertook research which analysed the key features and out-comes from a number of SCRs. Their research suggested that specific parental behaviours can place children more at risk of harm. Domestic abuse, parental sub-stance misuse and parental mental health were identified as being consistent features in a significant number of child deaths and child injuries. The impact of these behav-iours on families will be explored further in Chapter 4.

Categories of abuse

The *Working Together* 2015 guidance advises that there are four categories of abuse in relation to child maltreatment. Abuse is broadly defined in terms of:

- physical abuse
- emotional abuse
- neglect
- sexual abuse.

What is physical abuse?

Definition
A form of abuse which may involve hitting, shaking, throwing, poisoning, burning or scalding, drowning, suffocating or otherwise causing physical harm to a child. Physical harm may also be caused when a parent or carer fabricates the symptoms of, or deliberately induces, illness in a child.

(HM Government, 2015a: 92)

Prevalence

Radford et al. identified that approximately a quarter of young people had experienced serious child maltreatment during their childhood and 11.5 per cent had experienced severe physical abuse (2011: 119).

Possible indicators of physical abuse

- Frequent injuries or injuries which the child cannot explain, or explains unconvincingly.

- Injuries which have not been treated or have been treated inadequately.

- Bruising which reflects hand or finger marks, scalds, bite marks and burns.

- Broken bones (particularly in children under 2 years old).

- Fabricated or induced illness.

Behavioural signs to look out for

- A child is reluctant to have their parents contacted.

- Aggressive behaviour or severe temper outbursts.

- A child who runs away.

- A child who flinches.

- A child who is reluctant to get undressed.

- A child who appears to be depressed or a child who is excessively compliant.

(HM Government, 2015a)

ACTIVITY 2.2

Read and discuss the following statements.

Smacking a child is an absolute parental right.

It is OK to hit a child as long as you don't leave a mark.

Is it abuse if the child thinks that they deserve it, or where the physical harm is not pre-meditated?

Female genital mutilation (FMG) is acceptable in some cultures.

COMMENT

The issue relating to a parent's right to chastise their child is always a contentious area especially in relation to determining what constitutes reasonable punishment. If an adult assaults another adult or a child they have committed a criminal offence; however, if a

(Continued)

---

parent smacks a child no action will be taken if the action is deemed to be a reasonable chastisement. At what stage does 'reasonable' chastisement lead to excessive force and assault? In Scotland there is a much stricter definition of what constitutes reasonable punishment. The Criminal Justice (Scotland) Act 2003 (Section 51) made it illegal to punish children by: shaking, hitting on the head, using a belt, cane, slipper, wooden spoon or other implement.

If a child does not complain about the abuse that does not mean that it is acceptable. Abuse is never acceptable; it is important to remember that whether abuse is a result of commission or omission, whether the action is premeditated or not, the child has been subjected to abusive behaviour and as such the behaviour is unacceptable.

FGM is abuse: the Female Genital Mutilation Act 2003 has made it illegal for FGM to be performed and to practise FGM in the UK. It is also an offence to take young women who are British Nationals or permanent residents of the UK abroad for FGM whether or not it is lawful in that country.

What is emotional abuse?

Emotional abuse involves the ongoing emotional neglect of a child, making the child feel worthless and devalued.

Definition

The persistent emotional maltreatment of a child such as to cause severe and persistent adverse effects on the child's emotional development.

It may involve conveying to a child that they are worthless or unloved, inadequate, or valued only insofar as they meet the needs of another person. It may include not giving the child opportunities to express their views, deliberately silencing them or 'making fun' of what they say or how they communicate.

It may feature age or developmentally inappropriate expectations being imposed on children. These may include interactions that are beyond a child's developmental capability, as well as overprotection and limitation of exploration and learning, or preventing the child participating in normal social interaction

It may involve seeing or hearing the ill-treatment of another. It may involve serious bullying (including cyber bullying), causing children frequently to feel frightened or in danger, or the exploitation or corruption of children.

Some level of emotional abuse is involved in all types of maltreatment of a child, though it may occur alone.

(HM Government, 2015a: 92)

Prevalence

During their longitudinal research Radford et al. found that one in 14 young people (6.9 per cent) aged 11–17 had experienced emotional abuse during childhood. (Radford et al., 2011: 119). On 31 March 2014 there were 18,420 children in the UK who were the subject of a child protection plan under the category of emotional abuse, which is 33 per cent of all the children who are subject to protection plans (Jütte et al., 2015).

Possible indicators of emotional abuse

- A failure to thrive.

- Sudden speech disorders or appearing nervous.

- An unwillingness or inability to play.

- Fear of making mistakes.

- Self-harm.

- Lack of confidence and self-worth.

- Being withdrawn and anxious.

- An excessive need for attention and approval.

(HM Government, 2015b: 10)

Davies and Ward (2012) suggest that many children and young people do not come to the attention of statutory services, despite the fact that emotional abuse is one of the most common forms of abuse. It could also be argued that all types of child maltreatment will involve some level of emotional abuse. During the Laming Inquiry (2003) some of the health professionals who cared for Victoria whilst she was in hospital stated that they had a feeling that Victoria's relationship with her aunt may have been emotionally abusive, but staff failed to explore this concern sufficiently to enable a conclusion to be reached and appropriate action taken.

Unfortunately, existing legislation and guidance fail to provide a comprehensive definition of emotional abuse, and further confusion is caused by the use of different terms including emotional abuse and psychological abuse, which are often used synonymously or interchangeably. Psychological abuse is sometimes used to incorporate both emotional abuse and psychological abuse. Existing definitions do not state what emotional abuse is, instead providing a list of parental behaviours, such as domestic violence, mental illness, drug or alcohol misuse, which can make children more at risk of emotional abuse. The existence of these factors does not guarantee that emotional abuse will result and provides no information about the impact on the child. O'Hagan (2006) argues that most children experience one or more of the parental behaviours set out in the definitions without being emotionally abused, yet there is no guidance to establish where the threshold lies.

RESEARCH SUMMARY

Attachment theory and emotional abuse and neglect

According to Bowlby's attachment theory, emotional abuse can cause harm and have a negative impact in infancy on the baby's ability to establish a secure attachment with the parent/carer. The purpose of the attachment bond is to provide physical and emotional protection, which ensures the baby's survival. If a child has feelings of insecurity the role of the caregiver is to restore a sense of security and wellbeing. As this process is repeated the child learns how to trust, to relate to others and how to develop a positive sense of self.

Children are not slates from which the past can be rubbed by a duster or sponge, but human beings who carry their previous experiences with them and whose behaviour in the present is profoundly affected by what has gone before.

(Bowlby, 1951: 114)

In cases of emotional abuse, parents often respond in inconsistent, intrusive or rejecting ways, which can lead to the child developing a negative sense of self and others. Howe (2011) suggests that maladaptive behaviours can occur as a result of a lack of consistent attachment figure, which can result in children struggling to understand their own and other people's emotions. He proposes that 80 per cent of children who live in abusive and neglectful environments develop insecure attachment styles and behaviours. O'Hagan (2006) suggests that children who experience insecure attachments can find it difficult to recognise and respond to positive feelings which can result in a lack of empathy, an inability to develop consistent emotional responses and low self-esteem. However, if a child is removed from the abusive environment, the long-term outcomes could be improved through the introduction of an alternative positive attachment figure.

What is neglect?

Neglect is considered to be an inability of parents or carers to provide an adequate level of care and a failure to meet the basic physiological and emotional needs of a child.

Definition

The persistent failure to meet a child's basic physical and/or psychological needs likely to result in the serious impairment of the child's health or development. Neglect may occur during pregnancy as a result of maternal substance abuse. Once a child is born, neglect may involve a parent or carer failing to: provide adequate food, clothing and shelter (including exclusion from home or abandonment); protect a child from physical and emotional harm or danger; ensure adequate supervision (including the use of inadequate care-givers); or ensure access to appropriate medical care or treatment. It may also include neglect of, or unresponsiveness to, a child's basic emotional needs.

(HM Government, 2015a: 93)

Prevalence

Radford et al. found that 15 per cent of young people in their study had experienced serious absence of care and 23.7 per cent had witnessed domestic violence (2011: 119). The most common category of abuse reported when a child becomes the subject of a plan is neglect at 43.2 per cent, followed by emotional abuse at 33.7 per cent (Department for Education, 2014c).

Possible physical indicators of neglect

- Children who are living in a home that is indisputably dirty or unsafe.

- Children who are left hungry or dirty.

- Children who are left without adequate clothing, e.g. not having a winter coat.

- Children who are living in dangerous conditions, i.e. around drugs, alcohol or violence.

- Children who are often angry, aggressive or self-harm.

- Children who fail to receive basic healthcare.

- Parents who fail to seek medical treatment when their children are ill or are injured.

- Child thrives away from home.

- Child is constantly hungry and may scavenge for food.

(HM Government, 2015b: 10)

Possible indicators of emotional neglect

- Children who are excessively withdrawn, fearful, or anxious about doing something wrong.

- Parents or carers who withdraw their attention from their child, giving the child the 'cold shoulder'.

- Parents or carers blaming their problems on their child.

- Parents or carers who humiliate their child, for example, by name-calling or making negative comparisons.

(HM Government, 2015b)

ACTIVITY *2.3*

From the list identify the five behaviours which you consider to be the most damaging to a child. Outline your reasoning for your decision in each case.

- *Behavioural problems*

- *Lack of age appropriate toys*

- *Poor attendance at school or nursery*

(Continued)

- *Global development delay*
- *Frequent hospital admissions*
- *Poor concentration or learning*
- *Speech delay*
- *Not taken to the optician regularly*
- *Poor self-care*
- *Involuntary wetting*
- *Involuntary soiling*
- *Non-attendance for medical appointments*

COMMENT

Each of the behaviours could be harmful to a child either as an act of commission or an act of omission. Neglect is the failure to provide socially acceptable standards of care for a child, and each of the behaviours on the list above could represent examples of neglect. Establishing whether a child is experiencing neglect will be dependent on a number of factors which are largely reliant on professional judgement. However, as noted earlier, professional judgement can be subjective, and interpretations as to what constitutes 'good enough' parenting tend to vary considerably.

The Working Together *definition contributes to this professional subjectivity in that it introduces some ambiguous statements, e.g. the word adequate is used throughout the statement. Again, it is difficult to have a definition of adequate as we all have different life experiences and values; what one professional would deem as adequate, another may not.*

Where physical and sexual abuse are often characterised by significant and traumatic incidents in which the harm caused to a child is readily apparent, other forms of abuse may be more insidious and marked by persistent acts of omission, none of which may be sufficient to trigger a safeguarding intervention. However, the child may still be suffering harm.

Neglect is often a feature over the long term of a child's life; early childhood experiences of neglect can have long-term and devastating effects on a child. There is a growing body of evidence about the impact neglect and abuse can have on a child's brain development. In a report submitted to the government in 2011, Early Intervention: The Next Steps, *Graham Allen suggests that how the brain develops is largely shaped by the child's early relationships and the care within the first three years of his/her life. Brown and Ward (2013) suggest that during this period of rapid development the interaction between parent and child can impact on how the neural pathways in the brain develop. In an emotionally abusive environment, the child will learn that their needs are not met by their caregiver. Consequently, feelings of*

(Continued)

guilt, disappointment, criticism and not being valued may be reinforced. Both reports recognise the detrimental impact that maltreatment and neglect can have on a child's emotional and social development. Both reports highlight that early intervention is crucial to avoid the impact of neglectful and abusive relationships, and that practitioners need to act sooner, to recognise the impact and to improve the long-term outcomes for children.

Brandon et al. (2010) highlighted that neglect was apparent in 60 per cent of serious case reviews undertaken between 2009 and 2011. However, unless the threshold of significant harm is established there can be no compulsory legal mandate to intervene to safeguard and protect children and young people.

What is sexual abuse?

Sexual abuse involves introducing a child who is below the age of consent to take part in activities which result in the sexual gratification of the perpetrator. This abuse involves the misuse of power and trust and can lead to the grooming and exploitation of vulnerable children.

Definition

Child sexual abuse covers a wide range of behaviours leading to a lot of interpretation about what sexual abuse is; here sexual abuse is defined as:

Forcing or enticing a child or young person to take part in sexual activities, not necessarily involving a high level of violence, whether or not the child is aware of what is happening. The activities may involve physical contact, including assault by penetration (for example, rape or oral sex) or non-penetrative acts such as masturbation, kissing, rubbing and touching outside of clothing. They may also include non-contact activities, such as involving children in looking at, or in the production of, sexual images, watching sexual activities, encouraging children to behave in sexually inappropriate ways, or grooming a child in preparation for abuse (including via the internet).

(HM Government, 2015a: 93)

Prevalence

Between 2013 and 2014, 64,200 sexual offences were recorded by the police in England and Wales. Of these, 23,772 were carried out against children under 16 years. On 31 March 2014, 2,884 children were made subject to a protection plan under the category of sexual abuse (Jütte et al., 2015).

Radford et al. (2011) suggested that one in 20 children (4.8 per cent) has experienced contact sexual abuse and over 90 per cent of children who experienced sexual abuse were abused by someone they knew. More than one in three children (34 per cent) who experienced contact sexual abuse by an adult did not tell anyone else about the abuse. Four out of five children (82.7 per cent) who experienced contact sexual abuse from a peer did not tell anyone else about it.

Maikovich-Fong and Jaffee (2010) suggested that young women were more likely to be abused by a family member or someone known to them whereas young men were more likely to be abused by strangers.

Possible physical indicators of sexual abuse

Some of the following signs may be indicators of sexual abuse:

- children who display knowledge or interest in sexual acts inappropriate to their age;

- children who use sexual language or have sexual knowledge that you wouldn't expect them to have;

- children who ask others to behave sexually or play sexual games; and

- children with physical sexual health problems, including soreness in the genital and anal areas, sexually transmitted infections or underage pregnancy.

(HM Government, 2015a: 8)

A child or young person who is being sexually abused may exhibit behaviours such as lack of confidence and self-worth, disturbed sleep patterns and enuresis. They may be in receipt of unexplained money and be unwilling to explain where this money has come from, or they may exhibit self-harming behaviour, substance misuse and eating disorders. A child may or may not exhibit any of these behaviours but the information might represent the missing piece of the jigsaw which can indicate that a child is being abused.

ACTIVITY 2.4

Discuss the following statements.

People who download child abuse images are always a risk to children.

If you are homosexual you are more likely to have a sexual interest in children.

No one would abuse a really vulnerable child.

Women don't abuse children.

A child can consent to sexual activity.

COMMENT

Making, downloading or viewing sexual images of children on the Internet is a crime and involves the abuse of children. If a person downloads these images they are participating in the abuse of children.

(Continued)

COMMENT *continued*

Offenders are predominantly heterosexual men and the majority are known to the child, often in a position of trust.

The greater the vulnerability of the child the greater the risk of abuse; children with a disability are three to four times more likely to be abused.

Sexual abuse is not solely perpetrated by adult males. Women can also commit acts of sexual abuse, as can other children.

Sexual activity with a child under the age of 16 years is an offence, a child under 13 years cannot consent to any form of sexual activity. A child may not complain about the abuse because they are frightened or they may have been threatened and forced to keep the abuse secret. The key issues are the misuse of power and the issue of consent.

What is child sexual exploitation?

The term child sexual exploitation (CSE) is often used interchangeably with commercial sexual exploitation, internal trafficking and child prostitution. CSE is found under the category of sexual abuse but it could be argued that due to the nature and extent of this issue it could constitute an additional category of abuse. Child sexual exploitation is predominantly identified by a manipulative and deceptive 'relationship' between the perpetrator and victim that typifies exploitation and a power imbalance. It is a complex and hidden crime where victims are often loyal to their abusers, which can make detection difficult.

Definition

Sexual exploitation of children and young people under 18 involves exploitative situations, contexts and relationships where young people (or a third person or persons) receive 'something' (e.g. food, accommodation, drugs, alcohol, cigarettes, affection, gifts, money) as a result of them performing, and/or another or others performing on them, sexual activities. Child sexual exploitation can occur through the use of technology without the child's immediate recognition; for example being persuaded to post sexual images on the Internet/mobile phones without immediate payment or gain. In all cases, those exploiting the child/young person have power over them by virtue of their age, gender, intellect, physical strength and/or economic or other resources. Violence, coercion and intimidation are common, involvement in exploitative relationships being characterised in the main by the child or young person's limited availability of choice resulting from their social/economic and/or emotional vulnerability.

(DCSF and Home Office, 2009: 9)

However, despite the introduction of government guidance around CSE in 2013 Berelowitz et al. found that only 6 per cent of local safeguarding boards were implementing fully the recommendations from the guidance. Another key area of concern which was highlighted was the lack of effective multi-agency working. These issues will be explored more fully in Chapter 5 with specific reference to the increased vulnerability of children in the looked after system to CSE.

ACTIVITY 2.5

Read the SCRs for Victoria Climbié, Baby Peter and Daniel Pelka and list all the possible indicators of abuse which were missed by different professionals/agencies.

Critically reflect upon the material and statistics that have been presented so far: what further information might you need to know? Do you have any anxieties about working in this area of social work?

Categories of adult abuse

The *No Secrets* guidance defined adult abuse as '*a violation of an individual's human and civil rights by any other person or persons*' (Department of Health, 2000: 2). The Care Act 2014 defines the types of abuse applicable to adults in the UK and includes some significant developments from the types of abuse defined in the *No Secrets* guidance. Chapter 1 notes that the first area of abuse of adults that gained attention was that of the physical abuse of older people and subsequently sexual and physical abuse of people in long-term institutions. The concepts of psychological abuse, neglect and acts of omission and discriminatory abuse were subsequently acknowledged and formalised in the *No Secrets* guidance. The guidance also discusses the idea of institutional abuse in terms of repeated incidences of bad practice, abuse and neglect arising in care settings. The Care Act guidance urges authorities not to limit their view of what constitutes abuse and neglect and also recognises the theme of exploitation as common in different forms of abuse. While the guidance notes that abuse can be a single event or repeated acts it stresses the need to look for patterns of harm. The types of abuse identified in the Care Act are as follows.

- **Physical abuse** – including assault, hitting, slapping, pushing, misuse of medication, restraint or inappropriate physical sanctions.

- **Domestic violence** – including psychological, physical, sexual, financial, emotional abuse; so-called 'honour'-based violence.

- **Sexual abuse** – including rape, indecent exposure, sexual harassment, inappropriate looking or touching, sexual teasing or innuendo, sexual photography, subjection to pornography or witnessing sexual acts, indecent exposure and sexual assault or sexual acts to which the adult has not consented or was pressured into consenting.

- **Psychological abuse** – including emotional abuse, threats of harm or abandonment, deprivation of contact, humiliation, blaming, controlling, intimidation, coercion, harassment, verbal abuse, cyber bullying, isolation or unreasonable and unjustified withdrawal of services or supportive networks.

- **Financial or material abuse** – including theft, fraud, internet scamming, coercion in relation to an adult's financial affairs or arrangements, including in connection with wills, property, inheritance or financial transactions, or the misuse or misappropriation of property, possessions or benefits.

- **Modern slavery** – encompasses slavery, human trafficking, forced labour and domestic servitude. Traffickers and slave masters use whatever means they have at their disposal to coerce, deceive and force individuals into a life of abuse, servitude and inhumane treatment.

- **Discriminatory abuse** – including forms of harassment, slurs or similar treatment; because of race, gender and gender identity, age, disability, sexual orientation or religion.

- **Organisational abuse** – including neglect and poor care practice within an institution or specific care setting such as a hospital or care home, for example, or in relation to care provided in one's own home. This may range from one-off incidents to ongoing ill-treatment. It can be through neglect or poor professional practice as a result of the structure, policies, processes and practices within an organisation.

- **Neglect and acts of omission** – including ignoring medical, emotional or physical care needs, failure to provide access to appropriate health, care and support or educational services, the withholding of the necessities of life, such as medication, adequate nutrition and heating.

- **Self-neglect** – this covers a wide range of behaviour neglecting to care for one's personal hygiene, health or surroundings and includes behaviour such as hoarding.

(Department of Health, 2014: 233–4)

Patterns of abuse are also discussed in the Care Act, including serial abusing where the perpetrator seeks out and 'grooms' individuals. It is noted that sexual abuse sometimes falls into this pattern along with some forms of financial abuse. Long-term patterns of abuse are also highlighted in the context of ongoing family relationships, such as domestic violence between spouses or generations or persistent psychological abuse, and also patterns of opportunistic abuse such as theft occurring because money or valuables have been easily accessible. Patterns of abuse are also likely to emerge in relation to organisational abuse. While the types of abuse categorised in the Care Act are similar to earlier definitions, there are some notable additions. Specific additional categories of abuse identified are domestic violence, modern slavery and self-neglect.

Developments in understanding adult abuse

While there have always been close connections between safeguarding and domestic violence it is only relatively recently that the crossover between the two concepts has been considered more explicitly. In 2013 changes were made to the definition of domestic abuse, now defined as an *'incident or pattern of incidents of controlling, coercive or threatening behaviour, violence or abuse ... by someone who is or has been an intimate partner or family member regardless of gender or sexuality'*. This included: psychological, physical, sexual, financial, emotional abuse; 'honour'-based violence; female genital mutilation; and forced marriage. The 2013 changes also lowered the age range for domestic abuse from 18 to 16. A further key point was that domestic abuse is not just about intimate partners, but can include other family members, and that much safeguarding work that occurs in a private home environment is concerned with domestic abuse (LGA, 2013). These changes identified explicitly that domestic abuse approaches and legislation can be considered safeguarding responses in appropriate cases.

RESEARCH SUMMARY

Modern slavery

There has been a major increase in recorded incidences of modern slavery, which is an international crime affecting an estimated 29.8 million slaves around the world. Modern slavery includes people brought from overseas, and individuals at risk from the UK, being forced to work illegally against their will in different sectors, including brothels, cannabis farms, nail bars and agriculture. People at risk often face more than one type of abuse and slavery, for example if they are sold to another trafficker and then forced into another form of exploitation (see https://modernslavery.co.uk).

Silverman (2014) provides an exploratory analysis of the scale of modern slavery in the UK. The research acknowledges the hidden nature of modern slavery and the impact this has on achieving realistic estimations of prevalence. Many victims may remain in servitude or under the control of perpetrators. When victims do escape they may leave the country or start a new life without reporting their situation to authorities. Other factors which mitigate against effective estimations of prevalence are feelings of fear or shame in victims and the exploitation not being recognised and identified as such by victims themselves or professionals working with them. Using statistical estimation techniques, the research suggests that there were between 10 and 13 thousand potential victims of modern slavery in the UK in 2013.

In 2014 the government published a Modern Slavery Strategy with four components: prosecuting and disrupting individuals and groups responsible for modern slavery (Pursue); preventing people from engaging in modern slavery crime (Prevent); strengthening safeguards against modern slavery by protecting vulnerable people from exploitation and increasing awareness and resilience against this crime (Protect); and reducing the harm caused by modern slavery through improved victim identification and enhanced support and protection (Prepare) (HM Government, 2014).

Self-neglect

The concept of self-neglect has been an area open to considerable differences in interpretation and has been viewed from opposing standpoints as either a highly debilitating psycho-medical condition or a value judgement on individual lifestyle choices. The interaction between factors external and internal to the individual which are biological, behavioural and social are all relevant here as is the differentiation between inability and unwillingness to care for oneself. The central factor in determining the appropriate response is the capacity of the individual to understand the consequences of their own actions and it is an area which highlights the complex relationship between respect for autonomy and responsibility to preserve health and wellbeing. There is currently a lack of conclusive evidence on indications of causation and also around the effectiveness of particular interventions in relation to self-neglect (www.scie.org.uk).

The changes in categorisation of types of abuse in the Care Act reflect developments in the understanding of abuse and also changes in society. For instance, awareness of 'honour'-based violence and FGM has developed alongside the growth in cultural diversity in the UK population. Likewise modern slavery has become more significant with the increase in global and European geographical mobility. Continued developments in our understanding of and responses to types of abuse are most likely.

Discriminatory abuse

Within the category of discriminatory abuse, hate crime is a significant area of abuse defined as *'crimes committed against someone because of their disability, gender-identity, race, religion or belief, or sexual orientation'* (www.gov.uk/report-hate-crime). The term 'mate crime' has also been used to describe situations where adults with care and support needs are befriended by members of the community who go on to exploit and take advantage of them (see the Association for Real Change, at www.arcuk.org.uk). Almost nine in ten people with a learning disability surveyed have experienced bullying or harassment in the past year. Of these, 66 per cent were victims regularly and 32 per cent of people were being bullied on a daily or weekly basis. Forty-seven per cent of the people surveyed had suffered verbal abuse, and 23 per cent had been physically assaulted (www.mencap.org.uk). Serious case reviews, such as those into the deaths of Steven Hoskin and Gemma Hayter, have also highlighted the prevalence of these types of abuse in our society (Flynn, 2007; Warwickshire Safeguarding Adults Partnership, 2010). Hate crime and mate crime are types of abuse that are inextricably linked with the way that people with learning disabilities (and similarly mental health problems) have been treated historically and are currently treated in society. The 2005 ADSS guidance noted that:

> *Safeguarding Adults work is specifically aimed at a group of people who historically have been discriminated against within our society. This discrimination explains in part why the prevalence of abuse of people 'who are or may be eligible for community care services' is high.*

> (ADSS, 2005: 48)

ACTIVITY 2.6

Watch the video **Kelly and Sue's Story: Learning Disability Hate Crime.**

Available from www.mencap.org.uk/get-involved/campaigns/hear-my-voice/hear-our-voice-manifesto/hate-crime

Look back at the different categories of adult abuse and consider what different types of abuse you can identify in the video?

COMMENT

The abuse of adults with a range of care and support needs must be viewed within the context of discrimination and marginalisation. These attitudes which pervade in wider societal contexts also underlie other forms of abuse such as institutional. Awareness of this should inform approaches to safeguarding, and responses should reflect the wider context and causes of abuse. Between 2011 and 2013 there were 124,000 disability hate crimes recorded in the Crime Survey for England and Wales (2011/12 and 2012/13). Only 3 per cent of these were recorded by the police and only 1 per cent resulted in prosecutions. Since 2013, the number of disability hate crimes recorded by the police has been improving but this has not led to an increase in convictions. Issues of under-reporting have been identified and people with a learning disability felt that police officers often ignored them or did not know how to communicate with them properly (www.mencap.org.uk).

Prevalence of adult abuse

There are significant limitations in considering the prevalence of abuse in that reported and recorded statistics do not reflect actual numbers for any type of abuse. This is particularly compounded by the hidden nature of abuse and the marginalisation and powerlessness of those who have been abused in our society. Data collection itself is at a relatively early stage in relation to safeguarding adults. Councils have been urged to keep records since the emergence of *No Secrets* in 2000 but a lack of guidance on what should be recorded led to an absence of comparable information on a national scale. The Health and Social Care Information Centre (HSCIC) carried out a fact finding survey in early 2007. The results from this and work carried out by Action on Elder Abuse were used to devise a national collection about the abuse of vulnerable adults. This collection was piloted among 31 Councils with Adult Social Services Responsibilities (CASSRs) in 2008. From 2010 the data collections became mandatory and all CASSRs were required to submit adult safeguarding data to the HSCIC. The system of data collection has been reviewed in the light of changes in the delivery of social care and to ensure that the information collected is of use to both government and to councils. From 2013–14 onwards, safeguarding data have been collected through the Safeguarding Adults Return (SAR). Since the way the information has been collected has changed, direct comparison with data from any previous years is problematic.

The SAR data are recorded by adult safeguarding teams based in the 152 CASSRs and provide the following information.

- Safeguarding referrals were opened for 104,050 individuals during the 2013–14 reporting year.

- 60 per cent of these individuals were female and 63 per cent were aged 65 or over.

- 51 per cent of the individuals had a physical disability, frailty or sensory impairment.

- 24 per cent had a mental health problem.

- 18 per cent had a learning disability.

- 6 per cent had substance misuse issues.

- 1 per cent were described as other vulnerable people.

For referrals which concluded during the 2013–14 reporting year, there were 122,140 allegations about the type of risk.

- Neglect and acts of omission accounted for 30 per cent of allegations.

- Physical abuse accounted for 27 per cent of allegations.

- Financial and material abuse accounted for 18 per cent of allegations.

- Psychological/emotional abuse accounted for 15 per cent of allegations.

- Sexual abuse accounted for 5 per cent of allegations.

- Institutional accounted for 4 per cent of allegations.

- Discriminatory abuse accounted for 1 per cent of allegations.

There were 99,190 allegations made about the location of risk in concluded referrals.

- 42 per cent of allegations occurred in the home of the adult at risk.

- 36 per cent of allegations occurred in a care home.

- 22 per cent of allegations occurred in community services, hospitals or other settings.

The source of risk varied.

- 49 per cent of allegations were against someone known to the alleged victim but not in a social care capacity.

- 36 per cent of allegations were against social care employees.

- 15 per cent of allegations were against someone unknown to the victim.

(HSCIC, 2014)

The safeguarding data aim to support adult safeguarding policy development and can be used to estimate the amount and type of safeguarding activity taking place. It is likely that the very low reportage of sexual abuse highlights the particularly hidden nature of this type of adult abuse. Criminal statistics do not include information about whether the victim of a crime has care and support needs. HSCIC statistics only consider information around abuse in relation to the activities of the council. There is, therefore, a lack of information on the percentage of allegations of abuse which become the subject of a police investigation, and how many lead to court proceedings and subsequent prosecution of perpetrators. This is likely to be a very small percentage of actual adult abuse as research indicates a wide range of problems that individuals with care and support needs face in their dealings with the police and criminal justice system. Barriers are at the personal, societal and institutional level (Keilty and Connelly, 2001).

RESEARCH SUMMARY

The barriers to legal redress for disabled people

Sin et al. (2009) carried out a wide-scale literature review on disabled people's experiences of violence and hostility for the Equality and Human Rights Commission, which included an analysis of the issues around reporting and seeking redress. They identify a severe under-reporting of incidents. Disabled people have a tendency to report incidents to a third party rather than to the police but there is a lack of research about this type of reporting. The important preventative role of health and social care agencies, housing associations, local authorities and other agencies is highlighted. While examples of good practice exist, they identify the need for better inter-agency working.

A number of barriers to reporting and recording, particularly in relation to the police, are noted. These include physical, procedural and attitudinal barriers that discourage disabled people from reporting. The impact of these barriers may lead disabled people to feel that they are not being taken seriously or even being treated as if they are in the wrong. The relationship between the victim and the perpetrator can also impact on a disabled person's willingness and ability to report abuse. The research also found that sometimes disabled people blame themselves for what has happened to them, or accept incidents as part of everyday life. Legislative mechanisms to assist disabled people seeking redress against abuse are identified as insufficient and inconsistent in terms of awareness and application. The research also noted that disabled people themselves have low levels of awareness of their rights.

Indicators of adult abuse

The following guide to the indicators of adult abuse has been produced by SCIE and considers some of the possible indicators of some of the main types of adult abuse.

- **Physical abuse indicators**
  - No explanation for injuries or inconsistency with the account of what happened
  - Injuries are inconsistent with the person's lifestyle
  - Bruising, cuts, welts, burns and/or marks on the body or loss of hair in clumps
  - Frequent injuries

- o Unexplained falls

- o Subdued or changed behaviour in the presence of a particular person

- o Signs of malnutrition

- o Failure to seek medical treatment or frequent changes of GP

- **Domestic abuse indicators**

  - o Low self-esteem

  - o Feeling that the abuse is their fault when it is not

  - o Physical evidence of violence such as bruising, cuts, broken bones

  - o Verbal abuse and humiliation in front of others

  - o Fear of outside intervention

  - o Damage to home or property

  - o Isolation – not seeing friends and family

  - o Limited access to money

- **Sexual abuse indicators**

  - o Bruising, particularly to the thighs, buttocks and upper arms, and marks on the neck

  - o Torn, stained or bloody underclothing

  - o Bleeding, pain or itching in the genital area

  - o Unusual difficulty in walking or sitting

  - o Foreign bodies in genital or rectal openings

  - o Infections, unexplained genital discharge, or sexually transmitted diseases

  - o Pregnancy in a woman who is unable to consent to sexual intercourse

  - o The uncharacteristic use of explicit sexual language or significant changes in sexual behaviour or attitude

  - o Incontinence not related to any medical diagnosis

  - o Self-harming

  - o Poor concentration, withdrawal, sleep disturbance

  - o Excessive fear/apprehension of, or withdrawal from, relationships

  - o Fear of receiving help with personal care

  - o Reluctance to be alone with a particular person

- **Psychological abuse indicators**

  - o An air of silence when a particular person is present

  - o Withdrawal or change in the psychological state of the person

- o Insomnia

- o Low self-esteem

- o Uncooperative and aggressive behaviour

- o A change of appetite, weight loss/gain

- o Signs of distress: tearfulness, anger

- o Apparent false claims, by someone involved with the person, to attract unnecessary treatment

- **Financial abuse indicators**

  - o Missing personal possessions

  - o Unexplained lack of money or inability to maintain lifestyle

  - o Unexplained withdrawal of funds from accounts

  - o Power of Attorney or Lasting Power of Attorney (LPA) being obtained after the person has ceased to have mental capacity

  - o Failure to register an LPA after the person has ceased to have mental capacity to manage their finances, so that it appears that they are continuing to do so

  - o The person allocated to manage financial affairs is evasive or uncooperative

  - o The family or others show unusual interest in the assets of the person

  - o Signs of financial hardship in cases where the person's financial affairs are being managed by a court appointed deputy, attorney or LPA

  - o Recent changes in deeds or title to property

  - o Rent arrears and eviction notices

  - o A lack of clear financial accounts held by a care home or service

  - o Failure to provide receipts for shopping or other financial transactions carried out on behalf of the person

  - o Disparity between the person's living conditions and their financial resources, e.g. insufficient food in the house

  - o Unnecessary property repairs

- **Modern slavery indicators**

  - o Signs of physical or emotional abuse

  - o Appearing to be malnourished, unkempt or withdrawn

  - o Isolation from the community, seeming under the control or influence of others

  - o Living in dirty, cramped or overcrowded accommodation and or living and working at the same address

- o Lack of personal effects or identification documents

- o Always wearing the same clothes

- o Avoidance of eye contact, appearing frightened or hesitant to talk to strangers

- o Fear of law enforcers

- **Discriminatory abuse indicators**

  - o The person appears withdrawn and isolated

  - o Expressions of anger, frustration, fear or anxiety

  - o The support on offer does not take account of the person's individual needs in terms of a protected characteristic

- **Organisational or institutional abuse indicators**

  - o Lack of flexibility and choice for people using the service

  - o Inadequate staffing levels

  - o People being hungry or dehydrated

  - o Poor standards of care

  - o Lack of personal clothing and possessions and communal use of personal items

  - o Lack of adequate procedures

  - o Poor record-keeping and missing documents

  - o Absence of visitors

  - o Few social, recreational and educational activities

  - o Public discussion of personal matters

  - o Unnecessary exposure during bathing or using the toilet

  - o Absence of individual care plans

  - o Lack of management overview and support

- **Neglect and acts of omission indicators**

  - o Poor environment – dirty or unhygienic

  - o Poor physical condition and/or personal hygiene

  - o Pressure sores or ulcers

  - o Malnutrition or unexplained weight loss

  - o Untreated injuries and medical problems

  - o Inconsistent or reluctant contact with medical and social care organisations

  - o Accumulation of untaken medication

- o Uncharacteristic failure to engage in social interaction

- o Inappropriate or inadequate clothing

- **Self-neglect indicators**

  - o Very poor personal hygiene

  - o Unkempt appearance

  - o Lack of essential food, clothing or shelter

  - o Malnutrition and/or dehydration

  - o Living in squalid or unsanitary conditions

  - o Neglecting household maintenance

  - o Hoarding

  - o Collecting a large number of animals in inappropriate conditions

  - o Non-compliance with health or care services

  - o Inability or unwillingness to take medication or treat illness or injury

(SCIE, 2015a)

ACTIVITY **2.7**

Look back at the indicators of child abuse and compare them with the indicators for adult abuse. How similar are the indicators and are there any key differences?

COMMENT

Indicators of abuse at any life stage need to be approached with caution as they are only potential signs of more serious problems. Conversely, abuse or neglect can occur when there are no clear indicators present. There are some categories of abuse that are specifically applied to adults, such as discriminatory or financial abuse. This does not, however, mean that children do not suffer from these types of abuse, for instance, through misuse of child or disability benefits or mistreatment due to race, gender or disability. There are some clear differences in the categorisation of abuse and also some indicators of abuse that are specific to children or adults. There are, however, considerable similarities in terms of indicators. Indicators of physical abuse across the lifespan are highlighted in terms of frequency, or unexplained or unusual injuries. Sexual abuse can lead to inappropriate or changed behaviour, disturbed sleep patterns, withdrawal and physical injury whatever the age of the individual harmed. Emotional and psychological abuse again can cause withdrawal from social relationships and also anxiety, loss of confidence and loss of self-esteem. Indicators of neglect are lack of essentials such as food, appropriate clothing or heating, unclean environments, lack of attention to personal hygiene and lack of access to healthcare and treatment.

CHAPTER SUMMARY

Abuse is unacceptable and should always be challenged and addressed. It constitutes a violation of a person's human rights whether the person is 8 months or 80 years of age. Abusers can be:

- any age;
- male or female;
- from any social class;
- working in 'helping professions';
- apparent 'pillars of the community'.

Social workers and other health and care practitioners have a duty to protect people at risk across the lifespan. To do this effectively they need to be able to recognise and understand different types and indicators of abuse. Theories of causation of abuse can assist practitioners to understand and respond to abuse. Such theories need to be approached in terms of providing possible explanations as opposed to absolute answers and should be considered as part of a wider context which takes account of social and structural factors impacting on individuals and families. Some themes emerge in relation to types of abuse which are common to both children and adults across the lifespan, such as grooming, exploitation, abuse of power and the impact of wider societal factors. These will be considered further in subsequent chapters.

There are a number of behaviours which can increase the risk of abuse. The term 'toxic trio' has been used to describe the issues of domestic abuse, mental ill-health and substance misuse which have been identified as common features of families where there may be an increased risk of harm. The impact of these factors in relation to safeguarding children and adults in families will be explored further in Chapter 6. It is crucial that professionals develop a greater understanding of how information can be shared more effectively within and between agencies, to accurately identify the legal thresholds and to decide what constitutes the threshold for significant harm. Greater awareness of risk factors and the cumulative nature of risk for both adults and children is required to enable a better understanding of safeguarding across the lifespan. There are difficulties in establishing actual prevalence as opposed to 'reported/recorded' data on abuse as there is likely to be a significant difference between the two. The hidden nature of abuse in many contexts impacts on people at any life stage achieving protective measures and legal redress. The legal frameworks for safeguarding children and adults will be considered in Chapter 3.

FURTHER READING

Department of Health (2014) *Care and Support: Statutory Guidance Issued under the Care Act 2014.* London: Department of Health.

HM Government (2015) *Working Together to Safeguard Children: A Guide to Inter-agency Working to Safeguard and Promote the Welfare of Children.* London: Stationery Office. Available from: www.gov.uk/government/uploads/system/uploads/attachment_data/file/419595/Working_Together_to_Safeguard_Children.pdf

Local Government Association (LGA) (2013) *Adult Safeguarding and Domestic Abuse: A Guide to Support Practitioners and Managers.* London: Local Government Association.

Miller, D and Brown, J (2014) *'We have the Right to be Safe': Protecting Disabled Children from Abuse.* London: NSPCC.

Chapter 3

The policy and legal context for safeguarding practice

Introduction

The historical development of children's and adults' safeguarding has diverged both in the timing and the nature of changes, as discussed in Chapter 1. The legal framework for safeguarding provides the central context within which all work with people at risk is carried out. It also reflects the values and norms which support wider societal views about acceptable behaviour. There have been significant changes in the policy and legislation which underpin both children's and adults' safeguarding in recent years. These changes have occurred in the context of increased understanding of the impact of abuse and appropriate safeguarding responses. This chapter will consider the current legislative frameworks for children's and adults' safeguarding and some differences across the UK. It will also reflect on the impact of legal frameworks in terms of safeguarding individuals across the lifespan.

Safeguarding children and young people

Children have the right to be protected from all forms of violence; they must be kept safe from harm, and they must be given proper care by those looking after them.

(United Nations, 1989: Article 19)

This section will provide an overview of the main legal frameworks, policies and key principles which have been implemented to protect and safeguard the wellbeing of children and young people.

The Children Act 1989

The Children Act 1989 (CA 1989) is the primary piece of legislation in child care practice and it places the welfare of the child as the paramount concern of everyone who is involved in the care of children. However, to appreciate the significance of this piece of legislation it is important to consider the events which led up to its enactment.

There were numerous inquiries during the 1970s and 1980s into the deaths of children who were in the care and supervision of social services. In 1973 Maria Colwell died after being starved and beaten by her stepfather, despite the fact that there had been 50 visits to the family by social services. The inquiry into her death found that the greatest failure was the lack of communication and liaison between the agencies involved.

In 1984 Jasmine Beckford was starved and battered to death by her stepfather. She had been in the care of Brent social services for two and a half years before she died. In 1984 Tyra Henry died after being battered and bitten by her father. Lambeth Social services were involved with the family.

Also in 1984 Heidi Koseda was starved to death and the inquiry found that there had been a failure to investigate a complaint by a neighbour. In 1986 Kimberley Carlile, aged four, was starved and beaten to death. The inquiry found that four key social and health staff failed to apply necessary skill, judgement and care in her case.

In 1987 Doreen Mason died of neglect – she had been beaten and left to sleep on the floor. Doreen had been on the child protection at risk register. (For more information on these cases see www.theguardian.com/society/2003/jan/27/childrens services.childprotection)

The Cleveland Inquiry was also pivotal in relation to changes that were brought about within the child protection system. The inquiry was held in 1987 and highlighted concerns in relation to the overuse of statutory powers and to the appropriate balance between family autonomy and state intervention.

The CA 1989 came into force on 14 October 1991, making radical changes in the law relating to children and their families. Geoffrey Howe, former Home Secretary, described the Act as, *'The most comprehensive and far reaching reform of this branch of law ever introduced. It meets a long felt need for a comprehensive and integrated statutory framework to ensure the welfare of children'* (Hansard, 1989).

The Act aimed to provide a comprehensive framework for setting out the rights and responsibilities that should be afforded to children, bringing together a single legislative framework which encompasses both private and public law proceedings. Private law focuses on the resolution of disputes that can develop between parents or other family members in relation to the upbringing of a child. Public law, by contrast, concerns the relationship between the state and the individual, such as proceedings that are initiated by a local authority to safeguard a child. White et al. (2008) comment that the Children Act 1989 has *'a wide ambit covering both the private and public law relating to the care and upbringing of children and the provision of services to them and their families'*.

The Act represents a major piece of legislation for child care social workers, therefore it is essential to develop a comprehensive understanding of the Act especially in terms of how it impacts on social work practice. Social workers have a professional responsibility and legal mandate to identify and protect children who may be at risk of significant harm. Social workers are required to understand the legislation, guidance and local procedures, and keep records appropriately (HCPC Standard 10); whereas HCPC Standard 2.1 states that social workers must, *'Understand current legislation applicable to the work of their profession'*.

Welfare principles (Part 1)

The Act contains a number of welfare principles which a court should adhere to when making any decision in relation to the wellbeing of a child; Section 1(1) clearly establishes that the welfare of the child will always be the court's primary consideration. The Paramountcy Principle applies when a court is making a decision about a child's upbringing in both private and public law proceedings.

The No Delay Principle in s 1(2) aims to avoid long drawn-out court proceedings which are seen to be detrimental to the welfare of the child. The importance of avoiding delays within court proceedings has been reiterated by the Children and Families Act 2014, introducing a maximum 26-week time limit for completing care and supervision proceedings.

Section 1(3) of the CA 1989 introduces the welfare checklist, which provides a list of factors which the court should take into consideration when applying the welfare principles. According to s 1(3) (a) the court should consider the ascertainable wishes and views of the child when making any decision in relation to their welfare; however, the child's welfare will always be the court's paramount consideration.

Finally the Non Order Principle in s 1(5) stipulates that the court should only make an order if it considers that doing so would be better for the child than making no order at all.

Concept of parental responsibility

The Children Act 1989 introduced the concept of parental responsibility (PR) which is a central tenet throughout the Act. According to s 3(1) of the CA 1989, PR means, *'all the rights, duties, powers, responsibilities and authority which by law a parent of a child has in relation to the child and his property'* (www.legislation.gov.uk/ukpga/1989/41/section/3)

PR allows the parent to make decisions in a number of different areas of the child's life. One area in which they can exercise their PR is consenting to treatment on behalf of their child on the basis that the decision is in the child's best interests and for the purpose of safeguarding their welfare.

Private law proceedings (Part II)

Part II of the Children Act provides the framework for resolving disputes about a child's upbringing and the exercise of parental responsibility. It concerns the law applied in situations where the court is required to resolve a private dispute concerning children, and is largely related to cases that involve disputes between parents over the upbringing of their children.

Private law is based on the natural assumption that parents promote the welfare of their children, and therefore there is normally no need for the courts to intervene. The courts only become involved if there is a dispute and the parents cannot come to an agreement. Child arrangement orders were introduced into section 8 of the CA 1989 by the Children and Families Act 2014 and these allow the courts to decide where the child is to live, with whom, and who should have contact with the child. This order can be granted to more than one person whether they live together or not. If a child arrangement order states that the child will live with a person, that person will have parental responsibility for that child until the order ceases. All of these decisions are made according to the Paramountcy Principle and in the best interests of the child (www.legislation.gov.uk/ukpga/2014/6/schedule/2/enacted).

Although statutory social services do not automatically become involved in private law proceedings s 37 provides the court with powers to direct social services to investigate a child's circumstances if there may be concerns in relation to the welfare of the child.

Child in need and duty to promote welfare (Part III)

This part of the Act is focused on early intervention to provide support and assistance to families to prevent abuse or neglect and to reduce the need for care proceedings. The local authority (LA) has duties to assess and provide services to support children who are deemed to be in need.

Section 17(10) provides a definition of a child in need:

For the purposes of this Part a child shall be taken to be in need if—

(a) *He is unlikely to achieve or maintain, or to have the opportunity of achieving or maintaining, a reasonable standard of health or development without the provision for him of services by a local authority under this Part;*

(b) *His health or development is likely to be significantly impaired, or further impaired, without the provision for him of such services; or*

(c) *He is disabled.*

(www.legislation.gov.uk/ukpga/1989/41/section/17)

RESEARCH SUMMARY

The Family and Childcare Trust undertook research over a two-year period (2011–13) to assess the impact that the austerity cuts were having on families. Their report, Families in the Age of Austerity – the Impact of Revenue Spending Cuts on Children's Services, *has suggested that spending cuts have forced councils to refocus their resources and redefine their priorities towards more crisis intervention or specific programmes such as the Troubled Families Initiative. In 2012 the Early Intervention Grant was cut by £2.3 billion, with further warnings of a possible 20 per cent cut in the budget.*

An increase in the number of hours needed to claim Working Tax Credits from 16 to 24 hours will affect 205,000 families with children who currently work fewer than 24 hours per week. If they are unable to increase their hours in response to this change, they stand to lose £3,810 pa of tax credit entitlement. The freeze in the rates of Working Tax Credit . . . will affect 1.9 million families who will lose £210 pa by 2012/13 as a consequence. The reduction in the childcare element of the tax credit will take £381 million of support from the system, affecting 489,000 families.

(Family and Childcare Trust, 2013)

Since the election of the Conservative Party into government in May 2015 the issue of austerity and welfare reform has gathered more political momentum. The government has proposed further cuts of £4.4 billion to the tax credits system; however, on 26 October the House of Lords voted to delay the government's proposed plans until there was an analysis of the impact of the cuts (BBC News, 2015d).

ACTIVITY 3.1

Consider what impact the current climate of austerity and welfare cuts could have on the availability of preventative services. What impact could the policies of austerity have on effective social work practice?

Children suffering or at risk of significant harm – duty to investigate and significant harm (Parts IV and V)

Parts IV and V of the Act provide the legal framework for the protection of children and the legal mandate to intervene to protect a child at risk of significant harm.

Section 47 – duty to investigate

Section 47 places a duty on the local authority to investigate the circumstances where a child appears to be suffering significant harm, or is believed to be at risk of significant harm. The LA makes enquiries to establish whether action should be taken to safeguard or promote the child's welfare. Section 47 enquiries enable an LA to decide whether action should be taken to safeguard or promote the welfare of the child. Section 47(1) of the Children Act 1989 states that:

> *Where a local authority:*
>
> *(a) are informed that a child who lives, or is found, in their area (i) is the subject of an emergency protection order, or (ii) is in police protection; and*
>
> *(b) have reasonable cause to suspect that a child who lives, or is found, in their area is suffering, or is likely to suffer, significant harm,*
>
> *the authority shall make, or cause to be made, such enquires as they consider necessary to enable them to decide whether they should take any action to safeguard and promote the child's welfare.*
>
> (www.legislation.gov.uk/ukpga/1989/41/section/47)

Significant harm

The Children Act 1989 does not use the term 'child abuse'. It uses the words 'significant harm'. The court can legally intervene in order to protect a child only if the child is suffering from or likely to suffer significant harm. 'Significant harm' is the threshold which justifies compulsory intervention (Brammer, 2014: 253)

The CA 1989 introduced the concept of significant harm, which has become synonymous with the concept of child abuse – physical, emotional, sexual or neglect. Whilst the term 'significant harm' has never been given a detailed definition, it sets out the criteria by which local authorities and courts measure whether protective procedures need to be initiated and whether application should be made for specific court orders.

Section 31(2) of the Children Act 1989 defines harm as ill treatment or the impairment of health or development (where health means physical and mental health and development means physical, emotional, social, intellectual or behavioural development). The concept of harm was strengthened by the Adoption and Children Act 2002 when it amended the statutory definition of harm to recognise the harm that children can experience when living in households where domestic violence occurs. Section 31(9) of the CA 1989 now stipulates that hearing or seeing the ill treatment of others and witnessing violence can also constitute harm (Brayne and Carr, 2013).

This amendment is significant because it finally recognises the impact that domestic abuse can have on a child's health and development, a subject which will be explored further in Chapter 5.

In all public care proceedings the local authority must provide evidence that the harm is of a degree of severity high enough to meet the threshold criterion of significant harm. This can be done in different ways (for example comparing the current development of a child with the expected level of development typically displayed by other children of a similar age), but is left to the professional judgement of the assessing social worker, typically working within thresholds defined by their employing local authority.

ACTIVITY **3.2**

Try to identify what difficulties might occur in relation to defining what constitutes signifi-cant harm.

COMMENT

Although the phrase was intended to be broad and flexible enough to incorporate a wide range of circumstances, legislation and statutory guidance do not define the line between harm and significant harm (Humphreys and Stanley, 2015).

This lack of consistency in relation to the interpretation of significant harm can be further exacerbated by differing professional judgements as to what actually constitutes 'significant harm'.

ACTIVITY **3.3**

Significant harm and risk

Consider the following scenarios and decide which cases represent the highest level of risk. How would you prioritise the cases, and on what basis would you decide whether the children were at risk of significant harm? What action might need to be taken to protect the child in each case?

1. *Joanne is a 15 year old who has been drinking (in bingeing sessions) since the age of 12. She has been part of a crowd of youngsters who take drugs and drink regularly. Her family have been unable to manage this behaviour and have effectively lost control. She often comes home alone in a terrible state, not really knowing what she has been up to. Joanne is now five months pregnant, but has not changed her lifestyle. Last night she came home with scratches and bruises, drunk, and without any knowledge of where she had been or what she had been doing.*

2. *Jamie is aged 8 months. This morning his father was looking after him while his mother was at work. The father got so frustrated with Jamie's constant crying that he took Jamie out of his pram and shook him until he stopped crying.*

(Continued)

57

3. *Dawn lives with Peter. They met in a club some months ago. They are both regular clubbers, and admit to using drugs recreationally along with their drink. Dawn has two children, aged 7 and 3. Recently Dawn has been appearing at her mother's with bruises on her arms and back, complaining of pain. She says she has been arguing with Peter, upsetting him over silly things, and he has lost his temper. She says it is her fault. The 7 year old has told his nana that Peter hits his mam and that he tries to stop him, but gets shouted at. He and his sister hear the arguments and are frightened their mam will get hurt.*

4. *John and Sarah are 9 and 10 years old and they attend a local primary school. For the last two weeks their appearance has been deteriorating. They look unkempt and poorly dressed and appear hungry. Today they also look unwashed and as though they have been up half the night. They are close to tears and are loath to say what is happening.*

5. *Rachel is aged 18 months. She is regularly left alone whilst her mother goes to the pub. Rachel wakes up at night crying and calling for her mother.*

COMMENT

All of the children in the scenarios could be said to be at risk of significant harm.

1. *Joanne's behaviour is placing herself at risk of physical harm; she is also at risk because her behaviour is outwith parental control. If Joanne continued to participate in risk-taking behaviours a strategy meeting would be convened to assess how best to protect Joanne. SCRs have highlighted that 25 per cent of reviews concerned young people who took part in a range of risk-taking behaviours, making them more vulnerable to risk (Brandon et al., 2010). If there are concerns that an unborn child may be at future risk of significant harm, it may be decided to convene a pre-birth initial child protection conference. Child protection plans can be made after the 24th week of gestation, to secure the safety and wellbeing of the unborn child.*

2. *Jamie is at immediate risk of significant physical harm. The higher the level of risk the increased likelihood of more compulsory intervention; it is important to remember that shaken baby syndrome can lead to a serious brain injury or death. Jamie's age and vulnerability are critical factors to take into consideration; approximately half of all serious case reviews are undertaken in relation to babies who are under one year of age.*

3. *Both of Dawn's children are at risk of physical and emotional harm. SCRs have consistently highlighted the negative impact that domestic violence, substance misuse and mental health problems can have on the prevalence of abuse and neglect (Brandon et al., 2010).*

4. *John and Sarah may be at risk of harm due to the recent deterioration in their physical and emotional presentation.*

(Continued)

COMMENT *continued*

5. Rachel is at risk of physical, emotional harm and neglect. Age is a critical factor which increases her vulnerability to abuse and neglect.

Within the safeguarding arena there is a critical need for effective multi-agency working between different professionals and between children's and adult services. The challenge is ensuring people who come into contact with children and families are able to appropriately recognise the potential harm and report it (Corby et al., 2012).

Short-term protection of children

There are provisions in the Act for the courts to deal with situations in which children are, or may be, at risk of significant harm, and it will be possible for social services to seek, through the courts, orders for assessment and protection. These are compulsory measures of care which are ordered by the court, and include:

- Child Assessment Orders (s 43);

- Emergency Protection Orders (s 44);

- police protection (s 46).

Child Assessment Orders (s 43)

Before a local authority makes an application for a Child Assessment Order (CAO) they must demonstrate in evidence that they have *'reasonable cause to suspect that the child is or is likely to suffer significant harm'* and that an assessment of the child's health and development is required. If an application is successful the court will grant this order for a period of seven working days to allow the relevant assessments to be carried out. During this time if access to the child is restricted or denied the local authority may have grounds to apply for an Emergency Protection Order (EPO) which will be used to provide the child with immediate protection.

Emergency Protection Orders (s 44)

In accordance with s 44(1) an EPO can be sought in an emergency situation, to protect a child who is likely to suffer significant harm. A local authority applying for an EPO must demonstrate in evidence that they have *'reasonable cause to believe that the child is likely to suffer significant harm'.''*

An EPO would be used in a situation where it is necessary to urgently remove a child from the home, or when it is necessary to ensure that a child remains at the place where he/she is accommodated, such as a foster placement. If a child requires hospital treatment an EPO can be used to ensure that the child stays in hospital and receives appropriate medical treatment.

An EPO may also be sought in a situation where enquiries are being made, with respect to the child, under section 47 of the Children Act 1989, and where these enquiries are being frustrated.

An EPO can also be sought in a circumstance where the applicant believes that access to the child is required as a matter of urgency but is nevertheless refused this access.

The order lasts for eight days, but can be extended to 15 days. There is also an exclusion requirement to an EPO in which an alleged perpetrator can be excluded from the home, which avoids the trauma of the child being removed from home (s 44A, inserted by the Family Law Act 1996).

An EPO does not give power to:

- stop parental contact
- arrange medical examinations
- enter premises to look for a child.

It should be noted that an EPO does not take away PR from parents but does allow PR to be shared with the local authority, providing it with powers to protect the child.

If you are refused access to premises or the child the court can issue a warrant for police assistance.

Police protection s 46

Section 46 provides police with powers to remove a child into police protection, as a matter of urgency and without any application to court. This action is short term and can only last up to 72 hours. The police must also inform the local authority. This action is taken in genuine emergencies and does not provide the local authority with parental responsibility (www.legislation.gov.uk/ukpga/1989/41/section/46).

Longer-term protection, care and supervision

If it is deemed that parents are unable or unwilling to make the improvements required of them under the child protection plan the LA might apply to the courts for an interim care order (ICO) s 38 or a care order s 33. An ICO is a temporary arrangement, made when the court is satisfied that a child should be kept in care on a temporary basis, while decisions are being made about the child's future. ICOs are granted to allow time to establish whether there are grounds for applying for a care order (see www.opsi.gov.uk/acts/acts1989/Ukpga_19890041_en_1.htm).

Under s 31 of the Children Act 1989 the LA may apply to the court for a care order (s 33) or supervision order (s 35). A care order is a long-term option, and is sought in order to protect children and young people. The LA must demonstrate in evidence that '*the child is suffering or likely to suffer significant harm and this is attributable to the care given to the child, or the child is beyond parental control*'. If a care order is granted the LA acquires shared parental responsibility with the child's parents; however, it is the LA that determines where the child lives. A supervision order allows the child to remain at home subject to a period of supervision and support; the LA does not acquire parental responsibility.

If a court grants a care order the local authority has a number of duties in relation to looked after children and young people to:

- safeguard their welfare;

- promote contact;

- consult the child and others;

- provide suitable accommodation for children with disabilities;

- consider, race culture, language, religion and linguistic background;

- place a child with family or friend, if possible.

A supervision order does not give the LA parental responsibility for the child and allows the child to remain at home subject to a period of supervision and support.

The Children and Families Act 2014 has implemented changes to the application of care proceedings, such as the introduction of a 26-week timetable, beginning with the day on which the application was issued. The timetable can be extended but only if this is necessary to enable the court to resolve the proceedings justly. The court must always consider the impact on the child.

Each extension can last no longer than eight weeks, which effectively removes the eight-week time limit on the duration of initial interim care orders and interim super-vision orders, allowing the court to make interim orders for the length of time that is deemed appropriate. One of the key aims of the Act is to speed up the adoption pro-cess. However, as Natasha Finlayson, chief executive of the Who Cares? Trust, comments:

> *Although the reforms to the adoption system were long overdue, when Michael Gove first came into office his belief in a hierarchy of care that placed adoption at the top and residential care at the bottom was transparent and unhelpful. The effects of this belief on national policy seem to have diminished to some extent with important policy gains being made for children in foster care and renewed attention given to reforms in residential care after the Rochdale scandal.*

(Stevenson, 2014)

ACTIVITY 3.4

Consider the implications and impact of these new statutory guidelines on social work practice within the current climate of austerity and cuts to welfare.

Children Act 2004

The Laming Report (2003) made a number of recommendations following the death of Victoria Climbié; the report was particularly critical about the failures in the child protection system and the lack of multi-agency awareness of the process. During the inquiry, Neil Garnham QC suggested that there were at least 12 separate occasions where different agencies could have successfully intervened in Victoria's life.

As a result Lord Laming highlighted in his report consistent issues such as system failures and 'widespread organisational malaise':

> *We cannot operate a system where the safety and wellbeing of children depends upon the personal inclinations or ability or interests of individual staff. It is the organisations which must accept accountability.*

(Laming, 2003: 36)

The outcome of the Laming Report reiterated the policy shift towards a refocusing of services away from intervention to prevention within an overall framework of collaborative and multi-agency working (www.gov.uk/government/publications/the-victoria-climbie-inquiry-report-of-an-inquiry-by-lord-laming)

The Children Act 2004 introduced a statutory framework which established the new procedural changes to support the integration of children's services; the principal purpose being to safeguard and promote the wellbeing of children (Brayne and Carr, 2013). The Children Act 2004 also places a legal duty on local authorities to ensure cooperation and appropriate information sharing with relevant partner agencies (s 10), and to set up a Local Safeguarding Children Board (LSCB) with specific responsibilities (s 13, s 14).

Following the enactment of the CA 2004, safeguarding procedures were set out in the *Working Together* guidance (HM Government, 2006). This guidance clearly highlighted the importance of effective multi-agency collaboration. The documentation specified that everyone who came into contact with children and families, including practitioners who do not have a specific role in relation to child protection, had a duty to safeguard and promote the welfare of children; protection was to become a shared responsibility. This guidance has subsequently been amended in 2010, 2013 and more recently in 2015.

Working Together to Safeguard Children 2013 and the single assessment process

The *Working Together* guidance was amended in 2013 (HM Government, 2013) and introduced a more streamlined approach to safeguarding. It aimed to clarify inter-agency roles and responsibilities in relation to the safeguarding process, together with the adoption of a more child-centred approach. The guidance has replaced *Working Together* 2010 and the *Framework for Assessment of Children in Need and their Families* 2000. The key aims highlighted within the guidance include the following.

- The child's needs are paramount, and should be at the heart of the safeguarding system.

- Children are best protected when professionals are clear about what is expected of them.

- All professionals who come into contact with children and families should be alert to their needs and any risks of harm that individual abusers, or potential abusers, may pose to children.

- All professionals should share appropriate information in a timely way.

- All professionals should contribute to whatever actions are needed to safeguard and promote a child's welfare.

The single assessment process

The guidance confirms that significant harm should be the threshold for compulsory intervention into a family's life. When a referral is received by local authority children's social care, the social worker and their manager must decide on the next course of action within one working day. If action is required, a social worker will lead a multi-agency assessment under s 17 CA 1989. If professionals agree that a child is in need, then a Child in Need plan can be implemented to provide appropriate services to meet the child's needs. However, if there are immediate concerns for the child's safety, emergency safeguarding action will be undertaken, legal advice sought and if appropriate an application for an Emergency Protection Order will be made. If there are no immediate concerns, but a social worker assesses that a child is at risk of or has suffered significant harm, then the local authority should hold a multi-agency strategy meeting to decide if investigations should commence under s 47 CA 1989. If an s 47 investigation indicates that significant harm has occurred, then a social work manager must convene a child protection conference within 15 days of the initial strategy discussion. A core assessment must be completed within 45 days of receiving the initial referral; however, all agencies must act on whatever timescale is appropriate to ensure a child's safety.

Working Together: A Guide to Inter-agency Working to Safeguard and Promote the Welfare of Children

The introduction of *Working Together* 2013 received criticism in a number of areas. Dr Liz Davies of London Metropolitan University asks whether the complexities of multi-agency responses to child protection can in fact be represented effectively by the use of flowcharts. Also there is a limited focus on the impact of abuse of children with a disability, children from black and ethnic minority communities and children/young people who experience more complex forms of abuse (BASW England, 2015).

Working Together 2015 was introduced in March 2015 and has replaced all previous editions. It confirms the significance of early intervention, timeliness and systematic assessment. The updated guidance has introduced a number of amendments which stipulate that local safeguarding boards must commission services for children who have been or may be: sexually exploited, radicalised or subject to female genital mutilation. Assessments that are undertaken in relation to the needs of young carers must take account of whether the role is 'inappropriate' or 'excessive'.

In cases where there are concerns that an adult who works with children has acted in a harmful manner a designated officer will investigate these concerns; this role will be undertaken by a qualified social worker. Other changes include notifiable incidents involving the care of a child. A notifiable incident is an incident involving the care of a child which meets any of the following criteria:

- *a child has died (including cases of suspected suicide), and abuse or neglect is known or suspected;*

- *a child has been seriously harmed and abuse or neglect is known or suspected;*

- *a looked after child has died (including cases where abuse or neglect is not known or suspected); or*

- *a child in a regulated setting or service has died (including cases where abuse or neglect is not known or suspected).*

(HM Government, 2015a)

Working Together 2015 further states that *'if an incident meets the criteria for a Serious Case Review then it will also meet the criteria for a notifiable incident'*.

The definition of serious harm for the purposes of serious case reviews and child death reviews has also been clarified and now includes cases where the child has sustained, as a result of abuse or neglect, any or all of the following:

- *a potentially life-threatening injury;*

- *serious and/or likely long-term impairment of physical or mental health or physical, intellectual, emotional, social or behavioural development.*

(HM Government, 2015a)

ACTIVITY 3.5

Review Working Together 2015 and highlight the main changes that have been made to the content and format of the guidance. Do you think that the criticisms that were made previously have been addressed sufficiently within the 2015 guidance?

Knowledge of the relevant legislative frameworks is essential to inform effective practice. However, what other knowledge and skills do you feel that you would need to incorporate into your professional practice?

The Scottish legal context: safeguarding children

The Children (Scotland) Act 1995 is the main piece of legislation in relation to children, bringing together aspects of family, children's and adoption law. The Act introduced specific rights and responsibilities towards children and outlined the duties and powers that the local authority has in relation to children. There are three main principles which underpin the Act.

- The welfare of the child should be paramount.

- No order should be made unless it is essential to do so.

- Children should be given the opportunity to express their views in relation to matters that affect them.

There are a number of similarities between the Children Act 1989 and the Children (Scotland) Act 1995, especially in relation to support for children in need and the provision of emergency protection. The main differences relate to the application of compulsory measures of care and the treatment of young people who are involved in the juvenile justice system. In England and Wales the local authority makes an application to the court for care and supervision orders; however, in Scotland the court has a more limited input – the court will initially agree the grounds of referral but then refer the case to the Children's Hearings System. Similarly, the majority of juvenile justice cases are referred to and dealt with by the Hearings System. This system is unique and aims to provide a structure which promotes the safety and wellbeing of young people. Decisions are made by a lay panel with a clear emphasis on the welfare needs of young people. Most of the legal provisions governing the Children's Hearings System are now contained within the Children's Hearings (Scotland) Act 2011.

The Criminal Justice (Scotland) Act 2003 amended the law in Scotland and made it illegal for parents to hit their child on the head or with an implement, or to shake their child.

The most recent piece of legislation to be enacted is the Children and Young People Act 2014.The main purpose of the Act is to safeguard and promote the wellbeing of children but it has also incorporated some specific guidance which is set out in *Getting it Right for Every Child* (GIRFEC) (Scottish Government, 2015) which places a duty on different agencies to recognise the needs of children and young people to ensure that all children have the opportunity to access the appropriate support, at times when they need it:

> *We all have a role to play in making this happen – as families, as communities, as a society. We want to ensure that services are designed and available to children and families to give them the support they need in the right way, at the right time.*

(Aileen Campbell, Minister for Children and Young People, www.gov.scot/Topics/People/Young-People/gettingitright)

The Act proposes that a lead professional should be appointed to coordinate a multi-agency responsibility in relation to the needs of a child. The *National Guidance for Child Protection* was also amended in 2014 and includes practice information into key issues such as child sexual exploitation (for more information, see www.legislation.gov.uk/asp/2014/8/contents/enacted).

ACTIVITY **3.6**

Consider the similarities in relation to the two legislative frameworks. Which, in your view, has a greater emphasis on welfare, especially in relation to the treatment of looked after children and children who are involved in the youth justice system?

Adult safeguarding policy and legislation

There are substantial differences between the legislative framework for children's and adults' safeguarding. One of the most significant factors is that up until the present time there have been no laws which specifically address adult safeguarding, and practice has been organised around policy guidance. As discussed in Chapter 1, adult abuse has not attained the same levels of awareness within society as has child abuse, and developments in policy have been considerably behind those for children. It is only with the introduction of the Care Act 2014 that safeguarding adults' protocol has been enshrined in legislation in England and Wales. This is different from the Scottish context, where safeguarding legislation was introduced through the Adult Support and Protection (Scotland) Act 2007 (ASP).

There are extensive aspects of legislation and policy which apply broadly to safeguarding adults. Legislation and policy which focuses on supporting adults has a significant role in preventing initial or further abuse and clearly prevention is a central aspect of safeguarding. The legal framework for support and prevention has been complex and confusing over many decades and has been largely replaced by the Care Act 2014. Alongside the role of legislation to support adults, criminal law has a central role in providing protection and redress for adults who are abused. The *No Secrets* guidance emphasised the necessity for adults at risk to gain legal redress in the same way as other members of the public. In relation to each category of abuse, a range of criminal offences may apply. So, for instance, in relation to sexual abuse, the Sexual Offences Act 2003 provides a general framework and also highlights specific offences, such as sexual activity with a person with a mental disorder impeding choice, and sexual abuse occurring in violation of the special relationship that a care worker has. In relation to physical abuse, the Domestic Violence, Crime and Victims Act 2004 provides a legislative context and also introduced the offence of '*causing or allowing the death of a child or vulnerable adult*'. This was extended by the 2012 amendment to the Act to include serious harm of these groups of people (Brammer, 2014). It has been suggested that practitioners remain unaware of and under-use relevant legislation in adult safeguarding (ADASS and LGA, 2013). A comprehensive range of legal applications to adult safeguarding is provided at: www.scie.org.uk/publications/reports/report50.pdf

The Human Rights Act

The Human Rights Act 1998 (HRA) was implemented in 2000 and incorporated the protection of rights into domestic law, which had previously been only available through the European Court of Human Rights. It is one aspect of legislation relevant to both children's and adults' safeguarding. The application of all other legislation in social work should be compatible with the HRA and it therefore provides a backdrop to all practice. There are significant exceptions to this, such as where the authority is acting under primary legislation. An example would be an approved mental health professional (AMHP) carrying out a compulsory admission to a psychiatric unit which is a deprivation of liberty but one which is allowed under the Mental Health Act 1983 (as amended by the Mental Health Act 2007). The HRA applies to public authorities and there were significant gaps in the protection of human rights of people in private care homes until the Health and Social Care Act 2008 was implemented. Section 145 of the Act asserts that where someone is placed in a private care home under statutory provision the home is seen to exercise a public function and must comply with the HRA (Scragg and Mantell, 2011). For people without capacity the HRA would be considered alongside best interest decision making (see Mental Capacity Act 2005).

Guidance and policy

The *No Secrets* guidance (Department of Health, 2000) and *In Safe Hands* (National Assembly for Wales, 2000) have provided the principal direction for adult safeguarding since their implementation in 2000. Issued under section 7 of the Local Authority Social Services Act 1970, there has been a clear expectation that local authorities would adhere closely to such guidance and only deviate from it when there is considerable justification to do so (Brammer, 2014). It has been used widely by local authorities and independent organisations in developing safeguarding adults policies and procedures. *No Secrets* confirms the role of the local authority as the lead agency in responding to adult abuse but also highlights the need for effective inter-agency working at all levels. Key principles that were promoted in *No Secrets* include: the rights of the individual to make choices; empowerment; and the recognition that achieving these can involve risk.

While *No Secrets* set out information for agencies with 'responsibility' to investigate adult abuse, this does not carry the same level of enforcement as, for instance, the 'duty' to investigate suspicions of significant harm to children under the Children Act 1989. This has been a much criticised deficiency in adult safeguarding frameworks and one which is addressed by the Care Act 2014 which repeals *No Secrets* (Brammer, 2014). During consultation around a review of *No Secrets* (Department of Health, 2009) the limitations of policy guidance as opposed to legislation were further highlighted. The review updated the original *No Secrets* guidance to take account of personalisation and also, in line with the Mental Capacity Act 2005, the importance of involving people who lack capacity in safeguarding.

A national framework of standards of good practice in safeguarding adults was introduced in 2005 (ADSS, 2005) and this further emphasises the idea of service users as key partners in safeguarding. It also signified a move in terminology from 'protection of vulnerable adults' to 'safeguarding adults at critical and substantial levels of risk'. Further emphasis is placed on establishing accountable multi-agency partnerships and raising the profile of 'zero tolerance' to adult abuse and access to training, information and support. The *Safeguarding Adults* framework also sets out specific stages in the process of responding to abuse which have been adopted and interpreted in local authorities.

The coalition government produced a *Statement of Government Policy on Adult Safeguarding* (Department of Health, 2011) which asserted a commitment to placing Safeguarding Adults Boards on a statutory footing. The statement also set out key principles for safeguarding as: empowerment; protection; prevention; proportionality; partnership; and accountability. *Advice and Guidance to Directors of Adult Social*

Services (ADASS and LGA, 2013) has also been issued with a focus on people and the outcomes they want. The guidance also stresses the importance of responsive specialist services to support people with difficult decision making and addressing concerns proportionately.

Alongside government policy and guidance ADASS and LGA have introduced the *Making Safeguarding Personal* (MSP) (Lawson et al., 2014) initiative which aims to develop an outcomes focus to safeguarding work, and a range of responses to support people to improve or resolve their circumstances. A central focus of MSP is asking people about the outcomes they want at the beginning and middle of working with them, and then ascertaining the extent to which those outcomes were realised at the end. It is a significant initiative which represents a shift in culture and practice in response to what is known about what makes safeguarding effective from research involving people who have been the recipients of safeguarding interventions. MSP research has shown that previous practice has been highly focused on process and this has often meant that the service user and the outcomes they want become 'lost'. The initiative has directly involved various local authorities in pilot projects and provided toolkits and a range of other resources to support agencies to achieve person-centred safeguarding.

RESEARCH SUMMARY

MSP

In 2013–14, 43 councils agreed to take part in work to develop MSP policies. The types of changes implemented in the councils varied. Some enabled people needing safeguarding to be better informed about the safeguarding process and to identify what outcomes they wanted. Others enabled people to identify what outcomes they wanted and to influence the process that was followed by professionals. Some of the councils enabled people to negotiate both the outcomes they wanted and the process that would then follow. All 43 councils stated that there were real benefits for people using safeguarding services as well as better social work practice. Most participating councils said that introducing person-centred, outcome-focused practice to safeguarding requires a cultural change that needs to be seen in the context of social work practice as a whole. The majority of councils identified impacts on workload often in the initial stages of working with people but also reported opportunities to release time and resources at other stages of the process.

The central benefits of Making Safeguarding Personal *which were recognised by all 43 councils were that people felt more empowered and in control of their safeguarding experience when they and/or their representative were involved from the start. Benefits to social work practice were also identified including social workers feeling more positive, motivated and enthusiastic. The ability to assess effectiveness from the perspective of people who use services and utilise tools to support practice was identified as creating improved practice. Councils also noted that clearer, more transparent plans and recording were in place along with more clearly defined endings to safeguarding support (Lawson et al., 2014).*

Mental capacity and safeguarding

It is clear that any safeguarding action should usually be taken in consultation with the adults concerned, and that it should be taken in a manner that does not usurp their own choices or decision-making. It is also important that decisions made at any one time are not taken to be irrevocable and non-negotiable. Action must ensure that when adults with mental capacity take decisions to remain in abusive situations, they do so without intimidation, with an understanding of the risks involved and have access to appropriate services if they should they change their mind.

(ADSS, 2005: 21)

The Mental Capacity Act 2005 (MCA) has been a very significant legislative development in relation to safeguarding. It not only provides a framework for best interest decision making when someone is unable to make a decision but also supports individuals with capacity and their right to make unwise decisions. Section 44 of the MCA introduces a new offence of ill-treatment or neglect of a person who lacks capacity. The MCA offers a legal redress to earlier prevalent attitudes of paternalism towards adults with care and support needs. Such attitudes often assumed that opinions and preferences which fell beyond what was deemed appropriate by carers, families or support services should be overruled (Scope, 2009)

There are five key underpinning principles of the MCA.

1. **A presumption of capacity**

   Every adult has the right to make his or her own decisions and must be assumed to have capacity to do so unless it is proved otherwise.

2. **Individuals being supported to make their own decisions**

   A person must be given all practicable help before anyone treats them as not being able to make their own decisions.

3. **Unwise decisions**

   People have the right to make what others might regard as an unwise or eccentric decision.

4. **Best interests**

   If a person has been assessed as lacking capacity then any action taken, or any decision made for, or on behalf of that person, must be made in his or her best interests.

5. **Less restrictive option**

   Someone making a decision or acting on behalf of a person who lacks capacity must consider a course of action which least interferes with the person's rights and freedoms. Any intervention should be proportional to the particular circumstances of the case.

(www.scie.org.uk/publications/mca/principles.asp)

The process of establishing if a person can make a decision should consider if the individual has all the information needed to make the decision, such as the range of possible alternatives. The act also stresses that the communication needs of the individual must be taken into account and information presented in a way that is easier for them to understand. Family, friends and carers should be involved to support individuals and records should clearly explain how the conclusion was reached that capacity is lacking for the particular decision.

ACTIVITY 3.7

Consider the range of techniques that could be used by practitioners to support individuals at risk with decision making.

One of the most important factors about assessing capacity is that it must be time and decision specific. The test to assess capacity is a two-stage functional test. To decide whether an individual has the capacity to make a particular decision two questions must be answered.

Stage 1. Is there an impairment of, or disturbance in the functioning of a person's mind or brain? If so,

Stage 2. Is the impairment or disturbance sufficient that the person lacks the capacity to make a particular decision?

The MCA says that a person is unable to make their own decision if they cannot do one or more of the following four things.

* Understand information given to them.

* Retain that information long enough to be able to make the decision.

* Weigh up the information available to make the decision.

* Communicate their decision – this could be by talking, using sign language or even simple muscle movements such as blinking an eye or squeezing a hand.

The time and decision specific nature of capacity assessments is highly significant and acknowledges that many individuals will have fluctuating capacity. It also provides an opportunity for capacity building in decision making through providing the right information in the appropriate way and developing knowledge and skills of the individual to support them to make their own decisions.

Where someone is judged not to have capacity, professionals are authorised by the MCA to act in the 'best interests' of the person. Acting in what is considered to be the person's best interests has sometimes been a substitute for trying to establish a person's views and involve them in the process. Friends, relatives or carers of an individual do not have legal power to make decisions for an individual unless the individual has made provision for this in advance, for instance through an advance directive or an Enduring Power of Attorney. The best interest principle provides a framework for considering the needs, wants and rights of the individual impartially. The individual should still be involved as fully as possible in decision making, including past and present wishes, beliefs and values. Family, friends and carers should be consulted as widely as possible in coming to a best interest decision.

The MCA also provides an outline of good practice in relation to the use of an Independent Mental Capacity Advocate (IMCA). In situations where a person lacks capacity, it is good practice to involve an advocate to represent their interests. This is particularly so when adult safeguarding measures are being considered or taken and is enshrined in legislation through the Care Act.

ACTIVITY 3.8

Consider the range of techniques that could be used by practitioners to involve individuals as fully as possible in best interest decision making.

Deprivation of Liberty Safeguards (DoLS) were introduced through the Mental Health Act 2007 and aim to ensure that people in care homes and hospitals are looked after in a way that does not inappropriately restrict their freedom. The safeguards should make sure that a care home or hospital only deprives someone of their liberty in a safe and correct way, and that this is only done when it is in the best interests of the person and there is no other way to look after them. DoLS apply to vulnerable adults who have a mental health condition (including dementia), who are in hospitals and care homes, and who do not have the mental capacity to make decisions about their care or treatment. Deprivation of liberty depends on the individual circumstances of each and every case and is ultimately a matter for the courts to determine the law. Test cases in the European Court of Human Rights and in the UK have clarified which situations *may* constitute a deprivation of liberty, such as: an individual being restrained in order to admit them to hospital; medication being given against a person's will; staff having complete control over a patient's care or movements for a long period; and staff making all decisions about a patient, including choices about assessments, treatment and visitors (see www.alzheimers.org.uk).

Court judgments in 2014 have had very significant implications for practice. *The Supreme Court Judgement in P v Cheshire West Council and P & Q v Surrey County Council* clarifies the meaning of 'deprivation of liberty' in the context of social care and has both practical and legal implications. Two key tests of deprivation identified were whether the person is subject to continuous supervision and control and whether the person is free to leave. The focus is not on the person's ability to express a desire to leave, but on what those with control over care arrangements would do if the individual sought to leave. This has caused local authorities and other organisations to review arrangements in place for large numbers of individuals who were thought not to be deprived of their liberty because they were not objecting to their care arrangements. The MCA also introduced the Court of Protection (CoP), whose powers include making declarations about whether a person lacks capacity or whether an act is lawful, and making a decision on a person's behalf. The CoP can also appoint a deputy to make decisions on a person's behalf.

Research into the impact of the MCA suggests that there has been a divide between policy and practice with some care professionals taking decisions about vulnerable adults without properly assessing capacity or consulting them – in breach of the Mental Capacity Act's principles (Samuel, 2013). Strong support for the MCA has been identified among practitioners as a source of empowerment for adults at risk, a support to person-centred practice and an asset for safeguarding work (Manthorpe et al., 2013). The House of Lords Select Committee on the MCA (2014) suggested that the empowering ethos of MCA has not been widely implemented with capacity not always assumed and capacity testing not carried out sufficiently. It suggests that the concept of unwise decision making is obstructed by *'prevailing cultures of risk-aversion and paternalism'* (Department of Health, 2014: 8) and that the presumption of capacity is misused to support non-intervention. The Select Committee recommendations suggest that overall responsibility for implementation of the Mental Capacity Act should be given to a single independent body alongside a range of steps to raise the profile of the MCA, including being incorporated into Care Quality Commission (CQC) inspection procedures. It also suggests that DoLS legislation is not adequately written and should be reviewed and replaced with provisions more compatible in ethos with the rest of the MCA. This will be discussed further in Chapter 6.

An unwise decision or a decision taken under duress?

Assessing capacity can be particularly challenging in domestic abuse situations, where the person is cared for by, or lives with a family member or intimate partner and is seen to be making decisions which place them in danger. Skilled assessment and intervention is required to judge whether such decisions should be described as 'unwise decisions' which the person has capacity to make, or decisions not made freely, due to coercion and control, and therefore part of the abuse. If, for example, authorities decide on limited information and time spent with someone that the person has made an unwise decision for which they have capacity, the victim may then not be offered options which would enable them to disclose coercion and be safe. It is important to remember that judgements about capacity must be decision specific; for instance someone may have capacity to make one decision and execute it, but not another. Judgements should also take account of fluctuating capacity (LGA, 2013).

This area of practice is often one of the most complex issues to consider when working in the field of safeguarding adults experiencing domestic abuse. Recent case law has clarified that there is scope for councils (using the principle of inherent jurisdiction) to commence proceedings in the High Court to safeguard people who do not lack capacity but whose ability to make decisions has been compromised because of constraints in their circumstances, coercion or undue influence (see www.bailii.org). The Care Act aims to resolve previous ambiguity around domestic violence and safeguarding by including domestic violence as an additional type of abuse applicable to safeguarding.

The Care Act 2014

The Care Act restructures the way in which adult social care and support is provided and financed in England and repeals much of the wider legislation previously used in assessing and providing services for adults. The act focuses on the principles of well-being, independence, prevention, choice and control. It is potentially creating increased expectations for entitlement to assessment of need at a time when actual spending on adult social care has fallen significantly (see sticerd.lse.ac.uk) and there has been wider discussion around the political motivations behind certain aspects of the legislation.

Safeguarding has to date remained a non-statutory policy directive, discharged through assertive use of community care legal provisions (such as assessment and care planning), referrals between agencies and the use of lawful information sharing. The framework of public law, along with the Mental Capacity Act 2005 and Human Rights Act 1998, has formed the legal underpinning to adult safeguarding (Schwehr, 2014a) alongside the guidance given in *No Secrets*. The Care Act is the first piece of legislation to focus specifically on adult safeguarding and places Safeguarding Adults Boards on a statutory footing, with core membership from local authorities, the police and the NHS/CCG, (Clinical Commissioning Group) and with power to include other relevant bodies. If an SAB requests information from an organisation or individual who is likely to have information which is relevant to the SAB's functions, they must share what they know with the SAB (Department of Health, 2014).

Section 42 of the Care Act requires local authorities to investigate when they think an adult with care and support needs may be at risk of abuse or neglect in their area and to find out what, if any, action may be needed. This applies whether or not the authority is actually providing any care and support services to that adult. It also applies whether or not the individual has capacity. While the Act places legal duties on key agencies such as the police and health authorities, it is the LA which has been given the lead duty in relation to investigation. LAs are also required to arrange a safeguarding adults review (SAR) in certain circumstances, such as, if an adult with care and support needs dies as a result of abuse or neglect and there is concern about how one of the members of the SAB acted. SARs replace serious case reviews (SCRs) for adults, and the legal obligation to carry them out in specific situations is a significant step in moving adult safeguarding procedures towards those for children as they were previously a discretionary option. The exception to this has been the mandatory system for mental health enquiries. While there have been significant lessons learnt from certain higher profile adult SCRs, such as the review into the death of Steven Hoskins (Flynn, 2007), adult SCRs to date have not had as much impact on policy and practice, as SCR's for children. The *No Secrets* guidance asserted that adult SCRs *should* take place and there have been many requests for adult SCRs to be more consistent, and that the lessons learnt should be more widely circulated among social workers and other professionals (Department of Health, 2009). The legislative framework around arranging SCRs for adults has the potential to further support development in effective safeguarding practice.

The Care Act also widens and updates the types of abuse recognised. Previously, the categories of adult abuse highlighted were: physical, psychological, financial, discriminatory, organisational (institutional) abuse and neglect and acts of omission.

Under the Care Act the categories have been extended and now also include domestic violence, modern slavery and self-neglect. This is a significant development in response to updated knowledge of the forms of abuse that can occur. The Act acknowledges that it is difficult to be prescriptive in this area as often there are overlaps and multiple forms of abuse. The inclusion of domestic violence is a recognition that there are clear connections between this and adult abuse.

Local authorities are also required to arrange for an independent advocate to represent and support a person who is the subject of a safeguarding enquiry or an SAR, if they need help to understand and take part in the enquiry or review and to express their views, wishes or feelings. Again this strengthens previous good practice guidance in relation to the provision of advocates, where there has often been a shortfall (Department of Health, 2013). It also has considerable resource implications for the widespread availability of appropriate advocacy services.

The Care Act undoubtedly strengthens arrangements to safeguard adults and formalises systems that are already in place in most local authorities. The Act does not give local authorities any new powers to enter a person's property although this was identified as an important additional power by some. The police do already have powers available to enter property if a person is at risk of harm, and local authorities have other powers which can be used in safeguarding situations. Research suggests that even when there is full use of potential legal options, there are many situations where social workers are denied access to individuals suspected to be at risk by a third party (Ruck Keene and FitzGerald, 2014). The police have powers, under the Police and Criminal Evidence Act 1984, to enter homes to arrest a person for an indictable offence or for the purposes of 'saving life or limb'. Ruck Keene and FitzGerald (2014) argue that in some circumstances there would not be sufficient evidence that an offence had been committed and that the 'life or limb' justification sets too high a threshold for entry. Issues arise where social workers suspect, but lack firm evidence, that a person is being abused, the person has mental capacity to make relevant decisions and a third party is barring access.

Issues also arise in terms of accessing individuals in order to assess their capacity. In cases where there is evidence that an individual lacks capacity to make relevant decisions, social workers could apply to the Court of Protection for an order to gain access to them to conduct a capacity assessment. But in some cases, there would potentially be insufficient evidence that the person lacked capacity. Councils can apply to the High Court to make an order under 'inherent jurisdiction' to protect vulnerable adults in cases where statutory powers do not apply. It has been argued, however, that the opportunity to bring a case under inherent jurisdiction is more limited than would be the case if this had been legislated for under the Care Act, due in part to issues of access to the High Court (Ruck Keene and FitzGerald 2014; Samuel 2014). This issue highlights the complexities of adult safeguarding and the potential for uncertain areas between clearly capacitated decisions and lack of capacity being established. In these margins there are individuals subject to coercion and undue influence where it can be argued that the Care Act could have provided additional legal powers.

A further potential weakness has been highlighted in the Care Act guidance in that explicit discussion of the lack of coercive power is not included and an opportunity is missed to provide detailed guidance on alternatives. Councils will sometimes have no option but to resort to court when everything else has been tried, and court proceedings can lead to injunctive relief with a power of arrest and the threat of contempt proceedings. There have been precedents set in case law where a person has been imprisoned for such contempt (see the case of *Stoke City Council v Maddocks*). Schwehr (2014b) believes that guidance and knowledge around this issue is imperative, even if proceedings never reach the court stage, as it informs a more robust conversation with perpetrators. Guidance has been developed to help support practice in this area and can be found at: www.scie.org.uk/care-act-2014/safeguarding-adults/adult-suspected-at-risk-of-neglect-abuse/

While the Care Act provides a legal framework for adult safeguarding which goes some way to bringing it into line with children's safeguarding, it has been suggested that there is a lack of detail in the Care Act guidance. The Care Act aims to encourage creative and personalised solutions in safeguarding and enshrines some of the positive developments initiated through *Making Safeguarding Personal.* While one of the features of previous safeguarding work identified through MSP was an overemphasis on procedure, the Care Act could be seen as lacking in detail and guidance around procedure and legal proceedings are likely to follow to examine application of the Act in specific circumstances (Schwehr, 2014b).

ACTIVITY **3.9**

The Care Act asserts that: 'Safeguarding encompasses six key concepts: empowerment, protection, prevention, proportionate responses, partnership and accountability.'

Consider each principle separately in relation to the following questions.

How can this be achieved in day-to-day interventions in safeguarding adults? Can you give examples of what this could look like in practice?

How far do you think current safeguarding arrangements succeed in achieving the principles?

Are there any barriers you can identify?

While the Care Act 2014 is legislation enacted in England, a new act in Wales – the Social Services and Well-Being (Wales) Act 2014 – appears much more specific in its provision for what it calls 'adults at risk'. The law in Wales allows for adult protection and support orders to be applied for from a magistrate to properly investigate where there is risk of abuse against an adult (UKQCS, 2014). While timescales for developments are similar in England and Wales, the Scottish context for the development of safeguarding has been different.

Ill-treatment and wilful neglect

The offence of ill-treatment and wilful neglect, came into force under the Criminal Justice and Courts Act 2015 (see www.legislation.gov.uk) and was intended to address a gap in the law left by the Mental Health Act 1983 and the Mental Capacity

Act 2005. These laws created offences of ill-treatment or wilful neglect, for people with mental disorders or people who lack capacity to make relevant decisions, by care staff or people appointed to take decisions for them. The Criminal Justice and Courts Act 2015 aims also to protect service users who do not have a mental disorder and do not lack capacity to make relevant decisions. The offence applies to people who work in adult social care and health workers providing care for adults and children in England and Wales. The new offences will inevitably affect both children's and adults' safeguarding, and this legislation will be explored further in Chapter 6.

The Scottish legal context: safeguarding adults

The Adult Support and Protection (Scotland) Act 2007 (ASP) was developed to protect adults at risk of harm and has been in use since 2008. The statute is based on the following set of principles:

- that any intervention must provide benefit to the adult;
- that this benefit could not have been reasonably achieved without intervention;
- that any intervention is the least restrictive option to the adult's freedom.

The Act aims to provide the means to intervene to prevent harm continuing, to put in place strengthened measures to give greater protection for those at risk from harm, to improve inter-agency cooperation, and to promote good inter-disciplinary practice. Section 35 of the ASP allows for overriding the consent of the adult, with the agreement of a Sheriff, and through provision of a warrant, if there appears to be undue pressure being applied to the adult by an external source (e.g. the perpetrator of the suspected abuse and/or harm) to withhold their consent (www.scotland.gov.uk/Topics/Health/care/adult-care-and-support/legislation). While many of the principles of the ASP are reflected in the Care Act, the ASP goes a lot further in terms of strengthening powers of intervention and the role of the state in safeguarding adults.

The central role of the Human Rights Act

The Human Rights Act 1998 is central in considering the crossover between the child and adult legal context as it is relevant in both. Application of other legislation in social work should be compatible with the HRA and it therefore provides a backdrop to both children's and adults' safeguarding.

ACTIVITY **3.10**

Look at the articles of the HRA listed below and consider what different types of potentially abusive incidents they could apply to. Try to include examples for people living both at home and within care settings and also consider their relevance for adults and children.

(Continued)

ACTIVITY **3.10** *continued*

The Articles of the HRA particularly relevant to safeguarding are:

- *Article 2: 'Right to life'*

- *Article 3: 'Freedom from torture' (including humiliating and degrading treatment)*

- *Article 4: 'Right to freedom from slavery and forced labour'*

- *Article 5: 'Right to liberty'*

- *Article 8: 'Right to private and family life'*

- *Article 14: 'Right not to be discriminated against'*

Important points in relation to the HRA are that abuse will often breach more than one of the articles and there can also be conflicts between the different articles. But in essence it provides a central framework for practice in terms of both guiding workers' own actions and considering the actions of others.

CHAPTER SUMMARY

This chapter has considered the recent developments in policy and legislation for safeguarding children and adults. Perhaps the most central point in terms of connections between the two is that legal measures to protect individuals from abuse are a vital tool in any society which values the welfare of citizens, whether they are children or adults. In comparing adult and child legislation, it is worth noting that the Care Act is based around the central concept of *wellbeing* which is somewhat different from notions of the *welfare* of the child enshrined in children's legislation. The notion of wellbeing is not specifically defined in the Care Act and is left open to significant differences in interpretation. The principle of *best interests* can be seen to run through recent legislation relating to both children and adults lacking capacity. A significant difference lies in the fact that if there are concerns that a child is at risk of significant harm, then action will be taken in best interests, measures will be taken to promote the welfare of the child, and this will override all other factors. The complexity of adult safeguarding lies in the right of capacitated adults to make unwise decisions and the implications of this for safeguarding practice. The notion of adults' rights to make decisions and the importance of opportunities for positive risk taking should be at the very centre of safeguarding practice. The concept of not interfering with the right to make unwise decisions has at times, however, been a justification for lack of engagement in situations where abuse is occurring (Flynn, 2007).

While the legal protection for children can be considered to be more overarching than for adults, it could be argued that this is entirely justifiable in relation to the potential vulnerability of all children in contrast to the rights of adults with capacity to make individual choices. The Care Act has provided a legal framework for adult safeguarding which comes nearer to a parallel approach with children's safeguarding. Opportunities to consider safeguarding of both children and adults on a similar footing and make connections between the two are valuable in achieving a lifespan approach to needs.

ACTIVITY 3.11

Read the case studies below and consider what aspects of policy and legislation are relevant in each scenario.

Keira

Keira is a 3 year old toddler who currently lives with her mother Carole. Carole has a history of opiate dependency, and although she has stated that she wants to overcome her dependency she has experienced a number of relapses.

Keira's grandparents have contacted you because they have tried to see Keira but have been denied access to the house and Carole is refusing to answer any phone calls. The grandparents have advised that there have been incidences of domestic abuse. They explain that they are particularly worried because a neighbour has told them that Keira seems to have a cut above her left eye and is not attending nursery.

Tina

Tina is 20 years old and has mild learning disabilities and some mental health problems. She lives with her father in a private tenancy and has recently stopped attending her supported work placement. You arrange to visit Tina but when you arrive at the house her father says she doesn't want to see you and isn't interested in returning to work.

FURTHER READING

Brandon, M, Bailey, S and Belderson, P (2010) *Building on the Learning from Serious Case Reviews: A Two Year Analysis of Child Protection Database Notifications 2007–2009*. Research Report. London: Department for Education.

Davies, L, Kline, R, Douieb, B and Goodman, K (2013) *Working Together Revision Documents are not Fit for Purpose. A Critical Focus on Two Documents: 'Working Together to Safeguard Children' and 'Managing Individual Cases'*. Available at: http://graphic-room.com/lizdavies/wp-content/uploads/2012/11/REVISION_OF_WORKING_TOGETHER__RESPONSE_TO_CONSULTATION.pdf

Department of Health (2014) *Care and Support: Statutory Guidance Issued under the Care Act 2014*. London: Department of Health.

HM Government (2015) *Working Together: A Guide to Inter-agency Working to Safeguard and Promote the Welfare of Children*. London: The Stationery Office.

Laming, H (2003) *The Victoria Climbié Inquiry*. London: The Stationery Office.

Laming, H (2009) *The Protection of Children in England: A Progress Report*. London: The Stationery Office.

Local Government Association (LGA) (2013) *Making Safeguarding Personal: Executive Summary*. London: Local Government Association.

SCIE (2014) *Gaining Access to an Adult Suspected to be at Risk of Neglect or Abuse: A Guide for Social Workers and their Managers in England*. Available at: www.scie.org.uk/care-act-2014/safeguarding-adults/adult-suspected-at-risk-of-neglect-abuse/

SCIE (2015) *Adult Safeguarding: Sharing Information*. Available at: www.scie.org.uk/care-act-2014/safeguarding-adults/sharing-information/

Chapter 4
Safeguarding and the family

Introduction

Sociological theory around the role of the family often suggests that family groupings have evolved specifically to fulfil the function of providing nurture and support to family members, in particular those who are young or who have additional needs in relation to health and wellbeing (Cunningham and Cunningham, 2014). While family structures have varied and evolved both over time and between different cultures, the overriding perceptions are of families being safe and caring places for individuals. Regrettably, this is not always the case and across the lifespan individuals are more likely to be harmed by family members than by strangers. In the UK, while there are different political standpoints in terms of appropriate levels of state involvement in family life, there is a widespread consensus that the state should intervene when abuse or neglect occurs in family settings. Understanding of the prevalence and nature of abuse and appropriate responses has developed considerably over recent decades. This chapter explores the factors underlying abuse across the lifespan within families and considers safeguarding responses. Emerging themes that impact on safeguarding individuals at any life stage, such as abuse of power, will also be considered.

Safeguarding children within the family

The 'toxic trio' is a term that has developed to highlight the possible impact that domestic abuse, mental health and substance misuse can have on children and their family; each of these parental behaviours is considered to be an indicator of increased risk of harm to children and young people. In their analysis of the primary causes of child deaths or injury in serious case reviews, Brandon et al. (2010) found that in a great many cases, children were exposed to the 'toxic trio' of domestic violence, parental substance misuse and mental health issues. In a study of 338 social work files from six English local authorities, domestic violence featured in 60 per cent of the referrals, parental substance misuse in just over half (52 per cent) of cases, and both issues were present in a fifth (20 per cent) of cases (Cleaver et al., 2007).

Domestic abuse

Defining domestic abuse

In 2013 the Home Office produced an updated definition of domestic abuse which describes abusive behaviour as:

> *any incident of threatening behaviour, violence or abuse (psychological, sexual, financial or emotional) between adults who are, or have been intimate partners or family members, regardless of gender or sexuality. This definition includes so called 'honour' based violence, female genital mutilation and forced marriage, and is clear that victims are not confined to one gender or ethnic group.*

> (Home Office, 2013c)

Domestic abuse not only places victims at risk of physical violence but it is also the random, repeated and habitual use of intimidation to control a partner. This power and control over a victim may not only be physical and sexual but rather by way of a number of behaviours such as threats, psychological coercion, intimidation, isolation and humiliation. Controlling behaviour is defined as a variety of acts that are designed to make another person subordinate and/or dependent, denying them independence, resistance and escape, regulating their day-to-day behaviour by isolating them from sources of support, exploiting their resources and capacities for personal gain (Home Office, 2013c). Although the extended definition is not a legal definition it does now include 'honour'-based violence, FGM and forced marriage and also recognises that young people are at risk from domestic abuse.

Historically, domestic abuse was often considered to be a private issue, within matrimony. The social and political concept of domestic abuse changed in the 1970s following pressure from women's movements; refuges were established and legislation was introduced to criminalise abuse within domestic relationships. Institutional and agency responses began to change and there has been a gradual awareness by government of the need for policy solutions to the issue of domestic abuse (Harne and Radford, 2008).

Domestic violence is not itself a crime under English law, i.e. there is no specific offence of domestic violence. However the 1990s saw an extension of the civil law remedies to victims and criminalisation of those who breach civil law injunctions. The Domestic Violence, Crime and Victims Act 2004 further extended civil law remedies to domestic violence victims, making the breach of a non-molestation order a criminal offence with a penalty of up to five years. Common assault became an arrestable offence and s 5 introduced a new offence, *'causing or allowing the death of a child or vulnerable adult'*. However, the Domestic Violence, Crime and Victims (Amendment) Act 2012 has strengthened s 5, by extending the definition of the offence to include causing or allowing serious physical harm to a child or vulnerable adult (www.legislation. gov.uk/ukpga/2012/4/contents/enacted).

In March 2014, Domestic Violence Protection Orders were introduced by the Crime and Security Act 2010 s 24–s 33. A perpetrator can be banned with immediate effect from returning to a residence and from having contact with the victim for up to 28 days, allowing the victim time to consider their options and get the support they need.

However, as Laing et al. (2013) highlight, *'the traditional criminal justice system is poorly suited to dealing with domestic violence. The criminal law is incident specific, while domestic violence is constituted by an ongoing pattern of behaviours aimed at exerting coercive control, only some of which may be codified in the law as criminal acts'* (2013: 40).

Prevalence

There are no reliable national data on the general incidence of domestic violence in the UK. In February 2014, the Office for National Statistics produced the following statistics: Women were more likely than men to have experienced intimate violence across all headline types of abuse – 8.5 per cent of women and 4.5 per cent of men reported having experienced any type of domestic abuse in the last year (that is, partner/ex-partner abuse (non-sexual), family abuse (non-sexual) and sexual assault or stalking carried out by a current or former partner or other family member). This is equivalent to an estimated 1.4 million female victims and 700,000 male victims (Office for National Statistics, 2014).

Domestic abuse continues to represent a significant social problem which impacts on individuals, children, families and communities. One incident of domestic abuse is reported to the police every minute (Women's Aid, 2015).

ACTIVITY *4.1*

Are the following true or false?

1. *One in ten women experience domestic abuse at some point in their lives.*

2. *Once a victim leaves they are not at risk of abuse.*

3. *The majority of victims of domestic abuse are women.*

4. *Incidents of domestic abuse are hidden from children.*

COMMENT

1. *False – Domestic abuse affects one in four women in the England and Wales.*

2. *False – On average two women are killed every week by their current or ex-partner (Women's Aid, 2015).*

3. *True – The Crime Survey for England and Wales (CSEW) 2011/12 estimated that 31 per cent of women and 18 per cent of men had experienced any domestic abuse since the age of 16 (Dar, 2013). It is important to remember that domestic abuse can affect anyone regardless of age, gender, race and ethnicity. Although it is reported perpetrators of domestic violence are usually men domestic abuse takes place where the victim is a male or within same sex relationships. Dugan (2013) suggests that men are often reluctant to report abuse because of a sense of shame, and a concern that they will not be believed by police.*

4. *False – In 90 per cent of domestic abuse incidents children are believed to be in the same or next room. McConnell and Taylor (2014) suggest some fathers and mothers believed their children were not aware, were protected from domestic abuse or did not recognise their/their partner's behaviour as harmful.*

Impact on children

The impact of domestic abuse on children is multifaceted, having a detrimental effect on both physical and emotional health. The child may not be injured directly; however, the emotional impact of witnessing or hearing the abuse, whether this is an isolated incident or ongoing, can be extensive. An assessment of risk should be undertaken to establish whether the threshold criteria have been met; is the child at risk of significant harm?

RESEARCH SUMMARY

Brandon et al. (2012) undertook a biennial analysis of 139 serious case reviews in England between 2009 and 2011; domestic abuse was considered to be a risk factor in 63 per cent of all the reported cases, placing children at risk of significant harm.

(Continued)

The NSPCC (2013) highlights the difficulties in gaining a true representation of the prevalence of domestic violence via statistics, due to the nature of the under-reporting. However, Lord Laming (2009) reported that 200,000 children in the UK live in households where there is a known risk of domestic violence. He also reported that an analysis of serious case reviews found that past or present domestic violence was found in 53 per cent of cases; thus highlighting how domestic violence can pose significant harm to a child. Research from the Co-ordinated Action Against Domestic Abuse (CAADA, 2012) found that there are approximately 130,000 children in the UK living in households where there is domestic abuse assessed at high risk. Research shows that children are more likely to be physically harmed where domestic violence is present.

Risk of physical harm

Children might be injured or they might be harmed by accident, or if they try to intervene to protect the person harmed. Children are also harmed in indirect ways by exposure to parental domestic violence. Parents may not provide appropriate stimulation, toys or opportunities for play. Social isolation can occur where friends and family withdraw from the parents' support network, and children may lose contact with significant attachment figures or others who might have helped ensure their safety and wellbeing.

Risk of emotional, social and psychological harm

Witnessing domestic abuse can have an effect on children's development in several areas, most notably in relation to their social, emotional and psychological development.

These indirect consequences can have a significant impact on children's attachment patterns and their feeling of emotional safety and security. In 2014, CAADA undertook a piece of research with a sample of children who had been exposed to domestic violence: 52 per cent had behaviour problems; 39 per cent had difficulties at school; and 60 per cent were impacted emotionally by feeling that they were responsible for the violence. Domestic abuse could undermine a parent and child relationship and affect a child's ability to cope with traumatic events, such as living with domestic abuse. Mullender (2004) observed that children who witnessed domestic violence were much more likely to have social and emotional problems compared to children who have not witnessed domestic abuse. Moreover, Stanley (2011) reports that children who were exposed to domestic abuse were more likely to describe feelings of anger and frustration.

Domestic abuse and social learning theory

Social learning theory has been applied to domestic abuse to help explain how some people learn that violence is a way of solving relationship problems, irrespective of their gender or sexual orientation. It has been used to explain why some children display and actively use aggression and manipulation in their interactions with others, as the theory suggests that children learn through observation and imitation.

Social learning theory suggests that when children are repeatedly exposed to aggressive behaviour, such behaviour can become accepted as the norm. Stanley et al. (2012) found that children who regularly witnessed domestic abuse were much more likely to view this behaviour as normal and may resort to violence more willingly in resolving conflict, often mimicking the interactions they have observed. However, it is important to remember that not all children who experience high risk environments will develop aggressive behaviours. Moreover, some children and young people are able to develop an adaptive response to adversity.

Multi-agency working

Interventions in domestic abuse cases need to address the protection of children and adults at risk, the empowerment of victims and the accountability of perpetrators. A number of agencies may be required to respond to a domestic abuse case.

ACTIVITY 4.2

List of all the different agencies that might be involved with a family where domestic abuse is an issue.

COMMENT

The nature and extent of professional involvement will depend on the needs of the family and the level of risk that is presented. However, agencies such as housing, health, education, the police, the Crown Prosecution Service, Women's Aid, children's safeguarding, adult services, Child and Adolescent Mental Health Services (CAMHS) and the probation service may all be involved with a family. In cases of high risk, victims and their families may be referred to a multi-agency risk assessment conference (MARAC) which provides a coordinated response to domestic abuse. The role and responsibilities of MARAC will be outlined later in this chapter.

Implications for effective practice

There needs to be a move away from the engendered and oppressive practice which can result in women being 'blamed' for failing to protect their children. This type of response contributes to misunderstandings about the complexities which are involved in dealing with victims, perpetrators and children. Beckett (2010) suggests that within domestic abuse cases professionals tend to assess the victim's capacity to protect their children, which can lead to additional pressure, oppression and the ongoing fear that their children may be removed. Parents who are the victims of domestic abuse may worry that their children will be taken away from them and as a consequence may try to minimise or deny the existence of the abuse.

Mental health

Defining mental illness

Mental illness is a general term that refers to a group of illnesses affecting the mind, in the same way that physical illness refers to illnesses which affect the body.

Episodes of a mental illness can come and go through people's lives. Some people experience their illness only once and then fully recover. For others, it may recur throughout their lives. In 2015 the Royal College of Psychiatrists estimated that one in four people will experience some type of mental health issue; 68 per cent of women and 57 per cent of men who have a mental health issue are parents.

Although there are many parents who have mental health issues who are able to successfully parent their children research indicates that parental mental illness can adversely affect child development both on a short-term and a longer-term basis. Cleaver et al. (2011) suggest that some parents may experience difficulties in being able to parent effectively and meet the physical and emotional needs of their children. Research undertaken by the Department of Health in 2002 estimated that between a third and two thirds of children whose parents have mental health problems would experience adverse outcomes.

Impact on family and social relationships

Horwath (2007) suggests that an inability to provide emotional support, boundaries and a lack of consistency within a child's life can have a negative impact on a child's development. As previously discussed, children need to have their emotional needs met before they can develop positive and secure attachments. If a parent is psychologically unavailable and therefore unable to meet their child's emotional needs the child may develop insecure attachments which may prevent them from being able to adapt to their social environment, which in turn could lead to social exclusion. If a child assumes a caring responsibility for a family member this could have an impact on their availability to participate in educational or social activities.

Although a significant amount of research has focused on mental health issues and dysfunctional parenting, there are many parents with mental health issues who provide a loving and stable environment for their children. Extended family members and community support networks can also be protective factors which can enhance the strength and resilience of families. It is also important to recognise that there may be a number of other factors which can exacerbate parental mental health issues and contribute to poorer outcomes for children, such as social exclusion, poverty and employment:

> *Parental mental health problems can, but do not always, have a significant impact on children's social and emotional well-being by disrupting the attachment bond between infants and parents. A number of factors will determine how, and to what extent, parental mental health problems impact on a child's*

health and well-being. The severity of the diagnosis alone may not be a good guide because access to treatment, support, social and economic circumstances can have a significant impact on whether the child develops their own mental health problems.

(Social Exclusion Unit, 2004; cited in Stanley and Cox, 2009: 18)

Parental substance misuse

Substance use and alcohol do not inevitably have a detrimental impact on children; however, research does indicate that parental substance misuse can have an adverse effect on parenting capacity, which in turn can contribute to poorer outcomes for children (Ward and Davies, 2011). In 2003 the Advisory Council on the Misuse of Drugs (ACMD) published a report, *Hidden Harm*, which highlighted the impact that parental substance misuse can have on a child. The report estimated that between 250,000 and 300,000 children and young people live with a parent who is categorised as drug dependent (ACMD, 2003). Research carried out has stated that alcohol and drug problems feature in a substantial number of families. It is estimated that 30 per cent of children live with an adult binge drinker, 22 per cent with a hazardous drinker and 2.5 per cent with a harmful drinker (Manning et al., 2009). Serious case reviews have consistently identified substance misuse as a key factor in child deaths and cases of serious injury (Brandon et al., 2010). Problematic substance use can have an impact on a parent's ability to provide basic care to a child. There are three main types of drugs: stimulants, depressants and hallucinogens; all of these are psychotropic, which can contribute to an impairment of a person's judgement and increase the risk of exposure to harm. The effects of alcohol are also well documented in relation to the possible impact on a person's perception, mood or consciousness.

Maslow (1970) suggested that all humans have a hierarchy of needs; a person will only progress to the top of this hierarchy if their needs are met at each level. He suggested that a child will thrive when their basic physiological needs are met, within an environment where they feel loved and safe. Consequently, if a parent is unable to meet their child's basic needs there may be impact on their social, physical and psychological development. Substance misuse can also lead to financial difficulties within a family, especially if a parent incurs debts to fund their dependency (Manning et al., 2009).

Women who misuse substances during pregnancy may place their own health and the health of the unborn child at risk. Both alcohol and drug usage during pregnancy can affect the brain development of a foetus; other adverse effects can include lower birth weight and cognitive impairment. Heavy drinking during pregnancy can also lead to Foetal Alcohol Syndrome (FAS) which may contribute to physical, cognitive and behavioural difficulties (NSPCC, 2013). It is important to remember, however, that chaotic lifestyles, inconsistent support and socioeconomic disadvantage may also have a negative impact on women's health during pregnancy.

Unfortunately there is also a view that substance misuse is a personal and moral failing rather than a health issue that requires support and treatment. Within this context women who misuse substances or alcohol are often perceived to be irresponsible or deviant. What effect do you think this might have on parents' views of their own situation, and their willingness to engage with support? As a professional, how might you address this?

Political agenda

Parental substance misuse has been a key feature in recent political agendas. The *Drug Strategy* (Home Office, 2010b) states that social workers are required to *'respond to safeguarding concerns'*, but also emphasises the importance of keeping families together. The *Hidden Harm* report (ACMD, 2003) highlighted concerns about the lack of communication and information sharing between adult and child services. A further risk to consider is that professions may focus more attention on the needs and views of the parent and not fully consider the child's perspective. Historically professionals have been criticised for their lack of focus on the child, making the child almost *'invisible'* (Munro, 2011). This lack of awareness can ultimately lead to a minimisation of the risks that a child may face and was highlighted recently during the SCR into the death of Daniel Pelka:

> *Despite Daniel being the focus of concern for all practitioners, in reality he was rarely the focus of their interventions. Almost every child who has been the subject of a serious case review over the last 40 years was 'seen' by a professional within days (or hours) of their death. Simply seeing a child is not protection against harm. The child needs to be seen, listened to and heard.*

(Staffordshire and Stoke-on-Trent Safeguarding Children Boards, 2013)

Young carers

As stated previously, parental substance misuse or parental mental health issues do not always lead to safeguarding concerns or difficulties in parenting capacity; however, they can increase the likelihood of a child experiencing harm or neglect. Another issue to consider is the number of children and young people who assume the role of carer for their parent. The term young carer includes:

> *children and young people under 18 who provide regular or ongoing care and emotional support to a family member who is physically or mentally ill, disabled or misuses substances ... a young carer becomes vulnerable when the level of care-giving and responsibility to the person in need of care becomes excessive or inappropriate for that child, risking impacting on his or her emotional or physical well-being or educational achievement and life chances.*

(ADASS, The Children's Society and ADCS, 2012: 7)

Figures released from the 2011 census show a 19 per cent increase in the number of young carers aged under 18. The 2011 census identified 178,000 young carers in England and Wales alone; an 83 per cent increase in the number of young carers aged 5 to 7 years and a 55 per cent increase in the number of children caring who are aged between 8 and 9 years (www.barnardos.org.uk/what_we_do/our_work/young_carers.htm).

RESEARCH SUMMARY

Research indicates that children and young people who are in this situation may lack routine and live chaotic lives. They may be more likely to experience a poor diet and to miss health appointments. Young carers may also experience educational difficulties and are statistically more likely to miss school (ADASS, The Children's Society and ADCS, 2012). Research by the Carers Trust and the University of Nottingham found that almost a third of young carers surveyed (29 per cent) reported that their own physical health was 'just OK', and 38 per cent reported having a mental health problem. Despite the impact that caring responsibilities can have on children and young people, many young carers felt loyalty towards their parents and were often reluctant to disclose the full extent of their responsibilities in case they were removed from the family home (Sempik and Becker, 2014).

Silent Voices: Supporting Children and Young People Affected by Parental Alcohol Misuse (Children's Commissioner, 2012) highlighted key messages from young people about the impact of parental alcohol misuse. The report also identified the type of support that young people wanted from different professionals.

- Children want their circumstances to be recognised by someone who is helpful, caring and encouraging.

- Someone taking time to know the child and work at their pace, not just focusing on the parental substance misuse.

- Support can be about more than talking about the parental alcohol misuse. It can also be about talking about other things, not talking at all, or engaging in fun or other diversionary activities.

- Having practical help when it is needed.

- It can be very hard for children to talk about what is going on. Children need time to develop a relationship of trust, and to feel safe; they also need to understand confidentiality and what will happen to the information they share with others.

- Having consistency and reliability in the workers that they get help from – staff turnover, getting to know new workers, having to repeat their story (to new workers or to workers from different services) can be challenging for children.

- Professionals who understand the concerns held by many children about being separated from their parent(s) and who often remain extremely loyal to their parents).

The issues that many young carers face are finally being acknowledged within statute with the enactment of the Children and Families Act 2014 and the Care Act 2014. Section 96 of the Children and Families Act stipulates that the LA must assess the needs of young carers who live in their area, if it appears to the LA that this young carer may have needs which require support or if the LA receives a request from the carer or parent of the carer to assess the need for support (see Children and Families Act at www.legislation.gov.uk/ukpga/2014/6/section/96/enacted).

Approaches to safeguarding children

A number of approaches to safeguarding children have developed during the past 20 years which recognise that families are often sources of strength and resilience. The *Think Family* approach, Signs of Safety® and family group conferencing are all examples of approaches which focus on families and extended family members being able to adapt to challenges and to succeed despite experiencing difficulties. In the past services have often engaged only with the parents of a vulnerable child, rather than reaching out to wider family members which can have positive outcomes and avoid the need for the child to be taken into care.

Family group conferences

Family group conferences (FGCs) are a decision making and planning process where the wider family group makes plans and decisions for children who are at risk. The process is facilitated by a professional but is led by the family. FGCs are unique in that the main decision makers in the development of a plan at an FGC are family members. Children and young people will make a major contribution to the conference. The family group gets together with professionals, to make a plan and decide how to resolve the situation (NSPCC, 2009b). FGCs provide a different approach to traditional child protection case conferencing where activity is driven by professionals and agencies tend to have ownership of safeguarding plans rather than families. In 2011, 89.5 per cent of children referred to an FGC by social services found a safe home within their extended family (Hasted, 2012). Rapid response times are a further advantage of the FGC approach as the whole process usually takes a maximum of four weeks.

Signs of Safety®

Concerns have been expressed that the child protection process has become overly procedural and increasingly defensive (Munro, 2011). The Signs of Safety® approach was originally developed by Turnell and Edwards to work with the Aboriginal community in Western Australia (see Turnell and Edwards, 1998); however, the approach has now been developed worldwide. The Signs of Safety® model adopts a more collaborative approach in which professionals and families work in partnership to address child abuse. It is a strengths-based and solution-focused approach where assessment and planning documents are written in straightforward language that everyone involved should understand. The model covers four domains of enquiry which are: What are we worried about? What is working well? What needs to happen? How safe is the child? (On a scale of 0–10). It aims to develop a more constructive approach to safeguarding children while remaining attentive and realistic about risk.

A central aspect of the approach is the inclusion of resources that can be used with children to enable their voices to be heard. An example of a resource which can be used with children is the three houses tool.

1. House of Good Things: what is going well?

2. House of Worries: what are your worries/concerns?

3. House of Dreams: what are your dreams?

(Bunn, 2013)

(See also www.signsofsafety.net)

Think Family

Recent policy drivers, such as *No Health without Mental Health* (HM Government, 2011), the troubled families programme and *Think Family*, have emphasised the importance of supporting parents who have mental health issues. *Think Child, Think Parent, Think Family* was developed by SCIE in 2009 to help support parents with mental health issues and improve the outcomes for children and families. *Think Family* identified a number of factors which contributed to families 'falling through the net' and as a consequence missing out on supportive services. Stanley and Cox (2009) suggested that adult professionals did not always share important information with children's services, which can lead to an underestimation of the risk that can be posed to children.

Think Family adopts a multi-disciplinary approach and aims to establish whether services take into consideration the combined needs of parents and children. It is argued that a holistic stance should be adopted which is centred on the family and assessment processes should take into account the needs of both parents and children. Plans and interventions should identify risk, strengths and resources and all plans should be shared with the family.

ACTIVITY 4.4

How do you think a child or young person might feel when plans are made and implemented, without their own views and wishes being taken into consideration?

Bee et al. (2013) suggested that the views of children are not being acknowledged by professionals. Often children are not aware of what is happening to their parents and information is not being shared with them, which often results in children experiencing more anxiety.

Think Family supports a more diverse and flexible approach to working with families and supporting people whose capacity to parent is affected by their own issues. The approach highlights the importance of effective information sharing between adult and child services (SCIE, 2009). However, it is worth noting that despite the recognition that a more systematic approach is required, which in turn requires significant improvements in relation to multi-agency working and information sharing, the 2013 Ofsted report *What About the Children*? suggested that there continues to be a lack of coherence between adult and children's services (Ofsted, 2013a).

ACTIVITY 4.5

Think Family *case study*

Maureen and Joseph live in a community which has suffered from high unemployment and socio-economic hardship for many years. Both Maureen and Joseph have been unemployed for a number of years. There is a history of domestic abuse and, following one incident, Joseph received a short custodial sentence. The couple have separated but Joseph regularly visits the family home to see his children, Jennifer aged 10 and Tom aged 12.

Maureen has enduring mental health issues and often states that she struggles to cope with the care of the children. The family are in debt and are facing eviction from the family home. The children's school attendance has declined during the past couple of months and there are concerns about deterioration in their physical presentation. The children never attend any out of school activities and do not appear to have many friends.

You are asked to assess the family's needs.

- *What needs can you identify within the family?*

- *What are the strengths within the family?*

- *What outcomes might you expect to achieve from your assessment and intervention?*

COMMENT

Firstly you will want to establish whether the children are at risk of harm or are children in need. The scenario would suggest that the children are in need of support to address the current concerns. As a practitioner one of your first tasks would be to identify the needs of both the children and their parents. It is important to recognise the dynamic relationship between the parent and child where both affect each other's emotional state and ability to cope. How are you going to ascertain what other services might be working with the family? How are you going to ensure that information is communicated effectively and appropriately? Although your priority is always to ensure that children are safe it is also important to identify areas of strength and support which may exist within the family, extended family and community.

Safeguarding adults within families

For adult safeguarding referrals to local authorities which concluded during 2013–14, the alleged abuse most frequently occurred in the home of the adult at risk (42 per cent of allegations) and the source of risk was most commonly someone known to the alleged victim but not in a social care capacity (accounting for 49 per cent of allegations). Social care employees were the source of risk in 36 per cent of allegations and for the remaining 15 per cent the perpetrator was someone unknown to the alleged victim (HSCIC, 2014). It is clear from these statistics that although everyone should have the right to feel safe in their own home, whatever their life stage or circumstances, domestic settings are far from safe places for many people. The impact of domestic abuse on children has been well documented above. The range of factors which contribute to this has also been considered. While responses to safeguarding adults and children in family settings have been very different historically, in reality, many of the potential causes and contributory factors which lead to abuse within families are in evidence whatever the age of the person who is harmed. The impact of wider factors, such as poverty, stress, mental health and substance abuse on families has been highlighted and these factors also increase the likelihood of abuse and neglect of adults. Likewise, abuse of power and patterns of behaviour that have become established within families can also have negative results for both children and adults at risk.

Domestic violence and safeguarding adults

The Care Act includes domestic violence as a specific category of adult abuse. This highlights the fact that these are not separate issues and much abuse of adults with care and support needs could also be considered and responded to using domestic violence measures. Conversely, domestic abuse of individuals with care and support needs could be addressed using safeguarding measures. The language used and the way that abuse is categorised can undoubtedly impact on how it is responded to (Butler, 2011). It is therefore essential that those responding to abuse are clear about how abuse is framed and why specific ways of responding are the most appropriate. Clearly the most critical factors here are the expressed wishes and needs of the individual but it is crucial that they are given the widest range of information on potential options. The impact of domestic abuse in terms of the long-term health and emotional wellbeing of those affected cannot be overestimated (McGarry, 2008).

RESEARCH SUMMARY

Disabled women's experience of domestic abuse

Sixty per cent of individuals referred to local authorities for safeguarding concerns in 2013–14 were female and just over half (51 per cent) of the individuals had a physical disability, frailty or sensory impairment (HSCIC, 2014). There is, however, a lack of research around disabled women's experiences of domestic violence. Hague et al. (2011; Hague

(Continued)

and Bridge, 2008) suggest that over 50 per cent of disabled women may experience domestic violence in their lifetime and that they are twice as likely to experience domestic violence as non-disabled women. While there is a higher prevalence of domestic violence for disabled women, Hague et al.'s research shows that there is a lack of dedicated services in the UK for disabled women who experience domestic violence. The potential for isolation, discrimination and dependence on others for care and support that impact on the lives of individuals with disabilities can significantly exacerbate the likelihood and impact of domestic violence. While clearly not an issue which just affects women, it is important to consider the impact of structural oppression along gendered lines. Models of disability which highlight the social construction of disabling factors in society (e.g. Shakespeare, 2014) need to be considered in the context of the further structural power imbalances that are present for disabled women specifically. So disabled women have a greater need for services, together with much less specialised domestic violence provision.

Specific experiences of women with learning disabilities suffering domestic abuse suggest that they do not have access to support or that support options are inappropriate and that the experience of inadequate support intensifies the impact of the original abuse. Research also suggests that their experiences of abuse are marginalised because of being labelled as having a learning disability (Walter-Brice et al., 2012). Helpful service provision included advocacy, a domestic abuse support programme, and an empowerment group informed by feminist perspectives. Disabled women also experience distinctive forms of abuse linked to their care and support needs, such as withholding medication or support to mobilise (Robbins et al., 2014). The gendered nature of much domestic violence should not obscure the fact that men with care and support needs may also suffer abuse, and this aspect is even less researched than that of women. Butler (2011) makes the significant point that if disabled women are twice as likely to suffer domestic violence then this is likely to be similar for disabled men.

Older people and domestic abuse

During 2013–14, 63 per cent of referrals for adult safeguarding to local authorities were aged 65 or over (HSCIC, 2014). In the context of an ageing population, there is a steady increase in the number of older people who are dependent on family members and other informal carers for care and support. Elder abuse is an under-researched area of family violence which until relatively recently remained completely hidden. Likewise, awareness of the impact of ageism is a recent progression but a factor which undoubtedly affects older people's opportunities to maintain control over their own lives. This is compounded by the gendered aspects of elder abuse. Studies suggest that previous abuse is a risk factor for elder abuse, with some research indicating that one third of abuse had started before the age of 65, and that there was an increased likelihood for individuals living in extended family settings (Naughton et al., 2012). Further studies have also indicated that a life course perspective is relevant to understanding elder abuse in that abuse in childhood increased the risk of experiencing abuse later in life (McDonald and Thomas, 2013). There has also been a tendency to see domestic abuse and elder abuse as completely separate, with older women being marginalised in terms of domestic violence research and support services. The specific needs of older people have been masked by this and further exacerbated by traditional views around privacy and lack of awareness of support (McGarry et al., 2014).

Serious case reviews have demonstrated that services have failed to make the link between older people and domestic violence. In the SCR (Southend Safeguarding Adults Board, 2011) into the case of 81 year old Mary Russell, who was murdered by her husband, police, social services and health professionals had been alerted to injuries. A failure to recognise domestic abuse among the services is identified in the SCR, alongside poor communication and deficiencies in multi-agency responses (Robbins et al., 2014).

While the term domestic violence indicates abuse within the home, it is important to note that violence from partners, ex-partners and family members can occur anywhere. Robbins et al. (2014) also point out that other specific groups are often excluded from research and services, including migrant women and those in traveller communities. They also identify issues around forced marriage and 'honour'-based violence in terms of how these are labelled and therefore constructed by agencies. Psychiatric patients also appear to be more likely to suffer domestic violence but this is less likely to be detected by mental health practitioners. Between 40 and 62 per cent of women with a serious mental illness reported being the victim of domestic or sexual violence since age 16 (Pettitt et al., 2013). These points again highlight that while different terminology may be used in different circumstances, the categorisation of abuse and domestic violence is often one which results from service responses rather than the lived experiences of individuals.

RESEARCH SUMMARY

Risk factors in the domestic abuse of adults

In reviewing research into risk factors for elder abuse in domestic settings, Johannesen and LoGuidice (2013) identified factors relating to the older person themselves, the perpetrator, relationship and the environment as significant. For the older person factors such as cognitive impairment, behavioural problems, mental health problems, functional dependency, poor physical health or frailty, low income or wealth, trauma or past abuse and ethnicity were relevant. People with dementia are likely to be particularly vulnerable to abuse and also much less likely to be able to report this (Samsi et al., 2014). For the perpetrator, perceptions of caregiver burden or stress and mental health problems were highlighted as risk factors. In terms of the relationship itself, family disharmony, poor or conflictual relationships impacted and environmental conditions such as low social support and living with others were significant.

Stress and caregiver burden are contentious in relation to abuse and neglect. While some studies have linked higher levels of caregiver stress to abuse (Compton et al., 1997), a

(Continued)

direct link between carer stress and abuse has not been established. Other research has highlighted the complexity of caring relationships in relation to abuse. Caregiving can cause changes in physical and emotional health, finances, and time available to participate in other family, social, work, leisure or community activities. While caregiving can be stressful, people who perform the same or very similar roles may have very different experiences. Caregivers also experience different types and levels of stress over time (Brintnall-Peterson, 2012). Concerns have been raised that overemphasis on stress and burden as factors leading to abuse can mask other issues such as longer-term family dynamics and patterns of domestic violence (Johannesen and LoGuidice, 2013).

Clearly wider factors impacting on carers' lives also impact on their experiences of caring. Pressures created by cultural expectations of caregivers are also relevant and the link between social isolation and caring for some is a significant factor. Chow and Tiwari (2014) identify resilience, good service support and an appropriate environment for caring as critical in positive caring relationships. They also highlight the importance of access to social and community networks in terms of both physical and attitudinal barriers to opportunities to lead an ordinary life for carers. Looking at caregiver burden in relation to parents of (adult) children with learning disabilities, some recent studies have suggested that stress related to the caring role has been overemphasised as opposed to the impact of wider societal stigma and marginalisation. Parental concerns about the impact of wider societal factors are likely to be exacerbated by anxiety that they will not be there in future years to support their adult children (Thackeray and Eatough, 2015). Green (2007) argued that the trend towards focusing on the emotional burden of having a child with a disability has tended to obscure the impact of society's negative attitudes towards disability and also failed to recognise positive parental experience.

Financial abuse

Financial abuse is an area where knowledge and awareness are gradually increasing in terms of adult safeguarding in domestic settings and, as with other forms of abuse, perpetrators can be family members, informal networks, wider community or paid support. International research suggests that central risk factors among families are: family members having a strong sense of entitlement to assets, an older person having diminished capacity and being dependent on family for care (Wendt et al., 2013). Like other forms of domestic abuse, power and control within family relationships are factors that can predicate financial abuse. Likewise, cultural norms and understandings of privacy and respect within families are also relevant here. Studies have highlighted people with dementia as particularly vulnerable to financial abuse in relation to declining cognitive abilities and forgetfulness (Manthorpe et al., 2012). Responses will vary according to context, such as whether financial abuse occurs in isolation or alongside other forms of abuse. Appropriate behaviour in terms of supporting family members with money management is a contentious area. In many countries there are systems to regulate decision making when an adult does not have the capacity to do so, such as the Mental Capacity Act 2005 in England and Wales, through the appointment of a Lasting Power of Attorney (LPA) or court-appointed decision makers. However, even when systems are in place, misuse of a Power of Attorney can occur and constitute financial abuse and should be reported the Office of the Public Guardian (Samsi et al., 2014). Knowledge is also developing around the range of electronic fraud and other crimes that can be perpetrated through digital technology and the internet.

Abuse and paid carers

Research into older people and human rights in home care provision uncovered a range of abuse including physical abuse, theft, neglect and issues around privacy and dignity (EHRC, 2011: 111). This inquiry argues that problems are closely linked to local authorities' policies and practice in relation to the commissioning of home care and the way home care contracts are procured and monitored. Issues arising in relation to home care providers have included undervaluing of home care workers – in terms of both pay and conditions and training – and an overemphasis on quantity rather than quality of support provided, which directly impacts on the service received by individuals. Some LAs have become more aware of the dehumanising nature of very brief care visits; however, slots of 15 minutes or less are still being used by three quarters of councils (Donnelly, 2015). The way in which care work continues to be undervalued appears to be in direct correlation to the low status in society of many individuals with care and support needs.

Ensuring that people have greater choice and control over their own care has been one of the central aims of the personalisation of services in recent decades. While personalisation has been highly welcomed in terms of providing people with care and support needs with more control and choice in terms of how and by whom their needs are met, there have been ongoing concerns around safeguarding and managing risk (Fyson, 2009). Employing staff can be a daunting task and unless individuals are provided with appropriate support to set up and manage arrangements they can be open to abuse. Recent research, however, suggests that links between the personal budget model and higher vulnerability to abuse are not necessarily proven, with some data suggesting lower safeguarding referral rates for those receiving a personal budget. Early evaluations do, however, indicate that although personalisation and safeguarding are two of the most central priorities in adult social care for successive governments in the UK, they have tended to be addressed in parallel and that a more coherent approach to the two agendas is required (Manthorpe et al., 2015).

Approaches to safeguarding adults in the family

Collaborative working

Effective multi-agency working in safeguarding has already been discussed and is a theme which is highlighted consistently in SCRs and a range of policy developments across the lifespan. In terms of domestic violence, the multi-agency risk assessment conference (MARAC) process was set up in 2003 specifically to address high risk occurrences and provides a multi-agency forum for organisations such as the police, probation, local authority, health, housing, refuges and domestic violence support services. There are now approximately 260 MARAC groups operating in England and Wales and these are a key forum for key agencies to deal with domestic violence (Robbins et al., 2014). A further multi-agency forum which has developed over recent years to address safeguarding concerns is the multi-agency safeguarding hub (MASH) model. While there are significant parallels between the two models, the issues raised above in relation to how abuse is defined tend to impact on the routes deemed appropriate in specific cases. It is important that individuals supporting adults with social care needs are aware of the systems in place and the option of referral to MARAC where someone is experiencing significant levels of domestic violence.

Risk Identification Checklist

Co-ordinated Action Against Domestic Abuse (CAADA), which was recently renamed as SafeLives, provides a Risk Identification Checklist for domestic abuse which can be used to identify situations of extreme danger for people at risk. The purpose of the risk checklist is to give a consistent and simple tool for practitioners who work with adult victims of domestic abuse, stalking and 'honour'-based violence to help them identify those who are at high risk of harm and whose cases should be referred to a MARAC meeting.

Recommended referral criteria to MARAC are as follows.

1. Professional Judgement: if a professional has serious concerns about a victim's situation, they should refer the case to MARAC. There will be occasions where the particular context of a case gives rise to serious concerns even if the victim has been unable to disclose the information that might highlight their risk more clearly. This could reflect extreme levels of fear, cultural barriers to disclosure, immigration issues or language barriers particularly in cases of 'honour'-based violence. This judgement would be based on the professional's experience and/or the victim's perception of their risk even if they do not meet criteria 2 and/or 3 below.

2. 'Visible High Risk': the number of 'ticks' on the checklist. If you have ticked 14 or more 'yes' boxes the case would normally meet the MARAC referral criteria.

3. Potential Escalation: the number of police callouts to the victim as a result of domestic violence in the past 12 months. This criterion can be used to identify cases where there is not a positive identification of a majority of the risk factors on the list, but where abuse appears to be escalating and where it is appropriate to assess the situation more fully by sharing information at MARAC. It is common practice to start with three or more police callouts in a 12-month period but this will need to be reviewed depending on your local volume and your level of police reporting.

The risk assessment tool and guidance on its usage are available at: www.safelives. org.uk/sites/default/files/resources/Dash%20with%20guidance%20FINAL.pdf

Robbins et al. (2014) also suggest that, if appropriate, domestic violence concerns can be addressed both through MARAC and local safeguarding protocols and practice should not be forced down one particular route.

While formal multi-agency settings are a vital tool in collaborative working, Kharicha et al. (2004) suggest that informal practitioner-driven activity is as important to successful collaborative working as formal arrangements. They note that effective collaborative working requires individuals to identify and address differences in priorities and positions that they each hold. It requires practitioners to focus on relationship building and networking activity with a wide range of stakeholders.

ACTIVITY 4.6

Consider the range of skills required to achieve effective collaborative working. How might practitioners work towards addressing the differences in priorities and positions that they hold?

Making Safeguarding Personal

While effective multi-agency working is key in safeguarding, collaborative working with individuals and families is of central importance. Approaches and interventions which are not person-centred have the potential to cause further damage to individuals and to make situations worse. *Making Safeguarding Personal* (MSP) sees individuals as experts in their own lives and highlights the importance of work which focuses on the outcomes that they want to achieve (Lawson et al., 2014). This will depend entirely on listening to the individual. Research such as that carried out for the *Review of No Secrets* (Department of Health, 2009) demonstrates that although people do want to be safer, other things such as maintaining relationships may be of equal importance to them. In its simplest form, the intervention required involves working with individuals (and their representatives or advocates if they lack capacity) to develop a real understanding of what they wish to achieve and negotiating, agreeing and recording how best to achieve this. A further crucial step in this process is reviewing whether these outcomes are achieved at the end of involvement.

Traditional approaches to safeguarding adults in domestic settings have often left the adults involved feeling further disempowered by interventions and the MSP initiative provides a Toolkit of responses which can support person-centred working. The Toolkit can be accessed at: www.local.gov.uk/documents/10180/6869714/Making+safeguarding+personal_a+toolkit+for+responses_4th+Edition+2015.pdf/1a5845c2-9dfc-4afd-abac-d0f8f32914bc

Some of the approaches in the Toolkit include: supported decision making and freedom from undue influence; the use of advocacy and buddying; Signs of Safety®; attachment-based approaches; building resilience and assertiveness; family and network group conferencing and the use of restorative justice. There are clear parallels in many of the aspects of the Toolkit to approaches that have been used for some time in safeguarding children and young people which further highlights the connections between safeguarding at different stages of the lifespan. Family or network group conferencing, for instance, is an approach already discussed in relation to children which is highly adaptable to some safeguarding work with adults and will be explored further in Chapter 5. Some other aspects of the MSP Toolkit will be briefly considered here.

Personalised information and advice

At the most basic level, in order for individuals to have control and choice in safeguarding activity, they need to have access to information, advice, support and advocacy. All activity should be guided by the needs and circumstances of the individual and should focus on their preferred outcomes. Having the right information is an extremely important preventative tool but also essential in considering different options once abuse has occurred. Ensuring that information is available in the right format and that the pace and timing of decision making allow the individual to fully participate are central features of personalised responses to safeguarding. Previously, individuals have often felt disempowered and marginalised within safeguarding; clear information and negotiation about the process and the different options for support are essential.

Dealing with risk in caring relationships, including when employing personal assistants

In terms of addressing risk it is essential that individuals are seen in the context of their support networks and socio-economic circumstances. MSP highlights the importance of getting to know the person in order to fully understand their family situation and wider networks of support. Regular support is required for individuals and their carers in order to identify issues with care alongside work to reduce isolation and dependency on one person where there are risks and concerns in caring relationships. Some individuals in either paid or informal caring roles may harm a person they are caring for, which presents a very complex situation for the individual who is dependent on the abuser to meet their care and support needs. Some of these relationships will also go further and provide social and emotional support to the individual which they may be fearful of losing. The MSP Toolkit suggests that risk assessment models such as Signs of Safety® which consider danger, safety and strengths could be valuable here.

Signs of Safety® and wellbeing

As discussed earlier, this is an approach which came originally from children and families work but it has now been adapted for work with adults. It is a strengths-based approach which involves service users and their social and professional networks in developing intervention plans to improve wellbeing. It is highly adaptable to adult social care work and makes use of person-centred tools for assessment and planning. By mapping out the situation, those involved can identify strengths which could be built on to improve safety as well as clearly identifying risks and dangers.

Table 4.1 Using a Signs of Safety® questionnaire

An adult where there are concerns over their safety		
What are you worried about?	What's working well?	What needs to happen?
What has happened, what have you seen, that makes you worried about this adult?	Who are the people that care most about ___? What are the best things about how they care for ___? What are the best things about ___'s life? Who are the most important people in ___'s life? Have there been times when this problem has been dealt with or was even a little better? How did that happen?	What would ___ need to see that would make them say this problem is completely sorted out? What do you think is the next step that should happen to get this worry sorted out?
What do you think is the worst thing that could happen to ___ because of this problem?		Having thought more about this problem now, what would you need to see that would make you satisfied the situation is at a 10?
Are there things happening in ___'s life or family that make this problem harder to deal with?		

On a scale of 0 to 10 where 10 means this problem is sorted out as much as it can be and zero means things are so bad for the adult that professional or other outside help is needed, where do you rate this situation today? (Put different judgement numbers on a scale for different people, e.g. person themselves, safeguarding practitioner, family, GP etc.)

(Adapted from Stanley, n.d.)

Supported decision making and freedom from undue influence

The Mental Capacity Act requires that individuals are assumed to have capacity to make their own decisions unless there is evidence to the contrary. Many individuals with care and support needs will still require support with decision making to explain issues and convey their wishes to others. When an individual is unable to make a decision then best interest decision making should still involve them to the greatest possible degree and reflect their wishes and feelings throughout.

The MSP Toolkit discusses situations when individuals refuse interventions and there is reason to believe that this is as a result of undue influence or coercion. In such circumstances support may be required to allow the individual to make the decision free from these influences. Courts can intervene and apply their inherent jurisdiction to overrule a person's expressed wishes where there is coercion in order to restore choice and control in decision making (LGA, 2015).

ACTIVITY **4.7**

Case scenario: Mary

Mary is a white 76 year old woman who lives alone in supported housing and she has severe arthritis. She is unable to leave her flat without assistance and her son Tom collects her pension each week, does shopping and pays her bills. Previously she was an active member of her local Roman Catholic Church but she has gradually lost touch with people there since her health deteriorated. The warden at the supported housing has contacted social services as she is concerned that the flat is very cold and Mary has very little food in the kitchen.

(Continued)

She also seems to have lost weight recently and has some bruising on her arms. There are several reminders for bills in the house that Mary thought Tom had paid for her. When you visit, Mary becomes tearful and says she is not sleeping. She says that her son drinks too much and gets very angry with her if she tries to talk to him about not having enough food. Mary is afraid that Tom will be angry if he finds out she has talked to you and the warden about this. She also states that she would be distraught if she lost contact with Tom as she loves him dearly and she can't manage her money without him to help.

Look at the different aspects of the MSP Toolkit and consider how you would apply the principles and practice of MSP to Mary.

How in particular could a Signs of Safety® approach be used with Mary?

COMMENT

In Mary's situation it is clear that safeguarding activity would need to balance her wish to retain her relationship with her son while protecting her from abuse and neglect. It is also apparent that she is reluctant to accept support due to fear of reprisals from Tom. The fine balance between protecting individuals from abuse and the potential to override their choices has already been discussed. While the Mental Capacity Act 2005 has provided a framework for decision making in safeguarding there continue to be many grey areas in practice. Assessing capacity can be particularly complex where there is domestic abuse and an individual who has care and support needs is potentially making decisions which place them in danger (Robbins et al., 2014). While the Care Act encourages protection to be seen alongside other areas of wellbeing as opposed to overriding them, this has to be considered in relation to notions of coercion and undue influence. Robbins et al. (2014) make the important point that practitioners are in the position of holding contradictory notions of service users as, at the same time, both autonomous and also potentially requiring intervention to which they cannot consent. A key point here is that even if an individual is reluctant to accept support, if practitioners are too quick to decide that the individual is making an unwise but capacitated decision, then opportunities to offer further support and potential disclosure of coercion may be lost (LGA, 2013). The right to make unwise decisions is a central difference between adult and children's safeguarding and one which permeates all work within families and communities. Unwise decisions, however, do need to be considered in the wider context of the potential for abusers to exert power and control over individuals.

Balancing choice and risk has long been a source of debate and dilemma in supporting individuals to lead more independent lives. A central feature of the Care Act is ensuring that protection does not override other areas of wellbeing in terms of support planning and that individuals should have the right to manage their own risks in seeking a better quality of life. While there has been much discussion about the shift in risk management from the state to the individual and the political motivations behind policy initiatives, it is clear that risk averse practice can be just as damaging to people as abuse and that individual needs and priorities should drive support planning and safeguarding.

Approaches across the lifespan

In this chapter we have considered the range of factors that impact on the likelihood of abuse occurring in family and domestic situations to individuals from young childhood to old age. Some of the key approaches to safeguarding across the lifespan that have been discussed are *Think Family*, Signs of Safety® and *Making Safeguarding Personal*.

ACTIVITY 4.8

Look at the case scenarios below and consider how the principles and practice of Signs of Safety®, Think Family and MSP could be applied to them:

Donna lives with her 12 year old daughter Sarah and 62 year old mother Anna, who has early onset dementia. Anna attends a lunch club once each week which she really enjoys. The family live in inadequate housing which is damp and sometimes they have to leave the heat off to have enough money to pay for food. Donna finds she often loses her temper with Sarah and Anna and at different times has slapped both of them across the face. Things seem better for the family when Donna's Aunty Joan and Uncle Jim come and visit to help them out.

Alistair has been physically violent to his partner Jess since they moved in together four years ago. Jess has a 16 year old daughter Kate who also lives with them. Jess thinks about getting out of the relationship often and has twice spoken to someone at a local women's refuge. Alistair has been drinking very heavily over recent years and often is violent to Jess when he comes home late at night. Jess has a good friend at work who she sometimes confides in. One night when Jess is at work, Kate refuses to make Alistair a sandwich and he pushes her across the room. She falls and sustains a head injury.

COMMENT

In the case scenarios above, there is clearly a range of factors which are impacting on abuse perpetrated against both children and adults. Unless underlying causes are addressed it is likely that these factors will continue to impact on the people at risk within the family setting, whatever their age or life stage. There is clearly a need to address the abuse, with the use of the law where appropriate, and identify what is required to plan for safety of all family members. This should be approached in the context of the expressed outcomes of the individuals who are harmed and from a perspective which builds on the strengths and networks of support available. Access to a range of support services would be necessary in both scenarios.

CHAPTER SUMMARY

In this chapter we have considered a range of factors which can increase the likelihood of abuse to individuals across the lifespan in family and domestic settings. Key themes have emerged in terms of defining and looking at the potential underlying causes of abuse. While abuse at any age can be seen to be closely

(Continued)

linked to power and control in specific relationships, it is also very much connected to the position of individuals in wider society, which will be explored further in the following chapter. It is apparent that domestic abuse, substance misuse and mental health issues can have lasting and negative effects on both children and adults. However, adult and children's services are informed by different legislative frameworks, which has contributed to the development of specialisms within practice and a more separatist approach to safeguarding. The challenge for practitioners is to enhance their understanding of the types of issues that may affect the protection of children and adults rather than assessing them as separate issues. An example of this separatist approach within social work practice was highlighted by Forrester and Harwin:

> *In general, there appeared to be a strong institutional tendency towards under-responding to alcohol and drug misuse ... ... a pervasive sense that social workers did not know how to work with parental alcohol or drug problems... ... [they had] minimal training and often had limited supervision and support ... ... a toxic cocktail that is almost certain to produce poor practice. (2011: 116)*

Hidden Harm made explicit reference to the lack of information sharing between adult substance misuse services and children's services. This has been observed as a common feature in a significant number of SCRs when adult and children's services have not communicated appropriately or shared information. SCRs have also consistently highlighted that the misjudgement of risk can have fatal consequences for both children and adults.

Multi-agency working

The development of the MARAC model and *Think Family* has demonstrated how multi-agency working can lead to a more coordinated response to risk. A key component to effective multi-agency working is joint training and greater collaboration between and across professions. Practitioners need to be aware of the range of legal and therapeutic interventions open to them, and to engage in critically reflective practice which enhances the safety of children and adults. Workers need to develop knowledge and skills in relation to working holistically with families to enable a better understanding of the issues that may exist within the family. Complex issues require greater knowledge across services and a more coordinated response to the assessment of risk and need.

A separatist approach to meeting the needs of children and adults undoubtedly impacts on the chances of achieving real change in people's lives. Despite the high profile of the *Think Family* approach, there continue to be very few services which are explicitly organised to meet the needs of families across the lifespan. A more holistic approach to assessments with families is required with a focus on risks, needs and strengths. A key aspect of this is services taking a much wider view of their remit and developing more awareness of a 'no wrong door' approach which aims to ensure that anyone needing help can access it wherever their first point of contact may be.

Collaboration with individuals and families

A range of approaches which can support safeguarding such as *Think Family,* Signs of Safety® and *Making Safeguarding Personal* have been considered and key themes from these have been identified. Central to any

(Continued)

safeguarding activity is maintaining the individual and the family at the centre of the process. Ensuring that the voice of the child is heard parallels the need for adult safeguarding measures to keep the individual at the centre of actions which are based around their own desired outcomes. Likewise, all family members and wider networks who are involved need to be fully included in safety planning. Concerns around dangers and risks and what is expected of particular individuals in relation to this, need to be practical, clear and trans- parent. The use of plain language and people's preferred methods of communication is essential if people are to be fully involved in support and safety planning. Taking the time to go at a pace where individuals and families remain fully involved is essential. Building relationships to develop a real understanding of people and their support networks is also a key factor here.

A central focus of the approaches considered is the importance of a move away from a deficit model of working to a strengths-based approach. Explicit agreement needs to be reached among all stakeholders about risks, dangers and harm and how these will be addressed. This, however, needs to be done in the context of building on strengths and what has worked well or has the potential to work well in the future. Moves away from an individualised deficits approach can also be supported by continued and increased awareness of the wider structural factors which impact on individuals and families. Many of the points raised in relation to practice improvements require a well-resourced service context which allows good practice to flourish. The implications of this in relation to the climate of austerity will be reviewed in depth in Chapter 8.

The approaches to safeguarding children and adults that have been considered in this chapter require a shift from procedure-driven practice. Much safeguarding work to date has been highly focused on procedure, as a reaction to the anxiety around abuse and the potential for blame if harm occurs. Such anxiety has also fuelled models of practice which see the practitioner as the expert. The key challenge for safeguarding work is to build alternative models which see individuals as experts in their own lives and ensure that they are fully involved in safety planning. The breaking down of boundaries between different professions and with families is central to this process. Putting more emphasis on creative and preventative safeguarding is a further crucial factor in providing personalised responses. These aims are only possible if safeguarding is seen within the context of raised awareness and the involvement of wider communities.

FURTHER READING

Children's Commissioner (2012) *Silent Voices: Supporting Children and Young People Affected by Parental Alcohol Misuse*. London: Community Research Company.

Cleaver, H, Unell, I and Aldgate, J (2011) *Children's Needs – Parenting Capacity. Child Abuse: Parental Mental Illness, Learning Disability, Substance Misuse, and Domestic Violence*, 2nd edn. London: The Stationery Office.

Cooklin, A. (2014) *Parental Mental Illness: The Impact on Children and Adolescents: Information for Parents, Carers and Anyone Who Works with Young People*. Available at: www.rcpsych.ac.uk/health advice/parentsandyouthinfo/parentscarers/parentalmentalillness.aspx (accessed 27 October 2015).

Local Government Association/ADASS (2015) *Adult Safeguarding and Domestic Abuse: A Guide to Support Practitioners and Managers* , 2nd edn. Available at: http://www.local.gov.uk/publications/-/journal_content/56/10180/3973717/PUBLICATION#sthash.TGS1DVgU.dpuf

SCIE (2014) *Gaining Access to an Adult Suspected to be at Risk of Neglect or Abuse: A Guide for Social Workers and their Managers in England*. London: Social Care Institute for Excellence. Available at: www.scie.org.uk/care-act-2014/safeguarding-adults/adult-suspected-at-risk-of-neglect-abuse/

Turnell, A and Edwards, S (1997) Aspiring to partnership: The Signs of Safety approach to child protection casework. *Child Abuse Review*, 6: 179–90.

Chapter 5
Safeguarding and communities

Introduction

Social care policy and legislation from the mid-1900s onwards has reflected a growing awareness of the harm that can be caused to people by institutional forms of care and the potential for abuse in such environments. The community is now fully acknowledged as the rightful context for meeting the needs of almost all individuals at any stage of the lifespan and whatever their specific needs. The refocusing on care within communities, however, has not necessarily meant that communities are willing to undertake or indeed are equipped for this role. The potential for the wider community to harm individuals of all ages has been acutely highlighted in recent years in relation to, for instance, exposure of child sexual exploitation and incidences of hate crime against adults. Debate around raising awareness and the roles and responsibilities of wider community networks in terms of safeguarding from abuse has evolved even more recently in response to these themes. Cases of exploitation and abuse within communities are regularly reported in the media. At the same time, political rhetoric and social care policies are promoting the key role that the voluntary sector and informal networks within communities should play in supporting individuals with health and care needs in their localities. This in turn is occurring within the context of reduced funding for many charitable and voluntary community organisations. Chapter 4 reviewed risk factors and approaches to safeguarding within families. Clearly families do not exist in a vacuum but are situated within the wider context of communities. There are also many individuals within communities who do not live within any kind of family group. The role of communities as simultaneously potential protectors and perpetrators is therefore a complex one. This chapter explores the factors underlying abuse that occurs within communities to people of all ages and also the range of safeguarding responses. Themes that impact on safeguarding individuals at any life stage, such as citizenship, exploitation and marginalisation within society, will also be considered.

Children, young people and communities – child sexual exploitation

What is CSE?

Child sexual exploitation (CSE) is not a new phenomenon but represents a conceptual shift away from the term child prostitution. CSE is abuse of a child or young person and usually involves a grooming process which then leads to abuse. The relationship is manipulative, and exploits the imbalance of power between the child and the perpetrator. Media attention and public awareness have been raised during the past decade following a series of high profile inquiries into extensive and historical cases of CSE, in Rochdale, Rotherham, Oxford and Greater Manchester.

The following definition has been developed by the Department for Children, Schools and Families (DCSF) and Home Office (2009):

> *Sexual exploitation of children and young people under 18 involves exploitative situations, contexts and relationships where young people (or a third person or persons) receive 'something' (e.g. food, accommodation, drugs, alcohol, cigarettes, affection, gifts, money) as a result of them performing, and/or another or others performing on them, sexual activities. Child sexual exploitation can occur through the use of technology without the child's immediate recognition; for example being persuaded to post sexual images on the Internet/mobile phones without immediate payment or gain. In all cases, those exploiting the child/young person have power over them by virtue of their age, gender, intellect, physical strength and/or economic or other resources. Violence, coercion and intimidation are common, involvement in exploitative relationships being characterised in the main by the child or young person's limited availability of choice resulting from their social/economic and/or emotional vulnerability.*

(DCSF and Home Office, 2009: 9)

Age and CSE

The *Office of the Children's Commissioner's Inquiry into Child Sexual Exploitation in Gangs and Groups* found that the average age for children experiencing sexual exploitation is 15 (Berelowitz et al., 2013). However, there appears to be more evidence that younger children are being targeted. Following the Rotherham Inquiry, Jay (2014) reported that children as young as 11 years of age had been victims of CSE.

CSE is usually associated with young women but it also affects boys and young men; although there are limited data in relation to prevalence of CSE among these groups.

Grooming and CSE

What is grooming?

Grooming is a process where an emotional relationship is developed between an abuser and a child for the purposes of abuse and exploitation. Grooming can take place on a face to face basis or online but inevitably the process is manipulative and exploitative. There are various models of grooming that have been developed to try to encapsulate the complex processes of manipulation and abuse; grooming can take place where the child or young person is befriended and then is gradually exploited through a variety of different processes. The grooming process can involve a number of different stages including the following.

- Inappropriate relationships, which involve the perpetrator being in a position of power and control; there is often a considerable age gap between the victim and perpetrator.

- The 'boyfriend' model of exploitation and peer exploitation.

- The perpetrator befriends and grooms a young person often making the young person feel special, usually providing gifts.

- The perpetrator begins a sexual relationship with the child or young person, often introducing the child or young person to illicit substances such as alcohol or drugs. The perpetrator often then coerces or forces them to have sex with friends or associates.

- Organised/networked sexual exploitation or trafficking. Young people are often coerced into sexual activity with a multitude of groups of men, often being moved to different locations across the country. Young people may become involved in actively recruiting other young victims. *'Organised sexual exploitation is the sophisticated form of this abuse, based on links between abusers, and often involves victims being moved to other cities or towns for exploitation (referred to as 'internal trafficking')'* (Barnardo's, 2012: 4).

Online grooming

Online grooming is a process of online socialisation during which an offender interacts with a child in order to prepare him/her for sexual abuse (NSPCC, 2015). The popularity of social networks has increased the opportunities for perpetrators to contact young people online for the purpose of sexual grooming. Unfortunately, this process is difficult to police and monitor as perpetrators can easily conceal their identity. Offenders may try to conceal the relationship by moving possible victims to other sites (such as instant messenger) or using SMS to identify and meet children or young people. The Sexual Offences Act 2003 has been amended to introduce a number of new offences to try to tackle online grooming; it is an offence to meet a child following sexual grooming and befriending a child on the internet with the intention to initiate a sexual relationship (www.legislation.gov.uk/ ukpga/2003/42/contents).

CSE and risk indicators

Although it is recognised that any child could be at risk of CSE, the following factors may make a child or young person more vulnerable to being groomed or sexually exploited.

- Going missing for periods of time or regularly returning home late.

- Regularly missing school or not taking part in education.

- Appearing with unexplained gifts or new possessions.

- Associating with other people involved in exploitation.

- Having older boyfriends or girlfriends.

- Mood swings or changes in emotional wellbeing.

- Drug and alcohol misuse.

- Displaying inappropriate sexualised behaviour.

(Barnardo's, 2012: 5).

Children and young people who are vulnerable have low self-esteem and a poor self-image and are often identified and targeted by perpetrators. However, certain groups of children and young people are particularly vulnerable to sexual exploitation: disabled children and young people, young people who are trafficked or asylum seeking children and children who are looked after, who are often 'missing from care', are recognised as being much more at risk of being targeted. This subject will be addressed in more depth in Chapter 6.

ACTIVITY **5.1**

Consider the possible impact of CSE on the development and emotional wellbeing of a child. How might this impact be intensified if the child has communication difficulties, or if they are socially isolated?

RESEARCH SUMMARY

Children with learning disabilities are a group of young people who are at an increased risk of sexual exploitation. The report, Unprotected, Overprotected: Meeting the Needs of Young People with Learning Disabilities who Experience, or are at Risk of Sexual Exploitation was published in September 2015 (Franklin et al., 2015). The report suggested that children with learning disabilities are particularly vulnerable to CSE because the risk of exploitation is hidden or not recognised. children with disabilities do not meet the thresholds for statutory services and as a consequence do not receive support.

The report found that children and young people with learning difficulties were at an increased risk of sexual exploitation due to being overprotected and socially isolated. Young people with learning disabilities are vulnerable to CSE due to factors that include overprotection, social isolation and a reluctance to view disabled people as having a sexual identity. There was a lack of professional awareness of the sexual exploitation of young people with learning disabilities which tended to escalate the risk. This lack of awareness also meant that cases were not consistently referred to multi-agency arrangements for CSE. Young people with learning disabilities can face a number of challenges to disclosing CSE, including the negative responses of professionals.

'Young people with learning disabilities share many of the same vulnerabilities to CSE (Child Sexual Exploitation) that are faced by all young people, but there is evidence to suggest that they are more vulnerable to CSE than their non-disabled peers' (Franklin et al., 2015: 124). The report made a series of recommendations to help challenge the risk of children with disabilities from being exploited. It is suggested that children and young people with disabilities require specific resources and education to provide information on safe sexual relationships. The report also recommended that: children and young people need to be listened to by professionals; they need to be provided with support to meet their specific learning needs; and they need to have access to more specialist child sexual exploitation services (Franklin et al., 2015).

Unaccompanied asylum seekers

Unaccompanied asylum seeking children and trafficked young people are among the most vulnerable and socially excluded groups within society. An unaccompanied asylum seeking child is defined as, *'a child who is applying for asylum in their own right and is separated from both parents and is not being cared for by an adult who in law or by custom has responsibility to do so'* (Department for Education, 2014a: 3). Asylum seeking children have experienced trauma and distress, often fleeing persecution and violence. If they are unaccompanied and have been separated from their families or guardians then the local authority has a duty to promote and safeguard their welfare, according to s 17 of the CA 1989. In 2014 the Department for Education produced some statutory guidance for local authorities in relation to the care of unaccompanied asylum seeking and trafficked children. Local authorities have a duty to assess the needs of children and young people taking into consideration their physical and psychological health, religious and ethnic background, together with their accommodation and financial situation. There is also a responsibility to undertake an age assessment if it is deemed appropriate.

Section 20 of the Children Act 1989 provides that local authorities should accommodate unaccompanied asylum seeking children (www.legislation.gov.uk/ukpga/ 1989/41/section/20). However, Lay and Papadopoulos (2009) argue that although there may be some similarities between unaccompanied children and other looked after young people, unaccompanied children are vulnerable to abuse and exploitation due to *'their socio-cultural alienation and the challenges of acculturation, migration status, communication difficulties, absence of family in the UK, inappropriate accommodation and high levels of exposure to potential perpetrators'* (2009: 34).

Trafficked children and young people

What is trafficking?

The recruitment, transportation, transfer, harbouring or receipt of a child, by means of threat or use of force or other forms of coercion, of abduction, of fraud, of deception, of the abuse of power or of a position of vulnerability or of the giving or receiving of payments or benefits to achieve the consent of a person having control over another person, for the purpose of exploitation.

(Council of Europe, 2005)

Children are trafficked for financial and/or personal gain. Many children are trafficked as a result of abduction, some are threatened and others are groomed. As a result of trafficking, children and young people may be socially isolated, imprisoned or coerced into activities such as forced marriage, forced labour or sexual exploitation. In July 2014 the government initiated a campaign which aimed to highlight awareness of issues relating to modern day slavery including children and young people who might be trafficked (Children's Society, 2014). The Modern Slavery Act 2015 has a number of new civil orders to prevent slavery, forced labour and human trafficking; however, no separate offence has been proposed for child sexual exploitation (www.legislation. gov.uk/ukpga/2015/30/contents/enacted).

The Impact of CSE

CSE can have a detrimental effect on a young person's physical, emotional and sexual development, affecting all aspects of their health and wellbeing.

Short-term impact

Initially children may enjoy the attention that is given to them by the perpetrator; however, this attention is conditional and often leads to the child or young person being socially isolated from their family and friends. Once the grooming process has been initiated and the relationship enters into a more established pattern of abuse the child or young person may encounter coercion or threats to comply; threats can take the form of physical, emotional or sexual abuse. Threats are also often made towards the victim's family and friends. Children and young people are often introduced to drug and alcohol misuse and as a consequence may exhibit self-harm behaviours and substance dependency. There is also the risk that children and young people may be exposed to sexually transmitted diseases and continued threats of physical violence.

Longer-term impact

Research indicates that some victims of CSE can experience difficulties several years after they have been abused; a disproportionate number were victims of domestic violence, or had developed long-standing drug and alcohol addiction. Over 70 per cent of adults involved in prostitution were sexually exploited as children or teenagers (Pearce and Jago, 2008). The Jay Report (2014) found that some victims suffered post-traumatic stress and other emotional and psychological problems, while others experienced mental health problems (Jay, 2014).

The legal and policy context of CSE

Children are protected from abuse and harm principally by the Children Act 1989 and the Children Act 2004. The Sexual Offences Act 2003 introduced a range of new offences that recognised the grooming, coercion and control of children. The Act does not recognise the term 'child sexual exploitation'; however, the provisions of the legislation do allow prosecutions to be brought on a range of offences including: rape, sexual assault, sexual grooming, causing or inciting child prostitution or pornography and trafficking within the UK for sexual exploitation (Franklin et al., 2015). Unfortunately, however, the number of successful convictions remains low.

Safeguarding Children and Young People from Sexual Exploitation: Supplementary Guidance (DCSF, 2009) was introduced to provide statutory guidance on how organisations and individuals should work together to protect young people from sexual exploitation. The guidance aims to:

* develop local prevention strategies;

* identify those at risk of being sexually exploited;

* take action to safeguard and promote the welfare of particular children and young people who are being, or may be, sexually exploited;

* take action against those intent on abusing and exploiting children and young people in this way.

The United Nations Convention on the Rights of the Child 1989 provides a response to CSE on an international level. Article 19 stipulates that all children should be protected from all forms of violence: *'Children have the right to be protected from being hurt and mistreated, physically or mentally. Governments should ensure that children are properly cared for and protect them from violence, abuse and neglect by their parents, or anyone else who looks after them'* (United Nations, 1989).

Article 34 highlights that *'Governments should protect children from all forms of sexual exploitation and abuse. This provision in the Convention is augmented by the Optional Protocol on the sale of children, child prostitution and child pornography'* (United Nations, 1989).

ACTIVITY 5.2

Choose three of the reports below, read the summaries and recommendations and high-light the key issues and identify any recurring themes.

- Unheard Voices: The Sexual Exploitation of Asian Girls and Women, *report by the Muslim Women's Network on CSE in the Muslim community (Gohir, 2013).*

- *Parliamentary Inquiry into the Effectiveness of Legislation for Tackling Child Sexual Exploitation and Trafficking within the UK. Barnardo's report of Sarah Champion MP's inquiry (Barnardo's, 2014).*

- Independent Inquiry into Child Sexual Exploitation in Rotherham, 1997–2013 *(Jay, 2014).*

- Real Voices, *Ann Coffey MP's report on CSE in Greater Manchester (Coffey, 2014).*

- *The Sexual Exploitation of Children: It Couldn't Happen Here, Could It? Ofsted thematic review of local authorities' current response to CSE (Ofsted, 2014).*

- Report of Inspection of Rotherham Metropolitan Borough Council *(Casey, 2015).*

COMMENT

There were unfortunately consistent failings highlighted throughout all of the reports, including poor multi-agency working, information sharing and risk assessment. Another key theme that has emerged is the lack of professional responses to the victims of CSE.

Multi-agency responses

The lack of effective strategic multi-agency partnerships and planning between the police, education, health and children's services has resulted in failures in all services to identify and support young people who are at risk or who are experiencing CSE. The Child Exploitation and Online Protection Centre (CEOP) has stressed the need for agencies to be more proactive in the way that they identify and record cases of

CSE. The Children Act 2004 created Local Safeguarding Children Boards (LSCBs) which have a statutory duty to bring agencies together to safeguard and promote the welfare of children.

Jago et al. (2011) explored the extent and nature of the response of LSCBs to the 2009 government guidance on safeguarding children and young people from sexual exploitation. The research highlighted that only a quarter of LSCBs in England were implementing the guidance. In response to the Jay Report (2014) the government produced *Tackling Child Sexual Exploitation* (Cabinet Office, 2015). This acknowledged that whilst there may have been some improvements there are concerns that in some LAs the profile of CSE is still low. The report made a number of recommendations to promote a more effective and coordinated response to CSE. These recommendations include:

- Setting up a new national taskforce and a centre of expertise to help identify and respond more effectively to CSE.

- Consideration to be given in relation to extending the new 'wilful neglect' offence to children's social care and education services.

- Perpetrators of child sexual abuse will be given the status of a national threat.

- Finally the government has pledged to provide an additional £7 million to enable specialist organisations to support victims and survivors.

It is too early to establish how effective these proposals will be in relation to raising the profile of CSE and protecting vulnerable children and young people; however, barriers to effective practice must be acknowledged and addressed, and the rhetoric of policy needs to be translated at all levels, in all departments and across agencies.

A lack of a shared understanding of CSE and unprofessional responses

Although there have been changes in policy and more awareness of the impact of CSE a tension still exists in relation to whether young people are perceived as victims, or agents who are able to make their own decisions. Melrose and Pearce (2013) suggest that there is a tendency to view victims as consenting agents. As such, they were seen to carry responsibility for what happened to them, and consequently be blamed for the abuse that they suffered.

The inquiries in both Rochdale and Rotherham have highlighted that a number of different professionals made value judgements about the young people who sought support in relation to the abuse that they were experiencing. The report by the Office of the Children's Commissioner highlighted examples where children and young people who were being sexually exploited were frequently described by professionals as being 'promiscuous', 'putting themselves at risk', and 'asking for it' (Berelowitz et al., 2013).

ACTIVITY 5.3

Read the following case study and identify the main areas of risk. Are there any protective factors? Do you consider that Jane is at risk of CSE?

Jane

Jane has come to a direct access night shelter. She has been sleeping rough. The night shelter worker is concerned about her mental and physical health. Jane's friend has told the worker that Jane was recently in hospital following an attack when she was sleeping on the streets.

Jane was in care until the age of 15 when she ran away. She has spent the past couple of months living on the streets, in hostels or other insecure housing. Jane is eligible for support from the leaving care team but she is reluctant to meet any more social workers; however, she discloses that she is pregnant and is concerned about the impact that her substance misuse might have on her unborn child. Jane is heroin dependent. Jane has also stated that she has been involved with prostitution to fund her dependency.

History

Jane was made subject to care order when she was 11 years of age. Jane had been assaulted by her father on several occasions and left home alone frequently when her parents went on alcohol binges. Jane has a younger brother who is settled with foster carers.

Jane found it difficult to settle into foster care and had approximately ten different placements. Her behaviour was described as disruptive and at times aggressive, particularly after contact with her brother. Jane has had no contact with her father during the past couple of years. When Jane first ran away she went to stay with her mum but within two days they had a row which led to mum calling the police and Jane being charged with criminal damage and affray. Mum describes Jane as trouble and a 'dirty smack head'.

Jane changed schools seven times and was permanently excluded at the age of 13. She was referred to the local pupil referral unit for alternative educational provision, but rarely attended because she was bored.

- *What are Jane's needs? Prioritise these needs.*
- *Create a realistic plan to support and address these needs. Outline any barriers/ difficulties.*
- *What types of discrimination might Jane face?*
- *What knowledge and skills would you need to engage effectively with Jane?*
- *Decide how you might intervene to support Jane.*

(Continued)

COMMENT

First, it is important to recognise that Jane is a young person who may be at risk of signifi-cant harm and as such all agencies have a duty to promote her health, safety and wellbeing.

The following areas are important to help promote more informed practice:

- *listening to children and young people*
- *responding quickly to emerging difficulties*
- *ensuring effective management oversight*
- *better training and challenging and reflective supervision for professionals*
- *good commissioning arrangements*
- *competent assessments and care planning for children and young people*
- *effective joint working and information sharing across services.*

(Ofsted, 2014: 13–14)

Throughout your involvement with Jane, effective multi-agency communication and infor-mation sharing will be essential.

Multi-agency Child Sexual Exploitation (MACSE) meetings represent an example of effective multi-agency working. These meetings have been established to enable different agencies to work together to keep children and young people safe from sexual exploitation. The purpose of the meetings is to raise concerns, gather information and assess the risk that a young person may face in relation to CSE. Different agencies present information and agree a plan to determine how the case should be managed. The information will also be used to further inform investigations, and a strategy discussion must take place in every situation where there is reasonable cause to suspect that a child is suffering or is likely to suffer significant harm.

CSE continues to represent a significant challenge to safeguarding children and young people. The development of more effective processes for early identification and more coordinated intervention are key factors to achieving a more preventative approach to tackling abuse and exploitation. There should be more emphasis on recognising the needs and vulnerabilities of children and young people and a clearer differentiation between vic-tims and perpetrators. Finally there needs to be more emphasis on securing prosecutions, through the use of joint investigations and multi-agency responses. The significant change that needs to take place within CSE work is a conceptual shift from a victim needs led response to a much more child protection response which includes support for victims.

Adult abuse and the community

Ideas around care in the community emerged in the later decades of the twenti-eth century in response to the failings of institutional models of support. While the rights of individuals to live within communities are now fully acknowledged, there have been significant issues in terms of the nature and extent of support availa-ble to individuals. Themes arising have included the level and quality of paid support

(Equality and Human Rights Commission, 2011) and also whether individuals should have to be reliant on informal networks of support (Galpin, 2014). Recent governments have focused on the importance of informal support to individuals, with the coalition government introducing narratives around *the big society* to highlight the role of the community in providing support to those in need (Woodhouse, 2015). This focus on informal networks has continued and is a theme in current policy and legislation. Alongside this, media reports and serious case reviews have demonstrated that communities are often highly dangerous places where individuals with additional needs can be at risk of discrimination, mistreatment and abuse.

Hate crime and mate crime

Hate crime and mate crime have been discussed in Chapter 2 but are important to consider here in relation to safeguarding in a community context. These are closely linked to discriminatory abuse which is described in the Care Act guidance as including *'forms of harassment, slurs or similar treatment; because of race, gender and gender identity, age, disability, sexual orientation or religion'* (Department of Health, 2014: 234).

There have been many incidences of abuse and murder of individuals with learning disabilities, mental health problems and other care needs, many of which have resulted in SCRs, such as the inquiry into the death of Steven Hoskin (Flynn, 2007), who was tortured and killed by individuals who had 'befriended' him, and Michael Gilbert, who was tortured over a period of months, and finally murdered by people whom he had seen as friends (Flynn, 2011). The crimes committed against these people, among many others, have highlighted the very fragile nature of existence for many people who have 'fallen through the net' in terms of having little or no access to informal or formal support. Often those most at risk are people who are on the margins of eligibility criteria for services or have not engaged with the type of support offered. SCRs have highlighted a range of factors, particularly around the discrimination and social exclusion of people with additional needs. There are also significant grey areas where individuals may be assessed as having capacity and therefore the right to refuse support where they may be subject to undue influence or where further attempts need to be made to provide alternative or ongoing contact. The failures in multi-agency working and information sharing are also repeatedly highlighted, such as where individual agencies may have part of a wider picture of events that if put together would present a far more serious concern (Flynn, 2007; Warwickshire Safeguarding Adults Partnership, 2010).

RESEARCH SUMMARY

Landman (2014) refers to the human need for acceptance, validation, pleasure and support derived from friendships which can be so easily exploited. He suggests that hate crime has often been presented as bullying and harassment on the street; senseless and irrational crimes perpetrated by strangers. This is in contrast to much of the evidence from research which suggests that hate crime is more likely to be perpetrated by people known

(Continued)

very well to the victim in environments such as their own home and often in situations where the individual appears on the surface to be a willing participant (Sherry, 2010). Such abuse or 'mate crime' is often far more subtle than the traditional picture of hate crime and as such can be highly complex to uncover and respond to. Landman identifies some real incidences of mate crime collated from a range of sources, including:

- *multiple accounts of women with learning disabilities being pimped (sent to work as a prostitute) by their 'boyfriends';*

- *a man proposing marriage to a woman with learning disabilities and asking her for money to save for their wedding; the man had proposed to a number of women and was making a good living from these 'savings';*

- *multiple accounts of male paedophiles having relationships with women with learning disabilities with a view to abusing any resulting children;*

- *multiple accounts of people with learning disabilities having friends who only visit them on the day their benefits are paid, and persuade them to pay for pub visits, trips to the amusement arcade, etc.;*

- *a man with learning disabilities who was a low-level, mild drug user being befriended by the local drugs dealer, and being offered more, and harder, drugs;*

- *multiple accounts of people with learning disabilities being asked to look after, or store, suspicious packages by 'friends' or asked to hold bags on shoplifting trips.*

(2014: 357–8)

What interventions could support and protect the individuals who are being harmed? Consider the usefulness of the different approaches in the MSP Toolkit in each instance.

Available at: www.local.gov.uk/documents/10180/6869714/Making+safeguarding+personal_a+toolkit+for+responses_4th+Edition+2015.pdf/1a5845c2-9dfbac-d0f8f32914bc

How do these examples compare to abuse of other individuals such as children, young people, people with mental health problems and older people with care and support needs?

The criminal behaviour in the examples should be addressed wherever possible through the early involvement of the police and discussion of this with those at risk is an immediate priority. Messages from people who have been subject to safeguarding measures in the MSP

(Continued)

COMMENT continued

guidance confirms that safeguarding responses need to be based around what works best for the individual being harmed. Agreement about immediate and ongoing support from relevant agencies is needed. A central task would be to raise the awareness of the individual to the abusive nature of the perpetrator's actions and how they can, with support, protect themselves from this. For instance, the Signs of Safety® framework discussed in Chapter 4 could be useful here. The individuals may need to be supported to create real friendships and support networks within their local area. Further key areas are discussed later in this chapter.

While these specific examples refer to people with learning disabilities there are many examples of other vulnerable adults being subject to similar forms of exploitation. There are also significant parallels in terms of abuse of power and grooming behaviour over extensive periods of time to those displayed by perpetrators of child sexual exploitation. Concepts around grooming behaviour have more recently also been considered in relation to the targeting of individuals and families by extremist groups. These examples of abuse highlight the need to consider approaches to intervention within the wider context of community and society.

The links between social exclusion and abuse

A range of factors can make people with learning disabilities more vulnerable to mate crime, including fewer opportunities to make real friendships and the potential for isolation and lack of structure in their lives (Landman, 2014). Learned compliance, issues with communication and inexperience in relationships accompanied by increasing independence are also features for many people. Living outside social care systems of support and an increased likelihood of living in poverty are also key factors in social exclusion and increased risk of hate crime (Disability Rights Commission, 2006). Historical attitudes to people with disabilities and the normalisation of harassment and dehumanising treatment of individuals with additional needs are such that some disabled people have been conditioned to expect no better.

There are clear parallels between the abuse of people with learning disabilities in communities and other adults with care and support needs. Despite common media portrayals of people with mental health problems, they are much more likely to be the victims of crime than perpetrators. In a recent study 45 per cent of people with severe mental illness had been victims of crime in the previous year. Hate crime and mate crime against people with mental health problems are prevalent with a high risk of victimisation within communities (Pettitt et al., 2013).

While people with additional needs are much more likely to become the target of a range of exploitation and crimes against them, they are conversely less likely to receive appropriate legal redress. Responses to incidents of hate crime can be focused on protecting the individual by restricting their freedom, as opposed to providing access to justice (Hoong Sin et al., 2011). Also, evidence suggests that people with mental health problems are much less likely than the general public to have a satisfactory experience of reporting crime, including being disbelieved and blamed and also subject to a lack of understanding of their additional needs around this process (Pettitt et al., 2013). So responses to incidents of abuse can themselves cause further mistreatment to individuals.

Highlighting issues around hate crime, and the more specific features of mate crime, brings into focus the range of challenges that face people with care and support needs in their relationships with the wider community. These certainly do not present arguments against the rights of individuals to live ordinary lives but undoubtedly raise issues that need to be addressed in terms of supporting individuals in navigating their social relationships and community involvement. When people have the opportunities for full community involvement and to make real friendships, the opportunities for abusive relationships are reduced. Quarmby (2011) notes that of the hate crimes which have resulted in murder over recent years, most of the victims were estranged from their families and were craving social relationships to replace their family ties. This highlights the significance of social isolation as a factor in hate crime and the need to support individuals to build meaningful social networks.

Self-neglect

Self-neglect is included as a category of abuse in the Care Act, where it is described as *'a wide range of behaviour neglecting to care for one's personal hygiene, health or surroundings and includes behaviour such as hoarding'* (Department of Health, 2014: 234). Self-neglect itself is a contested issue which has been open to debate in terms of the parameters applied to it and the different perceptions of appropriate thresholds for intervention applied by agencies. The definitions applied have been seen by many to be subject to individual value judgements in terms of what are perceived as acceptable living environments. Achieving effective responses to self-neglect is a highly complex process and is continuing to evolve. Particularly challenging situations can arise when there are high risk situations but individuals with mental capacity refuse services, thus creating a dilemma between respecting autonomy and fulfilling a duty of care. Braye et al. (2014) note that in just over a quarter of local authorities self-neglect has featured in a serious case review.

RESEARCH SUMMARY

May-Chahal and Antrobus (2012) note the significant role of communities as referrers to services but also in defining what is accepted within neighbourhoods. Their research uncovered highly emotional reactions to situations and considerable concerns about the impact on neighbours, but also some extremely negative and abusive reactions. So the way in which people who self-neglect are perceived and treated in society can often reflect the stigma and discrimination faced by people with mental health problems or disabilities. In the context of safeguarding there is a clear need for individuals not only

(Continued)

to be supported with their self-neglect but also to consider the impact of wider public perceptions. May-Chahal and Antrobus propose a model for community intervention in relation to self-neglect which aims to achieve agreement on the lowest living standards community members feel able to accept, coordinating community resources, facilitating contact, and monitoring to fill resource gaps. Braye et al. (2014) highlight the importance of the relationship between the individual and practitioner and the need for understanding the life history of the person and how this relates to the current self-neglect. They also emphasise the need for interventions built on the specific circumstances of the individual including their motivations, relationships and networks. Creative interventions are required with key themes being flexibility and negotiation with a high level of multi-agency working. Like wider safeguarding issues, a clear sense of shared ownership between the agencies involved is required to achieve successful interventions.

Deception and scamming

The Care Act defines financial or material abuse as including:

theft, fraud, internet scamming, coercion in relation to an adult's financial affairs or arrangements, including in connection with wills, property, inheritance or financial transactions, or the misuse or misappropriation of property, possessions or benefits.

(Department of Health, 2014: 234)

Attempts to defraud people have been highlighted in recent years with increased incidents of people becoming victims of 'scams' and incurring debts, losing their savings and being persuaded into buying unwanted items. While older people are not more likely to be scammed than other groups, research shows that they lose more money when this occurs. People with dementia are particularly vulnerable with 15 per cent of people with dementia having been victims of cold calling, scam mail or mis-selling (Alzheimer's Society, n.d.). Initial research by the Centre for Ageing Studies at the University of Chester suggests that some older people are not able to identify a deliberate scam or feel coerced into buying goods or services (Kingston, 2015). The boundaries between criminal and unethical behaviour in this area can make it more difficult to address and respond to effectively, yet it does often lie within the definition of financial abuse in the Care Act. Whichever side of the criminal line these activities fall on, the impact on individuals is often immense and includes significant debt, loss of confidence, shame, mental health issues and family tensions (Kingston, 2015). Clearly these practices are highly exploitative and can often include targeting and grooming behaviours. There is, however, currently no national coordinated support to address this issue. Further forms of abuse linked to the internet such as internet scamming (financial abuse) and cyber abuse (psychological abuse) are also identified in the Care Act guidance.

Modern slavery, human trafficking and forced labour

The Care Act guidance describes modern slavery as encompassing:

> *slavery, human trafficking, forced labour and domestic servitude. Traffickers and slave masters use whatever means they have at their disposal to coerce, deceive and force individuals into a life of abuse, servitude and inhumane treatment.*

> (Department of Health, 2014: 234)

Human trafficking and forced labour are types of modern slavery which can sometimes overlap but are different. Human trafficking involves '*bringing someone into a situation of exploitation. It is a series of connected actions with the final purpose being a form of exploitation*' (Skrivankova, 2014: 4). Labour exploitation or sexual exploitation are often the purpose of human trafficking. Forced labour can be found in a range of work environments such as construction, cleaning, care work, agriculture and food processing where work is often temporary, low skilled and low paid. Although forced labour is a serious crime in the UK, legal responses can be unclear and disjointed which impacts on the potential for charging and prosecution. Skrivankova (2014) notes that the low risk of discovery combined with the potential for high profit and weak enforcement of the regulatory framework provides an environment in which forced labour is a lucrative business method. Forced labour often involves a range of abuses including financial, physical, psychological and discriminatory. Here again, the misuse of power and exploitation of individuals in vulnerable situations are key underlying causes.

Individuals exploited in these circumstances can be either migrants or from the UK. A range of individuals such as people with mental health problems, learning disabilities or those who have problematic substance use can be vulnerable to forced labour and exploitation. Immigration status forms another type of vulnerability and even when migrants have full rights to work in the UK they are open to exploitation due to additional vulnerabilities associated with their status, such as language barriers and lack of awareness of employment law.

Forced labour can include physical and psychological harms with fear and feeling powerless among the most frequently described experiences cited in research (Skrivankova, 2014). As well as the impact on mental health, untreated injuries or physically demanding work in dangerous and unhealthy conditions also create physical health problems. Forced labour is present across the UK and Skrivankova notes the structures that facilitate labour exploitation exist within regular industries that supply products and services on a daily basis to the UK public.

The Modern Slavery Act 2015 strengthens sentencing and also gives victims extra protection against prosecutions for offences committed as part of their exploitation (BBC News, 2015a). Forced labour cannot be addressed by a single agency but requires national and international cooperation and a multi-agency approach that fairly regulates business and ensures humane employment conditions for workers. The engrained nature of forced labour in daily life in our society, like other forms of abuse discussed in this chapter, also requires a raising of awareness and accountability within communities if it is to be addressed effectively.

Asylum seekers and refugees

The UK is home to less than 1 per cent of the world's refugees, out of more than 50 million forcibly displaced people worldwide (UNHCR Global Trends, 2013). The UKIP policies which have focused largely, if not almost exclusively, on negative themes around immigration have compounded the sense of disenfranchisement felt by many as a result of the recession and a climate of austerity in the UK. Immigrants have become a focus, fuelled by the tabloid press, as a scapegoat for the social problems such as unemployment and poverty that many people face. While there are wider issues about the negative misrepresentation of the impact of migrants and in particular economic migrants in the UK, the position of asylum seekers and refugees has become obscured within this debate. An asylum seeker is a person who has left their country of origin (due to fear of being persecuted) and formally applied for asylum in another country but whose application has not yet been concluded. In the UK, a person is officially a refugee when they have their claim for asylum accepted by the government. The likelihood that a refugee will be granted refugee status is variable depending on the country where they apply for asylum. In the UK in 2010, 25 per cent of the people who applied for asylum were granted it. In some countries, such as Switzerland and Finland, over 70 per cent of applications succeed (Refugee Council, n.d.).

RESEARCH SUMMARY

The experiences of refugees in the UK

Research by the Refugee Council demonstrates that most asylum seekers know nothing about welfare benefits and have no expectation of financial support when they come to the UK (Doyle, 2014). Once in the UK they frequently live in poverty, are unable to buy necessities and experience poor health. Despite common misconceptions, they do not queue jump for council housing and are nearly always allocated properties where other people do not want to live. It is estimated that one fifth of asylum seeking women who access therapeutic services through the Refugee Council have experienced sexual violence in this country. While more likely to be vulnerable to violence, asylum seekers fear detention and deportation so do not approach the police to report sexual and violent assaults. Such issues occur in a context where many people are subject to discrimination and forms of hate crime within their local communities.

The extreme vulnerability of unaccompanied asylum seeking children has been considered above. Alongside victims of domestic violence some other groups with specific support needs are less visible such as older refugees, young people in families and people with disabilities. A rights-based approach, considering the person as an individual and assessing their needs thoroughly, is essential as opposed to a focus on status and eligibility. Interventions must be based around the needs of the individual in relation to culture, race and the context of discrimination experienced. It is vital that social care services develop, sustain and engage with refugee and community organisations to advance appropriate

(Continued)

and coordinated interventions to safeguard asylum seekers and refugees (Sales, 2002). The role of wider communities in relation to this is crucial. There has been high profile debate recently over the role and responsibilities of the UK in the international response to the plight of refugees (Easton, 2015). More humane attitudes have come to the fore and the views of those who believe that local communities and the UK government should take a bigger role in addressing refugees' needs have been more widely reported in the media. While there may have been some change in opinion, many people will have always held this view. This has, however, highlighted the importance of communities and the individuals within them finding ways to demonstrate alternatives to the existing predominant discourse in relation to marginalised groups.

Approaches to safeguarding adults in the community

There are many overriding themes which link the types of people who require safeguarding responses within communities in the discussions above. These are often the most marginalised and excluded individuals and groups within our communities and while addressing their needs requires a personalised approach, attention needs to be paid to wider social factors. Thompson (2012) has provided a significant framework in his PCS (personal/cultural/social) analysis, which highlights that discrimination needs to be considered not just individually but in relation to cultural and social structures. So while it is central to look at the uniqueness of the individual it is also essential to consider the role of wider forces in shaping needs and solutions to these. Thompson (2015) has discussed this in terms of the simultaneous need for both individualisation and de-individualisation to ensure that people are viewed within their wider context. This is particularly pertinent when that context is the membership of oppressed groups.

Ola is 54 and lives with her son Tarek who is 23. They were granted refugee status after fleeing Syria last year with Ola's husband Adnan and their younger daughter Kamar. They had suffered several years of threats of and actual violence in their home and finally agreed to pay out all their life savings to be brought to the UK. Adnan and Kamar died on the journey which began on an overcrowded boat; it capsized and Adnan and Kamar drowned. Ola and Tarek were then forced to give all the money they had left to someone who smuggled them into the UK in the back of a lorry. Ola and Tarek have had both physical and mental trauma as a result of their experiences. They are both now suffering from Post Traumatic Stress Disorder and depression. They live in a council flat on a large inner

(Continued)

city estate where there are high levels of poverty and gang related crime. They are afraid to leave the flat as they are regularly verbally abused and have several times been hit with empty plastic bottles and cans. They pay part of their benefits to a 'protection' gang who say this will prevent more serious physical assaults and damage to their home.

Individualisation: What interventions could be put in place to support and protect Ola and Tarek?

De-individualisation: What could be done within communities to support people like Ola and Tarek who are targeted for abuse and prevent abuse or further abuse occurring?

COMMENT

Individualisation: *Work with Ola and Tarek has to be within the context of the range of abuse and exploitation that they have been subject to over a number of years in their home country and the UK. It also needs to take account of their individual needs in relation to their language and culture and the discrimination that they are facing. This may require a considerable amount of exploration by the practitioner to develop their own understanding of Ola and Tarek and their background. The central aspect of any work would be to build up a trusting relationship taking into account the impact of the range of abuse and exploitation that they have faced, including from perceived authority figures. A range of crimes have been committed and interventions need to fully involve the police, housing and mental health services to address the situation collaboratively but also in a way which does not put Ola and Tarek at risk of further abuse. All of this needs to occur within the context of what Ola and Tarek want, in other words, their expressed needs and the outcomes that they want to achieve. Expressing their needs and wishes not only potentially requires the use of interpreters but also the use of an advocate. Further therapeutic measures to address issues around self-esteem that could be a barrier to them asserting their views may also be required. It would be important to involve local community organisations that can engage support from other Syrian people and also organisations that can support them in relation to their refugee status.*

De-individualisation: *Through a collaborative approach involving statutory and non-statutory agencies and wider communities, awareness can be raised about the needs of specific groups in relation to safeguarding. Effective multi-agency working should address, through Safeguarding Adults Boards and other structured forums, the ongoing needs for protection and prevention within communities. Marginalised groups of people need to be supported towards more meaningful social inclusion by community-based work to build opportunities for them to share their experiences and develop networks of support. This can only be achieved by meaningful partnerships between statutory agencies, voluntary organisations and marginalised communities.*

Many themes here cross over from interventions to support individuals, which if implemented on a wider scale can further address the needs of marginalised groups. Some of these will be considered throughout the rest of the chapter.

Building resilience, confidence, assertiveness, self-esteem and respect

MSP notes that people need to be empowered to make their own decisions and take control in their lives and that support and interventions to achieve this should underlie all safeguarding work. Improving individuals' decision making and control often requires improvement of their self-esteem and self-worth, particularly when they have been abused. While resilience to adversity varies according to the individual and their circumstances, assessing needs from a strengths perspective, building on skills, abilities and supports, is central to improving their self-esteem. Much of this requires opportunities for direct work with individuals over time and within the context of a trusting relationship. Concepts around building individuals' capacity to make decisions, recognise signs of danger and find coping strategies are relevant to any marginalised groups who are at risk of abuse. Confidence and assertiveness are key skills in navigating social and community relationships for all individuals.

Peer support, survivors' networks and circles of support

One of the unintentional consequences of individuals with care and support needs being able to access more personalised options for support has been the potential for this to reduce their levels of contact with others in similar situations. As discussed earlier, there are also many individuals who may have needs which are not covered through eligibility for statutory support, and the isolation which this incurs can increase their chances of mistreatment from others. Peer support gives individuals the opportunity to share and validate ideas and concerns in a supportive context. It can also provide positive role models and the prospect of collective responses and solutions to situations. These notions are clearly also closely linked to the need to build self-esteem, which we have already discussed. There are many different contexts for peer support from informal to organised groups. Survivors' networks are particularly relevant when someone has been abused and feels that they would benefit from the support of people who have had similar experiences. Circles of support are based on person-centred principles with the individual deciding on group membership. The aim is for the group to provide support and friendship to the individual and act as a community around them to help them achieve their goals. The opportunity to have social contact with peers, in whatever form this takes, is not only relevant after abuse has occurred but can also be a factor in preventing harm and supporting disclosure where there are ongoing safeguarding concerns.

Advocacy

Advocacy is a central process in supporting individuals with decision making and ensuring that their rights are heard and upheld. Under the Care Act 2014, local authorities have a statutory duty to arrange an independent advocate in order to:

facilitate the involvement of a person in their assessment, in the preparation of their care and support plan and in the review of their care plan, as well as in safeguarding enquiries and SARs if two conditions are met. That if an independent advocate were not provided then the person would have substantial difficulty in being fully involved in these processes and second, there is no appropriate individual available to support and represent the person's wishes who is not paid or professionally engaged in providing care or treatment to the person or their carer.

(Department of Health, 2014: 113–14)

The role of the independent advocate is to support and represent the person and to facilitate their involvement in the key processes with the local authority and other organisations. Many of the people who qualify for advocacy under the Care Act will also qualify for advocacy under the Mental Capacity Act 2005. The same advocate can provide support as an advocate under the Care Act and under the Mental Capacity Act.

Alongside the statutory requirements for advocacy, there is a wide range of different types of advocacy such as self-advocacy and collective advocacy which people can access through different organisations. People First is one such example run by and for people with learning disabilities (http://peoplefirstltd.com) and Mind has a range of advocacy services for people with mental health problems (www.mind.org.uk). The most appropriate type of advocacy will depend on the needs of the individual but advocacy can be a central tool in increasing assertiveness and self-confidence particularly in relation to safeguarding.

Network group conferencing

Family group conferencing (FGC) is an approach which has been used extensively in childcare but which has been highlighted more recently in safeguarding adults (SCIE, 2012). This model aims to involve the wider network of family and friends in supporting individuals at risk of harm. This gives the individual at risk the opportunity to identify and involve the individuals who are significant to them, as opposed to imposing plans created by agencies involved. It is also a strengths-based approach which can harness extended family and wider community involvement to look at solutions to problems. Immediate family members may not be the most appropriate avenue of support for an individual or may even be the source of risk. In this case widening the circle of support may be a protective factor for the individual. Women's Aid advises against the use of FGC in situations where there is domestic violence and clearly the membership of the FGC needs to be carefully considered to ensure that those involved are able to provide a supportive role to the individual. In many situations identified earlier, where individuals have not had opportunities to develop meaningful relationships and are at risk within wider communities, then a network group conference could enhance available support. It is highlighted here as an example of the range of approaches that should be considered in terms of safeguarding adults in ways which maximise their potential for maintaining control over decision making about their own lives.

Safeguarding adults and citizenship

Much of the discussion above links issues around safeguarding adults in the community with rights to citizenship. Clearly if disabled adults are not being treated equally in terms of the respect they elicit from other members of society and the level of access to legal redress then they are not achieving full citizenship. Concepts of citizenship are based around the relationship between individuals and their society in terms of rights and responsibilities (Stewart and Atkinson, 2012). Despite ceaseless campaigning from pressure groups, some people continue to be excluded from full citizenship on the basis of age, class, disability, gender or ethnicity. As a result, these are often the individuals who are most likely to be abused and mistreated in our society. Those on the margins of citizenship, while not being given full human rights in wider society or equitable legal redress when crimes are committed against them, are also more likely to be subject to increased intrusion by the state under the notion of protection. So while the equilibrium between rights and protection is something of a balancing act, either too much or not enough support can infringe people's rights to full citizenship.

CHAPTER SUMMARY

There are significant contradictions in the role of communities in relation to safeguarding. While communities can be a significant protective factor in supporting people at risk of harm, individuals or groups within communities can also be perpetrators of grooming, exploitation and abuse. This chapter has looked at specific groups of people across the lifespan who are at risk of abuse within communities and how this links to prevailing attitudes, marginalisation and discrimination in wider society.

The themes of grooming and exploitation have been highlighted as relevant to a wide range of abuse and patterns of abuse in communities. Parallels have been drawn in this chapter between the patterns of grooming and exploitation seen, for instance, in child sexual exploitation and mate crime. It is apparent that, in previous reactions to CSE, service responses failed to recognise the grooming that had taken place over a period of time and that it was the precursor to abuse. Similarly many adults at risk in communities have been perceived as part of groups engaged in a range of anti-social behaviours and their position as the target for exploitation has been overlooked. It is essential that lessons are learnt across the lifespan in terms of the nature of exploitation and grooming and that perceptions shift away from notions of victim blaming and mislabelling certain individuals in terms of anti-social or promiscuous behaviour. When perpetrator actions are accurately identified and defined in terms of grooming and exploitation, then responses to people at risk are more likely to be appropriate in terms of support and protection as opposed to managing deviant behaviour. This is a concept which has more recently informed some of the debates around radicalisation, in that people targeted by extremist groups need to be perceived in terms of both grooming and radicalisation and discourse around appropriate interventions needs to start from this premise (Khan, 2015).

The role of the wider community in safeguarding is a central one in terms of both protecting individuals and being partners in wider understandings of and approaches to abuse. Public education campaigns

(Continued)

CHAPTER SUMMARY *continued*

alongside building awareness and assertiveness in people at risk themselves are central to protection and prevention. Information must be clear and accessible and support people to recognise inappropriate behaviour. This involves statutory services working not only with voluntary and community organisations but also businesses and work places. Access to effective and appropriate legal responses is a central factor in achieving full citizenship. Safeguarding boards for children and adults have a key role to play in recognising and responding to local needs and coordination with each other, other agencies and communities. It is easy for practitioners to become consumed in the day-to-day 'firefighting' activities of protection given the context of limited resources and high caseloads. Safeguarding, however, must be addressed within the wider context of social inclusion and prevention. This legitimises the need for a much wider role for safeguarding services in terms of work within communities to address the factors underlying marginalisation and exploitation.

FURTHER READING

Faulkner, A and Sweeney, A (2011) *Adults' Services Report 41: Prevention in Adult Safeguarding: A Review of the Literature.* London: SCIE. Available at: www.scie.org.uk/publications/reports/report41/files/report41.pdf

Franklin, A, Raws, P and Smeaton, E (2015) *Unprotected, Overprotected: Meeting the Needs of Young People with Learning Disabilities who Experience, or are at Risk of Sexual Exploitation.* London: Barnardo's.

Ofsted (2014) *The Sexual Exploitation of Children: It Couldn't Happen Here, Could It?* Manchester: Ofsted. Available at: www.ofsted.gov.uk/resources/140175.

SCIE (2015) *Care Act 2014: Commissioning Independent Advocacy.* London: SCIE. Available at: www.scie.org.uk/care-act-2014/advocacy-services/commissioning-independent-advocacy/files/commissioning-independent-advocacy.pdf

Chapter 6

Safeguarding and the care system

Introduction

The segregation of people with care and support needs characterised most of the service provision for those in need in the UK in the twentieth century. Although there has been a significant policy shift towards care within communities, residential care still offers care and support to some groups of adults and children. Institutional abuse and its impact was increasingly documented through the mid-twentieth century (Goffman, 1961; Townsend, 1962). The harsh and depersonalising regimes of large long-stay establishments led to the institutionalisation of the individuals who experienced them. The removal of people with support needs from their local environments to isolated facilities lacking privacy and dignity also provided a breeding ground for further forms of abuse and neglect. Growing awareness of the inadequacies and inhuman treatment under such regimes, alongside political concern to reduce expenditure and state responsibility for care, led to the growth and implementation of the community-based policies discussed in Chapter 1. Chapter 5 has considered safeguarding in relation to the current community-based options for most children and adults with care and support needs. Certain groups of children and adults, however, continue to live in residential settings and they are often the most at risk individuals with highly complex needs. While the majority of settings provide a high standard of care and support to the people they look after, there have been significant high profile examples of abuse and neglect across the lifespan in recent years.

Alongside commissioners of services, such as local authorities and the CCG, there are currently two organisations responsible for the regulation and inspection of care provision in England whether this is community-based or residential/hospital-based care. The Office for Standards in Education, Children's Services and Skills (Ofsted) regulates and inspects services involved in the care of children and young people, including local authority children's services, and services for looked after children, safeguarding and child protection. The Care Quality Commission (CQC) is the independent regulator of health and adult social care with equivalent agencies in the rest of the UK. Their role in safeguarding will be considered within this chapter. Factors underlying abuse of children and adults in residential settings will be explored alongside approaches to safeguarding and themes emerging across the lifespan.

Children, young people and the care system

The earliest examples of residential or institutional care for children can be traced back to the Poor Law. In 1834 the New Poor Law introduced a new system of relief for the poor; if a person was destitute and deemed deserving of support, the only right to welfare came in the form of the workhouse. A person had to lose all freedom and rights on entering the workhouse, the conditions were harsh and rigidly controlled, families were broken up, and children were separated from their parents. The introduction of the Poor Law saw a significant increase in the number of children who entered workhouses: in 1838 there were 42,767 children placed in workhouses, and two years later the number had risen to 64,570 (Davies and Ward, 2012).

ACTIVITY **6.1**

How do you think this policy affected social attitudes to poverty and the family?

Do you think these attitudes might still exist today, especially in relation to welfare provision and the concept of the deserving and undeserving poor?

Following concerns about the significant rise in the number of children entering workhouses, a board of guardians was established which transferred children away from the workhouse to 'workhouse schools'. The regime within the schools was still harsh and stigmatising; the philosophy which underpinned the system advocated that education and the acquisition of new skills could challenge poverty and pauperism.

In the 1860s voluntary children's organisations were established which led to the creation of residential homes for children. However, by the end of the nineteenth century there was a growing recognition that children in residential care were experiencing poorer outcomes and fostering began to be viewed as the preferred option for children who required care away from their families. Unfortunately this association between residential care and poorer outcomes is still echoed in the twenty-first century; in 2006 the Department for Education and Skills published the Green Paper, *Care Matters: Transforming the Lives of Children and Young People in Care*. It highlighted that many young people within the care system had lower educational achievements, and were more likely to be unemployed, to have substance misuse issues and to experience mental health difficulties:

> *Although outcomes for children in care have improved in recent years, there remains a significant and widening gap between these and the outcomes for all children. This situation is unacceptable and needs to be addressed urgently.*

> (Department for Education and Skills, 2006: 5)

Care Matters made a number of specific recommendations which were intended to address the failings within the care system and ultimately to improve the outcomes for children and young people. However, despite growing recognition of the association between care and negative outcomes for looked after children and young people, there continues to be a large evidence base which supports a link between care and negative outcomes compared to children in the general population (DfES, 2006).

In 2014 the Department for Education published the report *Children in Care: Research Priorities and Questions* (Department for Education, 2014b). The report aimed to identify gaps within current provision for looked after children and to highlight how research could help to inform more effective practice. The report concluded that despite improvements, children within the care system are still experiencing poorer outcomes in health, education and employment. Young people are at an increased risk of CSE, substance misuse, teenage pregnancy and mental health issues. They are over-represented within the criminal justice system and more likely to experience homelessness when they leave care (Department for Education, 2014b).

What does it mean to be in care?

In 2015, there were 69,540 children who were in the care of the local authority. Two thirds of looked after children are subject to care orders, according to s 31 of the Children Act 1989, and a third are accommodated under voluntary arrangements (s 20)(Department for Education, 2015a).

According to the CA 1989, *'a child is looked after by a local authority if s/he is in their care by reason of a care order or is being accommodated under s 20 of the 1989 Act for more than 24 hours with the agreement of the parents, or of the child if s/he is aged 16 or over'*. A young person ceases to be looked after when they reach 18 years of age. The court will take into consideration a number of factors before making a care order if the child is deemed to be at risk of significant harm and if this action is deemed to be in the best interests of the child. If a care order is granted the local authority assumes parental responsibility, which is shared with the child's parents or carers. A child can be taken into care on an emergency basis via an Emergency Protection Order (s 44) or be remanded in the care of the local authority (s 21). There is also provision according to s 25 which enables a child or young person to be placed in secure accommodation if they are deemed to be at risk to themselves or others.

The Children Act 1989 states that once a child is accommodated the local authority has a number of general duties which include:

- promoting and safeguarding a child's wellbeing;

- taking into consideration a child's wishes and feelings;

- taking account of a child's linguistic, religious, cultural and ethnic background;

- to place a child as close to home as possible and to endeavour to keep sibling groups together;

- all looked after children should be informed about their rights including the right to make a complaint.

Types of care

Children and young people can be placed with foster parents, at home with their parents with the supervision of social services, in residential children's homes or other residential establishments such as educational units or secure units. The majority of looked after children and young people live in foster placements; however, a sizeable minority are placed in residential care – 75 per cent of children are placed with foster carers and 9 per cent of children are placed in residential or secure units. Other types of placement can include children and young people being at home, whilst subject to a care order, and a child being placed with foster carers who are prospective adopters (Department for Education, 2015a: 1)

Residential care and historical abuse

Children and young people who are in the care of the local authority are often more vulnerable to abuse and exploitation:

> *It is wrong to assume all children in care are kept safe. A minority are at continued risk of abuse or neglect, including from their carers, other young people and those in the wider community who target them … Better support is needed to help these young people overcome the effects of the abuse and neglect they have suffered, and to enable them to realise their potential. Care must provide effective therapeutic support for children and young people and protect them from current and future harm.*

> (Radford et al., 2011)

Concerns have been expressed about abuse and the quality of the care system since the public inquiry into the death of Dennis O'Neill in 1947, a 12 year old boy who was murdered by his foster carers. Recommendations from the inquiry led to the implementation of the Children Act 1948 which established the care of children by local authorities and resulted in the development of children's departments.

Revelations about abuse in a variety of childcare institutions began to emerge in the 1980s, prompting a number of public inquiries into the nature and extent of abuse in residential childcare settings. Questions began to be asked about the effectiveness of residential care especially in relation to safeguarding and promoting the wellbeing of children and young people.

Pindown
In 1991 the Pindown Report (Levy and Kahan, 1991) was published, which suggested that a number of young people in residential care in Staffordshire were being sub-jected to excessive use of physical restraint and harsh regimes. Concerns began to be expressed about similar abusive practices in other residential establishments and the government requested an inquiry to be undertaken to identify the scale of the abuse.

Kerelaw
In 1999 a number of allegations were made by young people and staff from Kerelaw residential and secure unit. Allegations of abuse at Kerelaw spanned a period of approximately 25 years. Following an investigation and review into the allegations, two members of staff were jailed and a number were dismissed; the facility was finally closed in 2006. An independent inquiry was commissioned by the Scottish government to identify the factors that had contributed to the historical climate of abuse at the school and to make recommendations to prevent further occurrences of institutional abuse (Frizzell, 2009). The report highlighted a culture within the school which was secretive, controlling and resistant to change. It identified that:

> a toxic culture contributed to young people not being listened to and ineffective complaint systems; insufficient performance management; training and learning that was unsatisfactorily integrated.

> (Davidson, 2010: 406)

North Wales
In 1991 North Wales Police investigated a number of allegations relating to historical child abuse, in children's homes, during the 1970s and 1980s. Although there were eight convictions it was widely believed that the scale of the abuse was much greater than was being acknowledged. Following heightened political and public concerns the government ordered two separate inquiries into the allegations of abuse in the North Wales children's homes to be undertaken: the Utting Review and the Waterhouse Inquiry.

The Utting Review
William Utting was asked to review the adequacy of safeguards against the abuse of children living away from home and to make a series of recommendations to address the failings within the system. The Secretary State for Health, Frank Dobson,

addressed Parliament following the publication of the Utting Report, *People like Us* (Utting, 1997), and highlighted a number of key failings and concerns about the residential care system:

> *The report presents a woeful tale of failure at all levels to provide a secure and decent childhood for some of the most vulnerable children. It covers the lives of children whose home circumstances were so bad that those in authority, to use the jargon, took them into care. The report reveals that in far too many cases not enough care was taken. Elementary safeguards were not in place or not enforced. Many children were harmed rather than helped. The review reveals that these failings were not just the fault of individuals—though individuals were at fault. It reveals the failures of a whole system.*

(HM Government, 1998)

The Waterhouse Inquiry

In 1995 The Waterhouse Inquiry was set up to investigate the conduct of the children's homes and the social services departments in Gwynedd and Clwyd. In 2000, *Lost in Care* was published following the inquiry and made 72 recommendations to help improve the ways in which children and young people were protected whilst in care (Waterhouse, 2000). The findings from these inquiries led to an acknowledgement that the residential care system had failed to protect a number of vulnerable children and young people. A series of structural reforms were implemented, and more regulatory and inspection processes were introduced to help address the systems which had exposed a number of children and young people to abusive behaviour (Utting Report, 1997). The Quality Protects Programme was implemented to improve the services for children who were living away from home (Department of Health, 1998). The programme set targets to improve the lives and outcomes of looked after children by providing underpinning principles based upon holistic assessment. In 2002 national minimum standards for residential care were introduced with the aim of protecting rights and safeguarding children from abuse.

The Care Standards Act 2000 provided the legal basis for the regulation and inspection of children's homes and Ofsted was given the primary responsibility to ensure that every residential home meets the required statutory requirements. All homes must provide high quality care which is planned, safe and provides positive experiences for children and young people. (For more information on the Care Standards Act 2000, see www.gov.uk/government/publications?keywords=residential+care&publication_filter_option=all&topics%5B%5D=all&departments%5B%5D=ofsted&official_document_status=all&world_locations%5B%5D=all&from_date=&to_date=)

However, despite growing recognition of the association between care and negative outcomes for looked after children and young people, there continues to be a large evidence base which suggests increased negative outcomes compared to children in the general population (Stein, 2012). In 2012, following further historical allegations of child abuse, Operation Pallial was set up to review the cases and to establish the actual extent of the abuse that had taken place in North Wales. The investigation reported that the actual extent of the abuse had not been fully investigated and indicated there was evidence of 140 allegations of both sexual and physical abuse. It was reported that there had been elements of grooming, an absence of the duty to care for vulnerable children and young people, and evidence of systemic abuse across 18 different care homes (National Crime Agency, 2013b).

RESEARCH SUMMARY

Vulnerability and institutional abuse

Research suggests that children and young people who are looked after are more vulnerable to abuse. Sixty two percent of looked after young people were accommodated due to abuse and or neglect (Department for Education, 2015a). The Child Exploitation and Online Protection centre (CEOP) produced a report which looked at the risk of children being abused within institutional settings. The report suggests that children and young people are at risk of abuse from both perpetrators and staff who fail to report incidences of alleged abuse. The report highlights poor leadership, ineffective policies, a lack of accountability and cultures which collude with abuse (National Crime Agency, 2013a):

> The sexual exploitation and abuse of children is most likely when vulnerability meets power. Both vulnerability and power can take forms which are subtle, informal and – to a passive outside world – often barely visible … there is something about institutions that can amplify both vulnerability and power to a point where sexual abuse of children within them can become endemic. Institutions with children or other vulnerable people in their care, have special obligations to safeguard them. Where the risk increases, so do these obligations.
>
> *(National Crime Agency, 2013a)*

A study undertaken by Biehal et al. (2014) looked at allegations concerning the abuse or neglect of children in care, and found that although the majority of looked after children have a positive experience of care there is a sizeable minority of children and young people who do experience further harm whilst in care. Beckett (2010) suggests that there are a number of different factors which can interact together to make the care system more harmful to young people, such as excessive bureaucracy, staff shortages, overloaded professionals and cuts to resources which leave the system stretched and only able to respond to crisis. Stanley and Cox (2009) suggest that looked after children are one of the most vulnerable and socially excluded groups of young people because they have often entered care as a result of abuse and neglect. Children may be more vulnerable if they have experienced abuse, if they have not received adequate support and if they have not had the opportunity to develop resilience.

CSE and the looked after system

This increased vulnerability to abuse has also been highlighted more recently in relation to the increased risk of CSE among looked after children and young people.

The impact of multiple placements and failure of the care system to effectively plan for children has been consistently highlighted as a risk factor for children, increasing their vulnerability and reducing the opportunity to establish a secure base from which to make attachments and develop resilience.

RESEARCH SUMMARY

In 2013, following the inquiry into Rotherham, the Office of the Children's Commissioner's Inquiry into Child Sexual Exploitation in Gangs and Groups suggested that there was growing evidence that children in care are particularly vulnerable to child sexual exploitation, with a disproportionate number being groomed or sexually exploited (Berelowitz et al., 2013). The report suggested that there were approximately 16,500 children and young people who were at risk of CSE between April 2010 and March 2011 (2013: 53). The report highlighted that some residential homes were being specifically targeted by abusers as due to the high turnover of young people in care 'there is a constant flow of vulnerable children for perpetrators to exploit'. The findings also suggested that children who were exploited before they became looked after continued to be exploited, and were often at even greater risk of harm. Other children became exposed to sexual exploitation for the first time whilst they were looked after in children's homes, some children were 'introduced' to perpetrators by other young people who were also being exploited. The report makes a series of recommendations to address serious weaknesses in how care homes report and react to children going missing, in the checks made before children are placed into care homes, and weaknesses in staff skills and management quality.

The Coffey Report was commissioned following the Rochdale Inquiry in 2012, to highlight risk factors of CSE in Greater Manchester. The report found that of the 3,242 individuals reported missing to Greater Manchester Police, almost half of the reports were about children in care (Coffey, 2014):

> There is a significant risk of CSE of children who go missing from care, [as they] are very vulnerable children and are often preyed on by predators who understand this.
>
> *(BBC News, 2014)*

The Ofsted report, Missing Children, *published in February 2013, on local authorities' work in relation to children missing from home and care, highlighted a number of concerns (Ofsted, 2013b). The report highlighted that children and young people who are missing from their placements are particularly vulnerable to the risks of sexual exploitation. The report also suggested that approximately 25 per cent of children and young people who go missing are at risk of serious harm. It highlighted that the risk management plans for looked after children were often not developed or were incomplete; information in relation to children who were missing was not being routinely shared; and a key factor which contributed to children and young people running away from care was placement instability.*

ACTIVITY **6.2**

Try to imagine how a young person might feel if they have been taken into care to safeguard their wellbeing, only to be exposed to further abuse or exploitation from a system which is meant to protect them. Consider how difficult it would be for a child or young person to speak up or to challenge in a system where there are distinct power differentials and structures which can conceal abuse.

We need to understand the mechanisms which perpetrate abuse within institutions to be able to challenge and eradicate abuse and neglect. It is unacceptable that vulnerable groups can be subjected to further abuse in settings that purport to provide care and protection.

Investigations into historical child abuse

Operation Hydrant was set up in 2015 to investigate the links between historical child sexual abuse and approximately 1,400 prominent public figures. The investigation has highlighted significant links between child sexual abuse and institutional care. A total of 666 claims relate to institutions; of these, 154 are schools, 75 are children's homes, and 40 are religious institutions (BBC News, 2015c).

A new independent statutory review of historical child abuse cases in England and Wales has been established to investigate the failings of previous inquiries:

> *We will identify institutional failings where they are found to exist. We will demand accountability for past institutional failings. We will support victims and survivors to share their experience of sexual abuse. And we will make practical recommendations to ensure that children are given the care and protection they need.*
>
> (IICSA, n.d.)

In May 2015 the Scottish government announced that there would be a similar inquiry into historical abuse of children in care (for more information on this inquiry, visit www.childabuseinquiry.scot/).

Although there is a growing awareness that institutional structures can conceal and exacerbate abusive practices professional practice must become more proactive and actively listen to and acknowledge the expertise and views of children and young people. Unfortunately, if different professionals fail to listen or continue to 'blame' or 'judge' young people, the barriers to engagement and the failure to protect will continue.

An international perspective: social pedagogy

In the UK, during the past couple of decades there has been a reduction in residential childcare provision and residential care has become increasingly viewed as the last option associated with the most marginalised children and young people such as children who exhibit challenging behaviours, young offenders and children with disabilities. However, in Denmark and Germany residential care is considered to be the preferred option for children and young people. Once a child enters care they are allocated a social pedagogue who will work closely with them, providing a positive and supportive role model. The approach emphasises the merits of holistic working and the encouragement of personal growth for children who are in residential care. Children are encouraged to be active citizens who have a positive contribution to make. The model operates a common framework when working with children and young people, which recognises that the child is a whole person with his or her own distinctive experiences and knowledge (Petrie and Simon, 2006: 117). It is the role of the pedagogues to nurture the development of many emotionally damaged children and young people, and enable them to build strong relationships with others. Pedagogues support the child educationally, socially and emotionally to achieve positive change. They work closely with parents to help devise ways of addressing problems, improving parenting skills and rebuilding the family unit. This strengths-based approach has been adopted in a number of countries across Europe *'to achieve societal aims by means of social provision for children and young people'* (Moss and Petrie, 2002: 14). It was hoped that pedagogical principles could be adopted within the UK but the transition has been slow and restricted by the structures and values that exist within residential childcare. In Europe social pedagogy represents a long-established academic discipline where workers are trained extensively and respected by other professionals. Unfortunately this approach to practice has not been endorsed within the residential childcare services of the UK.

Safeguarding adults in care settings

The Care Act 2014 guidance states that when abuse or neglect by employees occurs in a regulated care setting such as a care home or hospital, the first responsibility to act is with the employing organisation as provider of the service (Department of Health, 2014). Once the employer is aware of abuse or neglect they have a duty to protect the adult from harm as soon as possible and inform the local authority, CQC and Clinical Commissioning Group (if the CCG is the commissioner of the service). CCGs were created following the Health and Social Care Act in 2012, and replaced Primary Care Trusts in 2013. CCGs are statutory NHS bodies responsible for the planning and commissioning of healthcare services for their local area. The local authority has a duty to make enquiries to decide what action needs to be taken and by whom when there is reasonable cause to suspect that an adult is experiencing or at risk of abuse or neglect. In such situations, the local authority needs to decide if the employer's response is sufficient or if further enquiry and action is required. This could include referral to the CQC and/or professional regulators such as the HCPC. The employer has a responsibility to investigate concerns unless: there is a conflict of interest (e.g. the owner is implicated in concerns); there is a history of previously ineffective enquiries by them; there are multiple concerns or matters that require police investigation. External enquiries should be governed by local multi-agency procedures and there are cross-agency guidelines on these roles and responsibilities (Care Quality Commission, n.d.). The wellbeing of the adult at risk is emphasised as the central principle and partnership working between commissioners and providers is highlighted to achieve best outcomes for those at risk. The role of the CQC in terms of raising standards and its enforcement powers alongside the use of referral to the Disclosure and Barring Service are also emphasised. There is a legal duty of an employer to refer an employee to the DBS. This is the case even if someone leaves a position to avoid a disciplinary hearing following a safeguarding incident if the employer would have dismissed them on the basis of the information they have (Department of Health, 2014).

This summarised explanation of roles and duties in relation to safeguarding people in care settings highlights the complex nature of the task and the range of individuals and agencies involved in protecting adults at risk from abuse. The number of different agencies that are required to work together effectively has already been emphasised in relation to safeguarding people across the lifespan in families and communities. The failures of collaborative working in those settings have been recurrent issues when serious harm has occurred and are equally central in relation to abuse in residential care and hospitals. Wider themes which have been much debated in this area of health and social care practice include where the appropriate distinction lies between poor practice and abuse or neglect. The use of agencies and practices that are designed for financial profit to provide care for vulnerable people is in itself a highly contentious issue but this business model has become engrained in policy and practice over several decades in the UK. Non-profit making organisations such as acute hospitals have also had significant incidents in terms of deficiencies in care, neglect and abuse of patients.

ACTIVITY 6.3

Think of a time when (or imagine that) you have visited a relative or friend in a hospital or residential setting. Write a list of what you want to see that will demonstrate that they are being well cared for.

COMMENT

There are likely to be a range of very basic requirements that are priorities in most lists, such as the quality of food, cleanliness and meeting healthcare needs. There are, however, many factors beyond the basic necessities that most people would also look for in terms of a caring manner and good communication skills in staff, and choices about food, clothing and activities. We are likely to be influenced by the demeanour and wellbeing of the person that we are visiting and also that of others being cared for. Wider factors such as well-organised practices and readily available information could also influence our overall impression. National minimum standards for care homes were created to include independent providers under the Care Standards Act 2000. The Dignity in Care *guidance has also been central in emphasising the features of good care for providers, practitioners and service users. It highlights the importance of wider factors that contribute to good*

(Continued)

COMMENT *continued*

care beyond the meeting of basic needs. The areas of Dignity in Care *are: choice and control, communication, eating and nutritional care, pain management, personal hygiene, practical assistance, privacy and social inclusion. (For more information on* Dignity in Care *visit www.scie.org.uk/publications/guides/guide15/index.asp)*

Family and friends can be in a good position to assess the quality of care that people are receiving and those most at risk are often people who do not have relatives and friends who maintain contact with them. This also suggests that people in the most isolated of care environments, such as locked wards, can be highly vulnerable to abuse and neglect. Some high profile examples of neglect and abuse in care settings will be reviewed here. Characteristics of the environment and of staff and residents will also be considered in relation to what creates the conditions for potential abuse and neglect.

Abuse in care settings

Mid Staffordshire NHS Trust and hospital care

The standards of care of patients in hospitals has been an area of significant concern over recent years. In 2006 Age Concern produced *Hungry to be Heard* (Age Concern, 2006), a report which found malnourishment and dehydration in hospital patients. Similar concerns were raised several years later (Age UK London, 2010). The Mid Staffordshire NHS Foundation Trust was the subject of investigations from 2009 culminating in a major public inquiry in 2013 (Francis, 2013) after it was found that poor care could have led to the deaths of hundreds of patients over a number of years as a result of maltreatment and neglect at Stafford hospital. The inquiry found appalling treatment of patients, including many patients who were left lying in their own urine and excrement for days, forced to drink water from vases or given the wrong medication. In 2013 a review into 14 other hospital trusts with higher than expected death rates led to 11 trusts being put into special measures for a catalogue of failings and fundamental breaches of care (Keogh, 2013). This has since led to special measures being extended to adult social care in 2015. Special measures include a timeframe of six months to demonstrate improvement to services and subsequent re-inspections. While data around mortality rates are themselves highly concerning, they have provided an indicator of much broader concerns about failings in acute hospital care. Such data also fail to reflect neglect that occurs without causing the deaths of those involved. Concerns have been evidenced not only from regulatory bodies and formal inquiries but also from voluntary and professional bodies, and patients and families. While a considerable amount of good care does exist, this is at one end of a continuum which includes significant amounts of poor care and ultimately abuse and neglect. Mandelstam (2014) notes that the assumption that NHS care must be safe and that all those involved are doing their best can in itself be a barrier to effective safeguarding.

The inquiries into events at Stafford hospital were highly critical of the emphasis by hospital managers, Department of Health civil servants and politicians on financial improvements, performance and targets which had obscured the central importance of good patient care. A negative culture was found within the hospital where clear causes for concern were minimalised and ignored at all levels of the organisation. There was a tolerance of extremely poor standards of care and isolation from wider medical practice. Poor governance, professional disengagement, staff intimidation and inadequate risk assessment of the impact of staff reductions were also identified. Poor standards of nursing care, including leadership, recruitment and training of staff were further issues. Patients and families were not listened to and ultimately there was a failure to put patients at the centre of the work of the hospital (Francis, 2013).

The *Death by Indifference* report (Mencap, 2007) investigated the deaths of six people with learning disabilities while they were in NHS care and highlighted concerns about the treatment of people with learning disabilities in hospitals and healthcare settings. This led to a wider investigation the *Confidential Inquiry into Premature Deaths of People with Learning Disabilities* (CIPOLD) (Heslop et al., 2013), which examined deaths of 247 people with a learning disability. Thirty-seven per cent of the deaths were found to be avoidable and linked to poor healthcare. Issues included inadequate communication, people not being identified as having a learning disability and reasonable adjustments not being made to take this into account. The inquiry also found that there were significant barriers to people with learning disabilities accessing investigations and treatments which amounted to institutional discrimination on the part of health services.

Orchid View and care of older people

Older people who live in residential care or nursing homes are likely to have significant care and support needs such as frailty, cognitive impairments and end of life care needs, and as such are especially at risk of abuse and neglect. As a result of the increased prevalence of a range of health issues in older age, older people have also been over-represented in the neglect and mistreatment uncovered in hospital settings (Mandelstam, 2014). The inquest into the unexplained deaths of 19 people at Orchid View nursing home, owned by Southern Cross in West Sussex, found that all of them had received 'sub-optimal' care and that neglect had contributed to the deaths of five residents (BBC News, 2013). This included many errors with medication and people being left soiled and unattended. The home had also run without a registered manager for most of the time that it was open. The subsequent serious case review (West Sussex Adults Safeguarding Board, 2014) made 34 recommendations, many of which reflected concerns in the mid Staffordshire hospital inquiries. The report highlighted the need for the independent sector to have similar standards of scrutiny as the NHS and be more fully accountable for effective management alongside suitability and appropriate training of staff. The poor communication with families and lack of information about concerns that statutory organisations had about the home were also criticised. The role of the CQC and its failure to effectively perform its regulatory functions with the home was a central concern. The wider concerns expressed were around financial profit being prioritised before the care of residents and the suitability of the private sector to care for the most vulnerable people in society.

Research into locked wards for people with dementia (Kelly, 2010) has highlighted abusive practice in such settings and indicates dehumanising treatment in some regimes.

Other forms of psychiatric inpatient care have also been heavily criticised for overuse of medication and punitive measures. Care which is not culturally appropriate to the individual has also been highlighted, further increasing the risk of abuse and neglect for black and minority ethnic (BME) people (Bowes et al., 2011).

RESEARCH SUMMARY

The experiences of BME people in residential care

Bowes et al. (2011) researched the experiences of BME people in residential care. They found that managing relationships well in care homes was important to help prevent mistreatment, neglect and abuse. In multicultural contexts, they found that racism, misunderstandings about cultural differences and problematic attitudes negatively affect all of those involved. They also note that for BME residents, being able to use their own language is central to identity and dignity but practicalities in care homes may make this difficult to attain. The research suggests that culturally competent care where practice is influenced by knowledge and understanding of cultural diversity needs to be included in staff training. Good links with local BME communities are seen as central here. They also note that BME experiences are influenced by migration and racism, as well as by cultural preferences, and this is part of the understanding required to provide the care that residents need. Bowes et al. also found that BME residents and families are likely to be inhibited from complaining about poor care due to negative experiences and that they may have low expectations of care which need to be raised. The research also suggests that the needs of multicultural staff groups who may also be subject to racism require recognition and support. For BME residents, culturally competent care can support identity, autonomy and the maintenance of self-esteem. In relation to relationships between residents they note that negative interactions may be more likely in multicultural environments. The authors also comment on the highly skilled nature of responding effectively to negative interactions. They also suggest that the skills in care and support required to provide high quality care in multicultural contexts must be appropriately recognised and rewarded.

RESEARCH SUMMARY

Overuse of psychotropic medication

Maguire et al. (2013) carried out a study in Northern Ireland that looked at how psychotropic drugs were prescribed for elderly people in the community and care homes. Psychotropic drugs are medicines that alter the level of certain chemicals in the brain, changing mood and behaviour. They include: antipsychotic drugs (used to treat psychosis), sedatives (hypnotics) and anxiolytics (prescribed for anxiety and agitation).

(Continued)

RESEARCH SUMMARY continued

Concerns have previously been raised that psychotropic drugs are overused in people with dementia. Antipsychotics in particular increase the risk of fatal conditions such as stroke if they are used long-term (NHS Choices, 2013).

The study found that more than 20 per cent of elderly people in care homes were given antipsychotic drugs, compared with just over 1 per cent of those living in the community. The most concerning aspect of the study was that prescription of antipsychotic drugs increased from just over 8 per cent before entering a care home to 18.6 per cent afterwards. People going into care homes could be more ill than those who continue to live in the community, and therefore may be more likely to be taking psychotropic drugs. Even accounting for this possibility, the researchers suggest that the increase in the prescription of psychotropic drugs for people in care homes cannot be fully explained by this. The research raises valid concerns about the overuse of very powerful antipsychotic drugs in care homes.

Winterbourne View

One of the most high profile failures in adult protection over recent years is the abuse of people with learning disabilities, autism and challenging behaviour at Winterbourne View private hospital. Despite a number of attempts to alert the CQC and health professionals about the abuse, it continued over several years until it was exposed by an undercover reporter on BBC's *Panorama* programme in 2011. The programme documented a harrowing range of abuse and degradation by different members of staff, six of whom were convicted of offences under the Mental Health Act 1983 (as amended by the Mental Health Act 2007) in 2012 and given custodial sentences. The serious case review (Flynn and Citarella, 2012) commissioned as a result of the programme highlighted problems with the commissioning of services, a complete lack of consultation with families, absence of advocacy, and failure to respond to whistleblowing and patient complaints by any of the organisations involved. The failures of the hospital itself and Castlebeck Ltd, the company that owned it, included: not attending to the mental and physical health needs of patients; physically restraining patients; not dealing with their complaints; issues with recruiting and retaining staff; leading, managing and disciplining its workforce; and not providing appropriate training and clinical governance. These factors among others were considered to have resulted in the violence and abuses that occurred. It was noted in the SCR that the policies, procedures and practices of the unit looked impressive on paper; however, inspection, oversight and responses to concerns had been entirely ineffective in uncovering the true picture. (For more information, visit: http://hosted.southglos.gov.uk/wv/report.pdf)

One of the central factors highlighted by the events at Winterbourne View was the inappropriate nature of isolated settings outwith local communities for people with learning disabilities or in fact any other type of care needs. While the unit was intended for 'assessment and treatment' many people had been at Winterbourne View for much longer periods of time. It is difficult to understand how such practices had been sustained so long after the original exposure of the negative impacts of long-stay institutions. In December 2012, the government made a commitment that, if a person with a learning disability and challenging behaviour would be better off supported in the community, then they should be moved out of hospital by June 2014. This target was not met and recent estimates suggest that the number of people in this type of setting has remained approximately the same largely due to the lack of appropriate alternative care settings within local communities (House of Commons Committee of Public Accounts, 2015).

The role of the CQC

The events at Winterbourne View, Orchid View and at Stafford hospital all highlighted the failure of the CQC to identify and respond to abuse and neglect. This led to a reform of the CQC and its inspection methods. The CQC announced in 2014 that it would re-inspect all care services and rate them individually and that inadequate care homes would be shut down if they were unable to comply with special measures within stated timescales. The inspection process has been restructured to provide more rigorous scrutiny including sector specific teams with appropriate specialist knowledge in each instance (www.cqc.org.uk). The CQC has produced *fundamental standards of care* below which care must never fall and which everybody has a right to expect when they receive care. These are reproduced here.

Person-centred care

You must have care or treatment that is tailored to you and meets your needs and preferences.

Dignity and respect

You must be treated with dignity and respect at all times while you're receiving care and treatment.

This includes making sure:

- *You have privacy when you need and want it.*
- *Everybody is treated as equals.*
- *You're given any support you need to help you remain independent and involved in your local community.*

Consent

You (or anybody legally acting on your behalf) must give your consent before any care or treatment is given to you.

Safety

You must not be given unsafe care or treatment or be put at risk of harm that could be avoided.

Providers must assess the risks to your health and safety during any care or treatment and make sure their staff have the qualifications, competence, skills and experience to keep you safe.

Safeguarding from abuse

You must not suffer any form of abuse or improper treatment while receiving care.

This includes:

- *neglect;*
- *degrading treatment;*
- *unnecessary or disproportionate restraint;*
- *inappropriate limits on your freedom.*

Food and drink

You must have enough to eat and drink to keep you in good health while you receive care and treatment.

Premises and equipment

The places where you receive care and treatment and the equipment used in it must be clean, suitable and looked after properly.

The equipment used in your care and treatment must also be secure and used properly.

Complaints

You must be able to complain about your care and treatment.

The provider of your care must have a system in place so they can handle and respond to your complaint. They must investigate it thoroughly and take action if problems are identified.

Good governance

The provider of your care must have plans that ensure they can meet these standards.

They must have effective governance and systems to check on the quality and safety of care. These must help the service improve and reduce any risks to your health, safety and welfare.

Staffing

The provider of your care must have enough suitably qualified, competent and experienced staff to make sure they can meet these standards.

Their staff must be given the support, training and supervision they need to help them do their job.

Fit and proper staff

The provider of your care must only employ people who can provide care and treatment appropriate to their role. They must have strong recruitment procedures in place and carry out relevant checks such as on applicants' criminal records and work history.

Duty of candour

The provider of your care must be open and transparent with you about your care and treatment.

Should something go wrong, they must tell you what has happened, provide support and apologise.

Display of ratings

The provider of your care must display their CQC rating in a place where you can see it. They must also include this information on their website and make our latest report on their service available to you.

(www.cqc.org.uk/content/fundamental-standards)

While the CQC inspections have undoubtedly become more rigorous, recent evidence suggests that the CQC has been unable to achieve its aims for improvement. The organisation has struggled to recruit enough staff to achieve its targets for re-inspection leaving considerable doubt as to standards of care in a wide range of settings (National Audit Office, 2015).

Organisational cultures

While abuse itself is caused by the individual behaviour of perpetrators, it is equally important to consider the conditions which create an environment in which abuse and neglect can occur.

ACTIVITY *6.4*

Look back at the examples of abuse and neglect in hospital and residential settings discussed above or consider other examples. What common factors have occurred in each setting to allow abuse to occur?

COMMENT

The Care Act guidance defines organisational abuse as:

including neglect and poor care practice within an institution or specific care setting such as a hospital or care home, for example, or in relation to care provided in one's

(Continued)

147

COMMENT *continued*

own home. This may range from one off incidents to on-going ill-treatment. It can be through neglect or poor professional practice as a result of the structure, policies, processes and practices within an organisation.

(Department of Health, 2014: 234)

The power imbalance that can be inherent in caring relationships has been highlighted in relation to care in domestic settings in Chapter 4. The potential for power imbalances in caring relationships within services is even greater. Hanley and Marsland (2014) comment that significant features of relationships between staff and service users in residential settings, such as non-mutual dependency, isolation and unequal decision making powers, create a climate where individuals are more at risk. The Care Act definition of organisational abuse emphasises the fact that abusive cultures of care are no longer unique to large institutions but can also be found in domestic and community-based services. On a wider scale, institutional or organisational discrimination is also found in state organisations such as health care or the criminal justice system and reflects wider discrimination and marginalisation in society towards specific groups such as disabled people.

In many of the high profile circumstances where abuse and neglect have occurred, there have been wide scale harms, as opposed to isolated individual perpetrators. It is likely that many of the staff who ultimately either became bystanders to or part of abusive or neglectful practice have done so despite coming into care work with good intentions. Prevailing attitudes and work practices can be passed among staff members and entrenched into the culture of the setting. Also, the environment and the organisational culture can create the opportunities for the actions of those predisposed to harming others to be tolerated or overlooked. These factors can result in a deterioration in work practices over time and can provide early warning signs to prevent abuse occurring or as indicators of more serious underlying problems.

Early indicators of concern in care settings

Marsland et al. (2015) carried out research to identify early indicators of concern in residential and nursing homes for older people and found that the themes which emerged were extremely similar to their earlier research into residential settings for people with learning disabilities (Marsland et al., 2007). Health and social care practitioners who had visited services in which abuse or neglect had occurred were asked about factors they had seen within the service which had caused them to become concerned. Marsland et al. categorise six key areas of concern in relation to organisational environments and cultures:

- *Concerns about management and leadership*

  Managers have a crucial role in creating and maintaining good practice and providing the central role model for the rest of the organisation. Factors which could provide early indicators of concern may include: lack of availability; frequent changes of manager; not responding to concerns or addressing identified risks; and not making decisions or setting priorities.

- *Concerns about staff skills, knowledge and practice*

  To provide good care staff need to understand the needs of the people they are caring for and to treat them in ways which maintain dignity, privacy and respect. Early indicators of concerns about staff may include: demonstrating a lack of understanding, knowledge and skills to support the individuals in their care; an inability to manage behaviours in safe and dignified ways; and the use of negative and judgemental language when speaking about residents.

- *Concerns about residents' behaviours and wellbeing*

  The way in which residents themselves present can be a crucial indicator of how well they are being cared for. Factors which may indicate cause for concern include: avoidable minor injuries; residents showing fear; changes in behaviour, mood or appearance; and different behaviour towards different members of staff.

- *Concerns about the service resisting the involvement of external people and isolating residents*

  Evidence repeatedly highlights how environments that discourage or prevent contact with people outwith the setting are a cause for concern. Indicators of services isolating individuals from external people include: physical isolation of residents, in their bedrooms rooms for instance; defensive responses to families and practitioners; resistance to external advice and guidance; and failure to report incidents to the appropriate external agencies or families.

- *Service delivery and planning*

  Effective planning and delivery of services is essential to achieving appropriate care. Some indicators of concern in this area may include: insufficient staff to provide the required level of support of residents; inability to deliver the type of support that it has been commissioned to provide; and accepting residents who have needs or behaviours that are different from those of the people usually accommodated.

- *The quality of basic care and the environment*

  Easily observable deficiencies within the setting can be a sign of serious risk or actual harm to residents. Indicators of concern around basic care may include: lack of support with eating and drinking; staff not checking whether people are safe and well; inadequate medical attention or support for people with health problems; and issues with essential equipment being absent, broken or not used.

Marsland et al. (2015) also noted that where indicators of concern are across three or more of the six themes there is further increased likelihood of risk of harm, abuse or neglect. This also highlights the need for action to address concerns over a range of areas if effective change is to be achieved. While patterns of concern do not prove that abuse is occurring they can be an indicator for further exploration.

Conversely, abuse may occur when there are no indicators present. The research emphasises the central role that practitioners have in identifying concerns in residential settings and the importance of those concerns being listened to and acted on. It also further highlights the importance of information sharing between agencies when there are concerns about a care setting to gain a fuller picture of the situation.

Clearly not all abuse in care settings is perpetrated by staff and abuse by other residents can be a particular risk in settings where individuals have challenging behaviours or cognitive problems. Such abuse is more likely to occur in settings where there is poor practice in terms of inadequate staffing levels or lack of training in the specific care needs of the residents.

Use of the law

The Mental Health Act

The MHA asserts that anyone detained under the Act, as were many of the people at Winterbourne View, has a right to an independent First Tier Tribunal to assess the lawfulness of their detention. While exercising this right may be unlikely for someone if they have limited understanding of their situation due to learning disabilities or mental health problems, there is a requirement that anyone who has not taken this up within the first six months of detention is referred for a First Tier Tribunal. After this, the requirement for a further tribunal is after three years, which is an extensive period to elapse without scrutiny of their circumstances. The tribunal also provides a forum for consideration of the wider aspects of the individual's care and as such can be a good forum for investigating issues around care. Green (2013) suggests that patients' rights could be further protected by more frequent use of the tribunal system and by including clauses in commissioning arrangements with private hospitals which require this.

People detained under the MHA also have the right to an Independent Mental Health Advocate (IMHA) who can speak for them in issues relating to care and treatment and exercising their rights. If someone lacks capacity to instruct an IMHA then the IMHA can provide non-instructed advocacy. IMHAs are in a pivotal position to provide external scrutiny in psychiatric care as they are likely to have access to wards and locked areas from which families have sometimes been excluded. They also in most circumstances see patients in private so can give people the opportunity to disclose information (Green, 2013).

The Mental Capacity Act

Chapter 3 looked at the range of legal and policy frameworks applicable to safeguarding and some of these are particularly pertinent to safeguarding in a residential context. The Mental Capacity Act 2005 (MCA), which has been considered in Chapter 3, provides a framework which not only clarifies how decisions should be made on behalf of people who lack mental capacity but also the central principle that the capacity of individuals should be assumed unless there is evidence to the contrary. While the principles of the MCA provide a robust framework to support decision making by and for adults in residential and hospital settings, the research reviewed in

Chapter 3 suggests that the empowering nature of the legal framework has often not been achieved in practice. Healthcare settings have been particularly criticised for not following the principles of the MCA and for low levels of understanding among staff of how it should influence practice (House of Lords Select Committee on the Mental Capacity Act 2005, 2014). The decision specific nature of capacity assessments is a key area where practice does not regularly comply with the MCA.

Research has further suggested that a finding of incapacity varies depending on the individual who is assessing and that people are more likely to be assessed as having capacity if they are in agreement with the organisation providing the care. Where there are concerns about risk, research suggests that all those involved in decision making, including judges, may feel drawn towards outcomes of capacity assessments that are more protective of the adult involved (Bartlett, 2014). Studies such as CIPOLD, discussed above, have found that lack of adherence to the MCA was a contributory factor in a number of deaths of adults and highlight the central role that adherence to the MCA plays in safeguarding. CIPOLD found that there was a lack of adherence to aspects of the MCA, particularly regarding assessments of capacity and best inter-ests decision making processes (www.bristol.ac.uk/cipold/). There was also a lack of understanding of specific aspects of the Act itself, particularly regarding the defini-tion of 'serious medical treatment' and in relation to resuscitation guidelines. Research also suggests that the link identified between poor understanding of, and adherence to, the MCA by health and social care practitioners and premature deaths may have a wider application beyond people with learning disabilities (Heslop et al., 2014).

The Deprivation of Liberty Safeguards

The Deprivation of Liberty Safeguards (DoLS) are a legal framework set up as part of the Mental Health Act 2007 to ensure that individuals who lack the mental capacity to consent to the arrangements for their care, where such care may be a 'deprivation of liberty', have the arrangements independently assessed to ensure they are in the best interests of the individual. A key element of the safeguards is that health and care providers must formally apply to their local authority and satisfy six different assess-ment criteria. The Supreme Court's judgment of March 2014 in the case of 'Cheshire West' clarified what constitutes a deprivation of liberty, as discussed in Chapter 3. The judgment vastly increased the likelihood of situations in care homes being clas-sified as a deprivation of liberty. The first annual official statistics report since the Supreme Court judgment gave new guidance on the use of the Deprivation of Liberty Safeguards saw a tenfold increase in DoLS applications received by councils between April 2014 and March 2015, compared with the previous year of data collection (www.hscic.gov.uk).

Alongside the impact of the court ruling, the House of Lords Committee report in 2014 was highly critical of the DoLS system, which was seen as overly complicated and not in keeping with the principles underpinning the MCA. Research suggests that there are various problems with the current system, including highly complex processes and paperwork, and lack of knowledge and confidence around navigating the system (Lennard, 2015). There also appears to be a sense of stigma felt by some care settings that seeking an authorisation is a negative event for the person or the care home or that if the application is not approved this is a criticism of the setting. Many of these issues would be resolved by improved systems of training to agencies although this could be unlikely given the current overstretched budgets of local authorities who oversee the DoLS system (Lennard, 2015).

The government has asked the Law Commission to draft a new legal framework for DoLS and draft legislation is expected in 2017 (Law Commission, n.d.). This will include deprivation of liberty in wider settings such as supported living where applications are currently made to the Court of Protection. The Law Commission aims to replace the current DoLS system with something which is simpler for practitioners to use while maintaining human rights protections. The House of Lords Committee recommended a body to have oversight of the DoLS system and in response to this the government has proposed an advisory board, the effectiveness of which is likely to have a major influence over the success or otherwise of the changes. Introducing safeguards earlier in care planning practice is one of the issues currently under debate alongside a more central role of advocates in the process.

Changes need to take account of wider European frameworks which are also constantly evolving. The UK has endorsed the United Nations Convention on the Rights of Persons with Disabilities (UN, 2006) which instructs member states to move away from notions of people as either having capacity or not, towards the increased use of supported decision making. The underlying concept of this is that a person never entirely loses legal authority to make decisions but assistance with decision making becomes stronger if functional ability reduces. Bartlett (2014) suggests that there is a fine line between people with and without capacity in care homes and that many people on the borderline of capacity in relation to specific decisions may not be protected by the current DoLS system in the UK. Moves to increase not only the involvement of the individual but also their family are likely (Bartlett, 2014). The reformed system has the potential to improve the quality of life for many people living in care settings if it can meet the challenge to provide a framework which enables the effective engagement of individuals, families and care providers in the process of protecting human rights.

Ill-treatment and wilful neglect
The offence of ill-treatment and wilful neglect came into force under the Criminal Justice and Courts Act 2015 (www.legislation.gov.uk) and was intended to address a gap in the law left by the Mental Health Act 1983 and the Mental Capacity Act 2005. These laws created offences of ill-treatment or wilful neglect for people with mental disorders or people who lack capacity to take relevant decisions by care staff or people appointed to take decisions for them. The Criminal Justice and Courts Act 2015 aims to also protect service users who do not have a mental disorder and do not lack capacity to take relevant decisions. The offence applies to people who work in adult social care and health workers providing care for adults and children in England and Wales. Separate charges apply under the Act to both care workers and care providers. The criminal charge for ill-treatment and wilful neglect carries a maximum jail term of five years (Stothart, 2014). The legislation does not currently apply to schools, children's care homes and childcare services; however, the

government is currently consulting on plans to extend the offence to such settings. The new offences allow the prosecution of both health and social care staff and organisations. The legislation came about as a direct result of the Mid Staffordshire hospital failings amid strong feelings that it was a necessary step to provide better protection to people in care settings. There have, however, been varied responses to the legislation including the suggestion that it focuses attention on the wrong areas by potentially highlighting failings of individual workers, as opposed to addressing wider themes in safeguarding (Bee, 2015). Concerns have been raised that the punitive approach of the legislation may make health and care staff less open to admitting when things go wrong and might lead to some employees being scapegoated when the failing was that of their employer to provide appropriate structures and training.

Whistleblowing

Good care environments require a culture where people are able to speak up about concerns and are encouraged to challenge bad practice. Conversely in poor care settings managers and care staff may be unwilling to listen to the concerns of others and staff may feel unable to voice their concerns. In cases where people are being abused or at risk of abuse the actions of those who have witnessed abuse or neglect have often been pivotal in protecting those involved. The events at Winterbourne View provide a stark example of someone raising significant concerns within and outwith the organisation, and ultimately with the CQC, and not being listened to. While there has been a much higher profile of whistleblowing over recent years, many people who do whistleblow have experienced intimidation or mistreatment within private care settings and within the NHS. Whistleblowing can be an isolating process with reprisals including counter allegations, disciplinary action and victimisation. A lack of support and lack of confidence in the process have also been highlighted, with negative effects on the whistleblower including loss of employment and personal and family breakdown (Smith, 2014). Some groups of people raising concerns have been identified in research as particularly vulnerable including locums and agency staff, students and trainees and BME groups (Francis, 2015). The Employment Rights Act 1996, which was amended by the Public Interest Disclosure Act 1998, asserts that where someone makes a protected disclosure, he/she has a right not to be subjected to any detriment by his/her employer for making that disclosure. The legislation largely provides measures which are reactionary after the individual has suffered losses as a result of speaking up, and despite initiatives to support whistleblowers there are still considerable issues around how whistleblowing is defined and who it applies to. A statutory *duty of candour* was applied to all NHS, adult social care and independent providers in 2014 (www.cqc.org.uk/content/regulation-20-duty-candour), intended to improve transparency with people using services and families along with specific procedures that must be followed when things go wrong with care and treatment. A review of whistleblowing in the NHS (Francis, 2015) has suggested that there is a need for further culture change, improved handling of cases and further measures to support good practice particularly for vulnerable groups of whistleblowers. The need for improved legal protection was also highlighted.

Approaches to safeguarding adults in residential settings

Making Safeguarding Personal

Chapters 4 and 5 have looked in some detail at the approaches advocated by *Making Safeguarding Personal*, and these are as relevant in residential settings as they are in families and communities (LGA, 2013). One of the significant features of many of the inquiries and SCRs into serious failings in health and care systems has been the over-riding sense that the individuals with health and support needs have been obscured within the settings and they have not been kept at the centre of their care. Indeed care has often not only failed to be person-centred but has ultimately dehumanised the individuals involved. Research by Redley et al. (2015) into safeguarding activity in relation to people in care settings has suggested that safeguarding lead officers tend to view their role in care settings as somewhat different from safeguarding in families and communities. Often, because concerns are around deficiencies in the quality of care, the focus is on service improvements such as changes to care plans or appropriate staff training and is less likely to directly involve the service user. Further approaches included addressing issues through councils' commissioning and contracting services (Redley et al., 2015). While these aspects are undoubtedly crucial in achieving good outcomes from safeguarding, they only represent part of the picture and potentially fail to address the more deep-seated problems in settings. If factors that put people at risk are considered in terms of a continuum with minor issues in standards of care at one end and intentional abuse and neglect at the other, then there are many people on this continuum who require direct support and intervention to explicitly involve them and their families in safeguarding responses. The factors that have been considered in relation to early indicators of concerns would also suggest that without a fully personalised approach to safeguarding interventions then it would be difficult for practitioners to be reassured that wider intervention to improve the service had rectified the problems, let alone addressed the impact of harms to the individual. Approaches which are purely reactive to failings in settings also negate opportunities for preventative work which are at the heart of MSP policy and practice.

Attachment-based approaches

Attachment theory has been a longstanding central feature in childcare and more recently its relevance to adults has been fully realised (Howe, 2011). The MSP Toolkit (LGA, 2015) considers the use of attachment-based approaches to support practitioners in understanding the motivations and behaviours of people within abusive relationships. Within the context of residential care, attachment as a crucial feature of human relationships can be a central concept in understanding motivations and achieving more compassion in care environments.

While there has been largely a reactionary approach to safeguarding, there is clearly a need for more fundamental, proactive work to address the negative cultures of care which can develop in settings and lead to or be an indicator of more serious abuse and neglect. Harbottle et al. (2014) discuss a model of leadership based on theories of attachment and parenting, which in turn is based on evidence originally from foster care settings, known as Total Attachment. The approach recognises the importance of attachment across the lifespan. It is a whole systems approach to leadership and care which is based around the notion that those providing care need to be cared for themselves in order to fulfil this role towards others. Worker detachment in care settings is seen as detrimental to both service users and staff and rooted in self-preservation for the worker.

Harbottle et al. use Schofield and Beek's (2006) model of nurturing through five dimensions of parenting as the basis for the compassionate leadership described in the model of Total Attachment. The five dimensions are:

* *acceptance*: leaders need to accept the strengths and limitations of staff and carers who do not feel accepted and valued may detach from relationships;

* *being available*: leaders being present and listening to staff which builds trust for stable effective workforces and continuity for service users;

* *responding sensitively*: sensitive leaders help carers to understand that others have feelings and opinions different from their own and if leaders or carers are too consumed by their own feelings detachment will occur;

* *cooperative care or being effective*: leaders make staff feel supported and appreciated within firm boundaries and a sense of working together. People in care may lack autonomy and self-worth and staff feelings of failure may be transferred to them if staff are existing in an uncaring culture;

* *membership*: both staff and service users need to feel a sense of belonging. Relationships need to demonstrate inclusivity, open channels of communication and involvement. Membership and collective sense of purpose allow compassionate practice to develop. In the same way that children benefit from secure attachment, it is also essential for adults in order to build trust, manage anxiety, and develop resilience and empathy for others. This is relevant in both the manager/worker and the worker/service user relationship and Harbottle et al. suggest that it is particularly important for people with physical or cognitive impairments and high dependency on others to meet their needs as the power imbalance in the relationship is extensive.

Ultimately, the aim of attachment-based approaches is for the care qualities of compassion, dignity and respect to permeate the whole organisation as modelled by leaders. Closely linked to this are the wider themes of staff in caring roles being valued through receiving suitable rates of pay, employment conditions and training which will be considered later in relation to care workers working with children and adults.

Community inclusion and reducing isolation

The geographical isolation of services has often been highlighted in relation to situations where abuse has occurred. This in itself can increase the risk of abuse and neglect but is particularly a cause for concern when people are placed a long distance from home, making it harder for relatives to maintain regular contact. While hospital-based forms of care may remain the best option for a very small minority of people, such facilities need to be more transparent and accessible to families and wider communities. The restriction of family and friends to visitor areas at Winterbourne View prevented them from seeing the reality of life on the locked wards. Green (2013) notes that legislation is in place requiring frequent unrestricted access to prisons by independent monitoring board members and suggests that a similar system would be beneficial in long-stay hospitals and assessment and treatment centres. This would provide more regular scrutiny than is offered through CQC inspection time frames alone. Isolating environments, however, can occur even within the close proximity of communities. Isolation of residents can be created by not just physical restrictions on access but poor communication and lack of consultation and transparency with families and friends.

Alongside initiatives to improve access of family and communities to residential settings, appropriate use of advocacy services can provide an essential check that people are receiving suitable standards of care and that their human rights are being adhered to. The statutory requirements to provide advocacy services have been extended in recent years to a wider range of people in different contexts through the MCA 2005, MHA 2007 and the Care Act 2014. Research suggests, however, that there are considerable difficulties in accessing advocacy services in some areas due to a lack of provision (Parson, 2015). Also, while high quality settings may be routinely accessing advocacy when required, it is likely that those most at risk in poor quality care may never be referred for such services. The purpose of advocacy is to provide a voice to people who require support to express their views and the most marginalised and isolated individuals are unlikely to be aware of their rights to such support. It is therefore dependent on statutory agencies commissioning and reviewing services to ensure that advocacy is accessed for those who need it. As commissioners of services, the NHS and local authorities have a pivotal role not only in ensuring that people are safe and well looked after but also in ensuring that care is meeting individual needs and stated goals. They are also accountable for ensuring that individuals do not experience isolating environments and negative cultures of care which create the conditions for neglect and abuse.

Prevention

The Care Act 2014 emphasises the concept of prevention in relation to safeguarding through the duty on local authorities to make enquiries where an adult with care and support needs is experiencing or *at risk* of abuse and neglect. The Care Act also places safeguarding adults reviews (SARs) on a statutory footing and encourages wider use of SARs to maximise learning and prevention opportunities. The risk factors around cultures of care where abuse and neglect can thrive have been reviewed and there is a widely recognised body of evidence around indicators of concern in care settings. While these can only act as a potential indicator in the context of informed judgements, they do provide a good basis for much preventative work. They are part of an approach which involves the opening up of closed environments to scrutiny by families and wider society who, if made more aware of such indicators of concern, are in a position to act on them.

Read the Winterbourne SCR, the Kerelaw Inquiry and the Coffey Report and identify any key themes which could contribute to the risk of abuse within residential settings.

COMMENT

The abuse of children and adults at risk has been prolific, often systematic and obscured through processes of social control and power. Cases of historical abuse have highlighted how institutional mechanisms can contribute to the concealment of abuse through silence and the collective misuse of power. Each of the inquiries identifies a number of common themes which are reflected in both adult and children's residential care. People enter care settings to safeguard their wellbeing and any abusive behaviour that occurs within these settings is unacceptable. It is a failure in our duty to care and represents a breach of human rights. People who are often looked after in residential settings are the most at risk members of society, such as those with complex mental health problems or behaviours that are challenging, disabled people and looked after children. These are people already marginalised in society who can become victims of abuse of power and the failure of agencies to listen to or acknowledge concerns. There are also situations where adults and children are looked after in settings which make them open to additional forms of abuse such as CSE, bullying and exploitation. Powerlessness and dependency can be reinforced through increased social isolation and society's ambivalence towards marginalised groups. A dominant theme that recurs throughout the reports is the lack of professional status and value that is placed on the role of residential care workers. There is often a failure to recruit suitably qualified staff and a reluctance to invest in consistent, good quality care and training. Devalued staff are likely to transfer this treatment onto those cared for.

CHAPTER SUMMARY

In this chapter various themes in safeguarding from abuse and neglect across the lifespan have been identified. While the principle of choice has been rightly prioritised in social care, this has created a system of provision which is challenging to regulate. The introduction of profit making businesses into the provision of care undoubtedly impacts on the priority given to factors such as quality of care, staffing levels and training. Many high quality care environments exist across sectors despite the high profile examples of neglect and abuse and the expansion of privatisation. However, even public bodies such as the NHS have suffered the overwhelming impact of dehumanisation of individuals to achieve financial targets. In 2015 Ofsted reported a decline in the quality of residential childcare (Ofsted, 2015). Matthew Coffey, chief officer at Ofsted, described this reduction in quality as, *'a cause for concern given the vulnerabilities of the children and young people they support'* (Donovan, 2015). Although residential provision which is run by the local authorities (public sector) achieves better ratings in comparison to provision run by the private sector, the public sector provision is currently being significantly reduced; it would appear that the cost of better care is becoming too expensive and being undermined by financial constraints.

(Continued)

CHAPTER SUMMARY *continued*

Safeguarding individuals in this context requires vigilance and a sense of ownership from all members of society. It requires commissioners and regulators of services to insist on regimes that are transparent and have open doors for wider agencies and communities to work in partnership. High standards of service monitoring and review are required from commissioners at a time when all areas of local authority and NHS resources are being stretched to the limit. Practitioners need to be able to have relationships with people in care which provide opportunities for them to listen to their experiences of care environments. Looked after children and the range of adults who live in residential settings have diverse experiences of marginalisation and historical segregation, but the impact of abuse and neglect on them all is undisputed. If individuals are undervalued in society as a whole then it is likely that they will be undervalued in care environments. Wider social change is required to address this. The likelihood that people in care will have more difficulties than most people in speaking up or being listened to when they are harmed means that opportunities to hear them need to be reconfigured and expanded. Improved legal redress and regulation are crucial to this. Service users and support networks such as families and friends need to be aware of channels for complaints and given a central role in partnership working. People in care settings need to be more fully involved in inspection processes and have their rights to advocacy fulfilled.

In some aspects of care, the stark lessons of institutionalisation have been obscured and institutional practices have infiltrated modern care settings across the lifespan. The principles of attachment and the need for compassionate relationships extend across service users and the care workforce. Relationship-based care models such as social pedagogy and Total Attachment are central to this. They are required to counter the inherent risks of non-mutual dependency and power imbalances in residential settings. Inclusion can only be achieved by more community-based forms of care across the lifespan and individuals require meaningful opportunities to be part of communities whatever setting they live in.

FURTHER READING

Davidson, J (2010) Residential care for children and young people: Priority areas for change. *Child Abuse Review*, 19: 405–22.

Howe, D (2011) *Attachment Across the Lifecourse: A Brief Introduction*. Basingstoke: Palgrave Macmillan.

Marsland, D, Oakes, P and White, C (2015) Abuse in care? A research project to identify early indicators of concern in residential and nursing homes for older people. *Journal of Adult Protection*, 17 (2): 111–25.

National Crime Agency (2013) *CEOP Thematic Assessment. The Foundations of Abuse: A Thematic Assessment of the Risk of Child Sexual Abuse by Adults in Institutions.* London: The Stationery Office.

Chapter 7

Skills for safeguarding and protection

Introduction

Due to the emergence of a 'think family' perspective there is an increasing need to consider safeguarding from both the adult and child perspective and for social workers from both disciplines to have interrelated knowledge of systems and resources across the lifespan. Serious case reviews focused on children have acknowledged that there is insufficient focus given to the role of the adult in caring for the children (NSPCC, 2014) and highlighted the crossover between community care assessments and referrals to children and families (NSPCC, 2014b). A focus on the processes of safeguarding children gained prominence in the early 1990s and has developed into a sophisticated framework which identifies concerns and outlines processes to be followed. Safeguarding has only gained prominence in adult social work in more recent years. Contemporary issues to emerge in safeguarding increasingly concern the safety of both adults and children, e.g. domestic violence, sexual exploitation, trafficking. Whilst it is still contested as to whether child sexual exploitation should be a separate category of abuse (Chand, 2014) it could be argued that adult exploitation is also a category of abuse although in real terms there is both abuse and criminal offence.

Chapter 2 identifies the low rate of prosecution of cases of both adult and child abuse. Training when delivered jointly with police on issues such as Achieving Best Evidence tends to focus on children's social workers although some universities are now expanding such modules to incorporate adult social workers. Until such a time as processes are harmonised and training is genuinely a joint venture between social workers (adults and children's) and police officers, it could be argued that prosecution rates will remain low.

The building block of positive outcomes for any individual in the safeguarding arena is a good assessment. Yet in all the serious case reviews reviewed a picture emerges of poor quality assessments which often do not focus on the subject of the assessment and in some cases the individual has never been seen by the social worker. Where sufficient and appropriate information is gathered there is a lack of critical thought, any systematic evaluation and analysis with poorly defined outcomes. Tools available to support assessments are insufficiently used and lines of enquiry are not followed through. As a result of these issues decision making by managers can be flawed with disastrous consequences. The whole process is hampered by the large caseloads carried by social workers who need more time to apply their skills to the process of gathering information, critical reflection and analysis.

ACTIVITY 7.1

Think about an assessment you have undertaken recently. Provide a brief outline of the situation. What was the aim of the assessment? Provide details of the outcome or decision. What knowledge was used to support the decision? What was the process you followed?

In considering the above you may have thought – I've done the visit, completed the assessment form, discussed with my manager and developed a care plan. When talking about 'doing an assessment' in practice it can be in terms of gathering information and completing the assessment form. During initial social work training emphasis is given to assessment in terms of how to do one, theories of assessment, and skills in gathering information – but then there is a leap to analysis of information and how it is used to inform decision making. This is not an intuitive process but one that should be a considered and reasoned activity using high level skills.

Any social work assessment is complex but none more so than when there are safeguarding issues. Each aspect of the assessment is complex: the service user's/child's needs; the capacity of others to protect and respond to needs; the environment in which they find themselves. For many reasons those involved will not want to be identified as perpetrators or as being involved in any way and will seek to mislead and confuse. Therefore, decisions need to be made with often incomplete and conflicting information to determine the best outcome for the service user/child. As decisions are arrived at they need to be supported by evidence and sound reasoning which can be clearly conveyed to others.

Critical thinking

Critical Thinking is a capacity to work with complex ideas whereby a person can make effective provision of evidence to justify a reasonable judgement. The evidence, and therefore judgement, will pay appropriate attention to context.

(Moon, 2008)

Wilkins and Boahen (2013) maintain that through the application of critical thinking skills time can be better managed and put to more effective use. Developing and using critical thinking skills throughout the assessment process offers the ability to focus on the aim of the assessment so that all the thought, work and process can be orientated to that aim. Social workers are familiar with the terms and practice of critical reflection, and this is part of the underlying process of critical thinking which enables a more holistic view of any situation to be provided. However, critical reflection is focused on your own practice, whereas in this discussion it is proposed that critical thinking is applied to the processes you are undertaking.

The term 'critical' is often misunderstood as a word with negative implications. In this context we do not set out to criticise but to be focused on the information needed so that we can arrive at a situation where we can get to the truth of the matter and aid decision making. It is about having 'creativity and curiosity' (as mentioned in the PCF), questioning, seeking alternatives and understanding motives.

ACTIVITY **7.2**

Think again about the assessment you reviewed in Activity 7.1 and identify the skills you have used.

The skills used during an assessment are many and varied. The skills of information gathering are well documented and acknowledged; in this chapter, whilst recognising the centrality of interpersonal skills in developing rapport, empathy and understanding of the individual, we will focus on the skills aligned with critical thinking. These include:

- focus;
- development of hypothesis;
- reflection;
- analysis and synthesis;
- awareness of risk;
- knowledge;
- ability to make decisions.

Focus

The purpose of an assessment is to make decisions. There is a fundamental need to establish WHY the assessment is being undertaken and WHAT you want to achieve. Vague statements of intent do not help to gather the relevant or even the right information.

Consider the following two statements.

- I'm assessing the individual's/child's needs.

- I'm carrying out an assessment to establish if the individual/child can remain safely in their home.

The second expressed outcome enables the social worker to focus on what information is needed to arrive at a decision.

There may be more than one outcome or purpose to the assessment which will require separate statements and consideration. This should be established at the earliest possible stage. In doing so you are beginning the process of thinking critically and developing an *'analytical mindset'* (Wilkins and Boahen, 2013). As assessment is a dynamic process, it may change once more information comes to light. Using the aim and the referral it is then possible to think about what might be happening and develop some hypotheses about the situation.

ACTIVITY **7.3**

Return to your assessment from Activity 7.1. Did you have a clear aim? Can you identify what influence that had on the gathering of information?

Development of hypothesis

Using what information you have enables you to develop your thinking about what might be happening. In many cases this will involve thinking the unthinkable. What questions are springing to mind? What do you need to know to support or disprove your hypothesis? No matter how hard we try when we first see something written down an often unconscious perception arises and intuition kicks in. An example of this is a case study used as the basis for an assignment.

CASE STUDY

Yesterday Polly turned up at school wearing a baseball cap and when she removed it her head had been shaved. When her teacher asked her what had happened she said her mum had done it as she was being naughty, telling lies and needed to be taught a lesson. Her brothers, aged 14 and 16, had grabbed and held her by the arms on a chair while

(Continued)

---

mum had shaved all her hair off. There are no other obvious injuries but she says her wrists are sore from being held. The teacher asked what lies she was telling and Polly got very upset saying they weren't lies – her brothers did get into her bed during the night.

School made a referral to social services. Subsequent discussions with the police led to a forensic medical examination and preparation for a video interview. Results from the medical examination indicated vaginal penetration with significant bruising in the genital area.

Within the assignments, 25 per cent of students assumed Polly had been raped; 50 per cent assumed she had been sexually abused, which implies that 75 per cent of the cohort did not consider any other explanations for her injuries. All assumed the injuries had been perpetrated by her brothers. This intuitive thought has a place when a very speedy decision is needed (Munro, 2008) but there still needs to be a more systematic examination of the probabilities following the action.

Return to your assessment from Activity 7.1. What hypothesis did you make initially? Was it proved or disproved?

When developing any hypothesis it must be remembered that it is only that – your mental representation of the *'picture of the situation'* (O'Sullivan, 2011: 111) and as such it is subject to change. Care must be taken to avoid 'confirmation bias', that is only looking for that which will support your hypothesis. Each new piece of information, each new observation should be considered and your hypothesis reconsidered.

Reflection

A period of reflection on the information gathered can enable fresh perspectives or interpretations of the information. Lack of time is always an issue but spending time in this valuable way can not only save time later but also make for better and more reasoned decision making. Much has been written about reflection and critical reflection (see, for example, Knott and Scragg, 2013) but it is clear that periods of critical reflection are an integral part of this process and essential for rational decision making.

What at first may not be apparent can become acknowledged during this period, offering further insight into the situation. Whilst reflection-in-action will be taking place during the process of gathering information, this is a period of time to reflect on the information as a whole. It can enable the identification of gaps in knowledge and other sources of information you may not have considered.

ACTIVITY 7.5

Consider how you reflect:

- *alone;*

- *in supervision;*

- *in a group.*

What are the strengths of each approach?

Perhaps for you reflection alone is the preferred option. Reflection-in-action is usually a sole activity and some people also like to reflect alone so as to be sure of what information has been collected and how the individual is interpreting it. Using reflection in supervision has been a key theme over the last decade. It has the advantage of allowing the individual to verbalise the information which can bring new meaning to that information; it allows the exchange of ideas; it involves managers at an early stage in the decision making process and it can feel safer for the individual. Group supervision can bring a diverse range of knowledge and skills together and when applied to a situation can enable a variety of perspectives to be considered.

Analysis

Up until this point the focus may have been on obtaining information about specific situations but it is now time to think about the information as a whole. Many people view analysis as turning their attention to detail but, as Wilkins and Boahen (2013) put it, '*critical analysis means taking a questioning and enquiring view of* [all of] *the information to hand and obtaining a good understanding of a given situation*'.

So analysis is about understanding what the information is telling us. It could be about considering a chronology or a historical narrative to identify any emerging patterns or cycles of behaviour. Or it could be about 'joining the dots' to see a fuller picture. Consider the following:

- You notice that recorded on the assessment form is the statement: 'the child is inappropriately dressed'. You might begin to ask yourself questions such as 'inappropriately dressed for what?' and also 'why?'. Using this statement alone would lead to decision making that may be unachievable.

- Also noted on the assessment form is the information that 'there has been a house fire and the children's clothing was destroyed'. This, taken together with details about the family's income ('parents are on benefits') may lead to a conclusion that the parents are unable to afford to replace the clothing. This would lead to an entirely different decision being made.

The events leading up to a referral and an understanding of the situations can help to determine a way forward. For example, if we take the first piece of information given above and then add 'the parents are unable to provide basic necessities for their children due to their high level of expenditure on cigarettes and alcohol', this is likely to lead to another entirely different decision.

So analysis begins and continues throughout an assessment. There will be analysis taking place while the information is being gathered, in terms of what information is sought and what more is needed.

This leads into another aspect of analysis: Do you give the same amount of weight or credence to all the information? Is some more relevant than others? There needs to be some consideration of the sources of the information obtained. Information from parents for example may carry less weight than information from a medical professional in a given situation. Other information may need to be 'tested'. A prime example of this may be found in the SCR of Baby P, where information was accepted by the social worker from the mother and was never corroborated by others or questioned or alternatives considered (Haringey Local Safeguarding Children Board, 2009).

Knowledge

In a complex assessment there needs to be some thought and reflection on the knowledge used to enable an understanding of the situation. Using theory and evidence from research not only enables you to make sense of the situation but also gives an insight into how the person can be better protected and helped. The term 'evidence-based practice' can be confusing, as it can be interpreted in many ways. Gambrill's (2006) approach is useful here: *'What's the fuss about? Everyone holds knowledge gained from experience, study and personal lives. We all know about theories BUT we don't use them.'* Practice has to be based not only on experience but on theory. Without theory and the knowledge from theory our decision making will be flawed and could harm rather than help our service users.

ACTIVITY 7.6

Return to the assessment you thought about in Activity 7.1.

What theories or knowledge did you draw on and at which stages in the assessment?

It is easy to get drawn into the fast pace of social work practice and intuitively use the theories you are familiar with, and for less complex situations that may be acceptable. However, in complex situations where decisions need to be taken often without complete information a detailed rationale is required for how the decision has been arrived at.

CASE STUDY

Mrs B has been referred by her family who want her to be placed in a residential home. The assessment shows that she meets the criteria for admission although she wishes to remain in her own home. The team manager advises that a residential placement should be sought.

Using systems theory and an ecomap the social worker is then able to identify that two of her four support systems have broken down; the day care centre has closed and her daughter has moved away from the area. She still has home care input and help with shopping from her son. This enabled the social worker to return to her team manager and suggest that a referral to a luncheon club and a meals delivery service, and regular visits by the community nursing service, would be sufficient at this time to enable Mrs B to remain in her home.

Risk management

In developing a clear understanding of the situation through the previous processes the risks can be articulated. Using the above example there are clearly risks to Mrs B staying at home. It could be argued that she would have more company in a residential home and risks being lonely at home. She would have immediate assistance in the residential home if she fell, whilst at home she risks lying for long periods of time. There are books written about risk and risk management (see Further reading) but in this context I am suggesting that the risks uncover themselves as a focus is clearly set, a hypothesis is explored, analysis considers the risks, and theory and knowledge are applied to the situation. Using a decision making process the risks are identified and various courses of action can be identified and considered. This is about forward thinking and a touch of clairvoyance – what could happen? Is it likely to happen? How can these risks be managed?

ACTIVITY *7.7*

Return to your own assessment and think about the risks you identified.

What theories supported your thinking?

Often risks are thought about in terms of physical risk but using a theoretical approach other risks can be considered as well.

CASE STUDY

Charlie, aged 8, is showing signs of an insecure attachment to both his parents. There are known to be low levels of domestic violence within the household but it is felt that there is no physical risk to Charlie.

(Continued)

In terms of Erikson's lifestages (see Walker and Crawford, 2014), Charlie is possibly facing the challenge of industry v inferiority. Due to the situation at home and an insecure attachment it is therefore unlikely that Charlie will have the focus to concentrate fully on his education or activities open to him. There is therefore a risk that he will not resolve this challenge successfully and that he will enter his teenage adolescent years with lower self-confidence.

Attachment theory would suggest that insecure attachments in childhood that are left without resolution will influence the future development of relationships in adolescence and adulthood (Walker and Crawford, 2014).

Supported by this information it may not be appropriate to leave Charlie in that situation given the long-term impact this could have. Here, the decision making process is supported by the skill of identification of risk, and the use of key theory.

Decision making

Increasingly there is emphasis on how social workers arrive at decisions. Following a process and using the skills described above it is possible to arrive at a decision for which there is a clear rationale and evidence to support it.

But, it is likely particularly in social work that there is no clear-cut decision as there are so many variables and unknowns in any given situation. And this is where professional judgement is so important. Everything discussed so far provides the support for professional judgement to be used and decisions to be taken. What is likely to happen is that a number of options present themselves. In Charlie's situation the options may be:

- leave him at home with supervision;

- place him with a family member;

- place him in foster care.

There are many models used to assist professionals in arriving at a decision, which are becoming increasingly recognised as relevant to the social work profession. A decision making tree is recommended by Munro (2008) for use in child safeguarding situations but can be applied to any situation. This allows for an exploration of the options and the possible outcomes of each option, along with any possible inherent risks. In *Effective Child Protection* (Chapter 7) Munro provides detailed guidance on how to apply and use a decision making tree. This can be fully used for highly complex situations where time is available or as an overview or framework where there is less complexity and time.

Emerging from decision theory, a decision tree can be a visual representation of the decision to be made and the options available. In the example above the decision to be made is where Charlie should live. The options are: (a) leave him at home; (b) place him with a family member; or (c) place him in foster care. Visually this would be represented as shown in Figure 7.1.

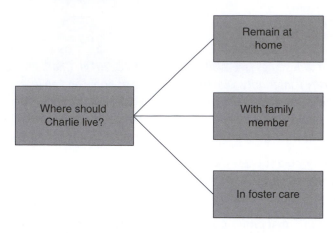

Figure 7.1   Decision tree for deciding on the appropriate option for Charlie

It is now possible to consider each of these options and think about what the outcome of each might be, what the risks are and the likelihood of the risk occurring. It is likely in less complex situations that this is sufficient exploration to enable an informed and rational decision to be taken. In more complex situations a mathematical approach can be followed whereby a numerical value is allocated to both the probability of an outcome occurring and the desirability of such an outcome. This gives a numerical weighting to the various options and can assist in providing a clear rationale for decision making.

Other models for decision making exist but are more scientific in approach and not easily applicable to the social, complex and often messy situations social workers work with. Having explored all the options, a social worker ultimately has to exercise their professional judgement. Standing (2011: 7) defines professional judgement as: *'Informed opinion (using intuition, reflection and critical thinking) that relates observation and assessment to identifying and evaluating alternative options.'*

ACTIVITY 7.8

Apply a decision making tree to the assessment you started in Activity 7.1. What are the options generated? What did you take into consideration in the exercise of your professional judgement in making the final choice of option?

You may find that you arrive at the same decision as your colleagues. However, when asked to explain and support that decision you will be able to do so with clarity and confidence. This saves time in the longer term both for managers who supervise social workers, and in writing reports for courts and conferences as there is a clear rationale and evidence for the decisions and recommendations. It may also bring to light alternatives that had not been previously considered. The process could provide the service user with more choice and more independence and the social worker with more curiosity.

CHAPTER SUMMARY

In conclusion the use of a systematic way to develop understanding, analysis and interpretation of information, exploring all the options, and use of a decision making process can only lead to better, more informed use of professional judgement. Social workers will readily admit to not consciously applying theory to their work, but when they do it could provide much more insight into service users' situations and the competing alternatives available to them.

Focus	What do you what to achieve?
Hypothesis	What is going on?
Reflection	What do you think about it?
Analysis	What is it telling you?
Knowledge	What can help you understand and predict?
Risk management	What are the risks and the likelihood of them occurring?
Decision making	What options are available and what are the likely outcomes of each?

FURTHER READING

Hothersall, S and Maas-Lowit, M (2010) *Need, Risk and Protection in Social Work Practice.* Exeter: Learning Matters.

Munro, E (2008) *Effective Child Protection,* 2nd edn. London: Sage.

O'Sullivan, T (2011) *Decision Making in Social Work.* Basingstoke: Palgrave Macmillan.

Taylor, B (2013) *Professional Decision Making and Risk in Social Work.* London: Sage/Learning Matters.

Wilkins, D and Boahen, G (2013) *Critical Analysis Skills for Social Workers.* Maidenhead: Open University Press.

Chapter 8

Key themes for safeguarding practice: challenges and priorities

This chapter will help you to develop the following capabilities from the Professional Capabilities Framework:

- **Professionalism:** Identify and behave as a professional social worker committed to professional development.
- **Values and ethics:** Apply social work ethical principles and values to guide professional practice.
- **Diversity:** Recognise diversity and apply anti-discriminatory and anti-oppressive principles in practice.
- **Rights, justice and economic wellbeing:** Advance human rights and promote social justice and economic wellbeing.
- **Knowledge:** Apply knowledge of social sciences, law and social work practice theory.
- **Critical reflection and analysis:** Apply critical reflection and analysis to inform and provide a rationale for professional decision-making.
- **Intervention and skills:** Use judgement and authority to intervene with individuals, families and communities to promote independence, provide support and prevent harm, neglect and abuse.

It will also introduce you to the following standards as set out in the 2008 social work subject benchmark statement:

5.1.3 Values and ethics
5.1.4 Social work theory
5.1.5 The nature of social work practice

This government will not cut [the] deficit in a way that hurts those we most need to help, that divides the country, or that undermines the spirit and ethos of our public services.

(David Cameron, at the launch of the Conservative Party's manifesto in Milton Keynes, 7 June 2010)

I say to those watching today and who are genuinely sick, disabled or who are retired. You have nothing to fear. This government and this party don't regard caring for the needy as a burden. It is a proud duty to provide financial security to the most vulnerable members of our society and this will not change. This is our contract with the most vulnerable.

(Iain Duncan Smith, October 2010; http://conservative-speeches.sayit.mysociety.org/speech/601437)

Today the infrastructure of welfare support is under attack. Social security is deemed too costly; the principles of mutual support and solidarity are being replaced by selfish individualism. People in poverty are labelled and are made to feel ashamed to claim the welfare support they need. Negative attitudes are reinforced by sensationalist media and opportunistic politicians, and the nasty and divisive public rhetoric that has emerged demonises those living in poverty in ways that are reminiscent of the early 1940s.

(www.theguardian.com/commentisfree/2015/apr/27/poverty-study-uk-bad-1940s)

ACTIVITY *8.1*

How would you define what austerity is? Is austerity inevitable or a political choice?

Consider the ways in which the people with whom social workers work have been impacted by the austerity agenda. Discuss what impact this is having upon service users, social workers and social work.

Introduction

This chapter sets out to wrestle with the issue of how far social workers can still protect service users and carers at a time when their incomes are being cut and when many of the state-run services they rely upon are being reduced or withdrawn. It argues that the so-called 'austerity agenda' is impacting disproportionately on many of the most vulnerable people that social workers work alongside. The chapter contends that the impact of austerity places people at an even greater risk of physical and mental ill health and risks increasing feelings of insecurity, social isolation and even a loss of meaningful identity. Austerity can and is impacting adversely on the overall wellbeing of individuals, families and communities. Within this climate, social work faces many challenges but as a profession it must try to ensure that the rights and needs of service users are protected and promoted.

Safeguarding in a climate of austerity

In May 2015, the newly elected Conservative government reiterated its intention to implement £12 billion of social security cuts every year up until at least the year 2018.

It can already be anticipated that this is going to continue to have a deeply disproportionate effect on the lives of people within our society who already have the
lowest incomes. Diminishing state resources and cuts in funding for the third sector have already had the effect of marginalising vulnerable people who rely on their
services even further. Communities are being impacted adversely as a range of
services are being threatened or withdrawn. The third sector, so often reliant on
funding from local authorities, has often been able to work in partnership (and com-
plement the state sector) in providing services and projects for a range of service user
groups. Today charity and voluntary groups are under ever greater financial pressure.
In many local authorities, services that have been provided by voluntary organisations, such as play schemes, family support services, early years centres, daycentres
and day clubs are under threat or have been withdrawn.

At the time of writing, people are still living under the impact of the worldwide economic crisis of 2008/9. Bankers, who were evidently to blame for the worldwide
financial crash, were in effect bailed out by western governments using money that
came from general taxation. UK citizens, much like other European citizens, were
told by their elected politicians that public services now needed to be cut on a huge
scale. It was inevitable, some governmental figures argued, that people who were
reliant on welfare benefits and state services would have to suffer losses to both.
None of the major political parties opposed this thinking with much vigour. The 2010
Conservative–Liberal Democrat coalition government subsequently embarked on a
programme of cuts which has had a major impact on public services and upon social
work – upon social work settings and how they are expected to operate, on the roles
of social workers themselves, and on the lives of the service users and families they
seek to serve.

The next round of welfare cuts from the newly elected Conservative government
has for some been seen as a concerted attack on the principles of the welfare state.
One respected campaigning organisation, Church Action on Poverty, has argued that
these cuts undermine the principle of the state 'safety net' which is there to protect
the most vulnerable people in society (Perry et al., 2015). There is certainly a danger of losing the important 'policy principle' that was hard won with the birth of
the welfare state and enshrined in the now (interestingly just repealed) 1948 National
Assistance Act. The welfare state fostered the idea that it was the state's duty to
provide a safety net from the cradle to the grave, and it is too often forgotten that
before this time many families had to shoulder the responsibility of caring for family
members regardless of whether they had the means or the ability.

It is therefore crucial to emphasise that any questions around safeguarding and risk
need to be located within the social, economic and political context of the society
in which they take place. Discourses that seek to limit recognition of that are not
only inadequate but also dishonest and dangerous. Social workers must always be
attentive to the impact that political and economic decisions have on the lives of the
people with whom they work. Social workers also need to be aware of how ideolo-
gies and discourses influence thinking around needs, rights, approaches to issues of
risk and safeguarding.

It is fair to say that discourses around safeguarding and risk have become much more prominent since the 1980s as wider public services have been 'rolled back' in order to discourage so-called 'dependency'. Indeed there is a case for saying that consideration of risk has replaced considerations of need as the key determinant in welfare provision. Social workers know that when people's needs are not being met they will generally be at more risk from many things. Yet despite massive budget cuts from central government, local authorities have been expected to retain their duties to meet need. Implicitly acknowledging they cannot do this, their strategy has at least been to ration services and to manage situations where people are judged as being at the greatest risk.

Since the late 1970s, successive UK governments have also tended to accept and adopt the ideology of neoliberalism and this, combined with managerialism, has resulted in social workers having much less autonomy in the management of their caseloads (Ferguson, 2009). This has moved the primary focus of social work away from people and towards considerations of targets and outputs, with increasing emphasis on considerations of money and resources. The neoliberal approach to policy also promotes the idea that it is legitimate and desirable for state services to be contracted out to the private sector. No areas of the public sector now seem to be safe from this philosophy and this has been seen very recently in considerations of outsourcing child protection services to independent companies (Jones, 2015). In tandem with this runs an emphasis on 'responsibilism' (the idea that individuals and families must take more responsibility whilst the role and responsibilities of the state are underplayed). Within such discourses there is a great danger that issues around risk will be further decontextualised and individualised, with issues around risk and safeguarding couched in terms of individual actions that might be taken by people or families or communities, rather than within a structuralist framework that recognises issues around social injustice and inequality.

In addition to this, neoliberalism puts additional stresses on social workers as they come under increasing surveillance and are compelled to meet targets and outputs over which they have little control. A discourse is propagated around the need to save money, and the reduction of the care packages of service users becomes legitimised. This approach often risks the health and wellbeing of social workers themselves, who become stressed as a result of having their professional integrity questioned. Social work staff are told they have to effectively cut care packages but too often have to be disingenuous with service users about why this is. This adds to increasing levels of stress among staff and a sense of disconnection between the values social workers try to uphold and what they are being asked to do. Workers feel under pressure to act in the interests of saving money as opposed to working for the real needs of their clients. This clearly can damage the social work and service user relationship, so crucial to effective social work.

Discourses that promote social solidarity and mutual responsibility towards others are also currently being marginalised in favour of discourses that stress self-sufficiency and the labelling and stigmatisation of those who are unable to cope. Government language argues that people need to be enabled to do 'more for themselves'.

173

Yet this discourse gives the impression that people are self-sufficient rather than interdependent beings. As earlier chapters have highlighted, individual people live in families, groups and communities and their needs are best met when these are thriving and are complemented by properly funded universal services. The concept of the 'common good' is a highly important one for social work in that it fosters the idea that people have responsibilities towards one another. The less connected human beings are to other people the more vulnerable they often are. There has been a tradition in social work that has fostered the belief in mutuality and collectivism and the idea that as moral agents all human beings have a collective responsibility towards one another. Social work has to be aware of the dangers of individualising people's problems and failing to relate the issues they face to wider political and economic decisions and policies. To fail to do so risks labelling people and misunderstanding the issues, struggles and discrimination they too often face.

It is important to focus on ways in which the so-called austerity agenda is already impacting upon groups of people who are generally considered to be the most vulnerable citizens in society. These include older people on low incomes, children within low income families, people with mental health problems and people with physical and learning disabilities. Social workers also need to recognise that some people often fall into more than one subscribed service user category and are vulnerable in many ways.

Older people, especially those already on low incomes, have been put particularly at risk from reductions in income and public services. Local authorities have been forced to look at ways that they can ration the services they provide. Tightening rules around eligibility criteria within social care has been seen as a legitimate way of saving money. The new Care Act 2014 actively promotes the idea of keeping people out of the care system for as long as possible. The emphasis is now upon trying to delay people's need for care and support. National eligibility criteria introduced under the Act have effectively meant that the threshold for receiving state services has been raised. Whilst preventative approaches are to be welcomed and social workers do need to recognise and value the role that community services can provide, the range of preventative services and projects outside the state sector is diminishing. This is despite the concerns expressed by the (recently closed down) College of Social Work as well as other bodies working with older people. Discourses which suggest that in the past many service users have been over-reliant on state help need to be questioned.

According to Age UK (2014a) more than £1 billion has been slashed from council budgets for social care since 2010 and this has amounted to a drop of 10 per cent in real terms funding. This is in spite of a growing older population which is often used as a smokescreen to explain why services are under pressure. In terms of actual provision, day centres and resource centres (crucial for many older people in terms of accessing resources and alleviating social isolation) have been cut heavily in many local authorities. For many older people this has meant the loss of important sources of support and increased the difficulties such people already have in terms of maintaining social networks. The report emphasises, for example, the impact that closing day centres can have. Day centres often provide older people with a nutritious meal which they may not cook at home. Consequently malnutrition becomes more of a concern among the older population with all the risks that this poses. There is also evidence of local authorities now having to increasingly charge for meals on wheels services, which results in some older people not taking these services up. New additional charges for other services have also been implemented with the same result and the sizes of domiciliary care packages and personal budgets have been restricted.

Age UK also reports that cuts in home care services or increased charges for those people using these services have also impacted adversely on many older people. Many older people are having to reduce the levels of home support they receive. Moreover, cuts in funding for services that seek to provide older people with a collective voice (e.g. older people forums) have also increasingly been marginalised and this reduces older people's ability to influence services and to have their voices heard. Wider cuts in other important public services that are valued by older people (e.g. library services, Post Offices, adult learning and leisure services) also increased the likelihood of social isolation, as have cuts in supported bus services.

Whilst it can be difficult to say exactly what the relationship is between wellbeing and income, a relationship does exist. Benefit cuts for older people such as a reduction in the winter fuel allowance and cuts in housing benefit do result in increased worries and stress, and even deaths, among older people. Deaths from hypothermia are a real risk. It is also important not to see older people as one homogeneous mass, and to recognise that some people are at greater risk of harm than others. Specific groups within the older population are at even more risk because of reduced services, and these include people from black and minority ethnic groups (for example in the reduction of interpreter and translator services) and single older women on low incomes.

One government discourse in recent years with regard to older people has tended to emphasise the concept of *'re-ablement'* (SCIE, 2013). Funding was allocated in many local authorities to enable people to return to their homes from hospitals as opposed to entering residential care. The motives for this were not always in accordance with the value base of social work (the cheaper cost of these services was clearly one factor in the implementation of this approach), although this policy was often couched in the language of 'positive risk taking' and 'empowerment'. Re-ablement services have tended to be narrowly defined with a stress on people being able to cope within the home rather than re-abling people to live a fuller, life-giving and interconnected life within their local communities. However, even some of these services are now under threat or have been withdrawn (Brindle, 2015). Age UK (2014b) has stated that 40 per cent fewer people now are receiving help with equipment such as handrails and stairlifts. Family carers are being expected to do more and more and whilst the Care Act extends the right to have an assessment of needs, there is no guarantee that needs can or will be met. Once again this is likely to result in increased social isolation, depression and mental health problems among carers, the majority of whom are women.

Another group of people who have been hardest hit by austerity have been adults with disabilities. Even government figures show that substantially more people with disabilities live in poverty than other sections of the population with at least one fifth of the disabled already live in poverty (Office for Disability Issues and Department for Work and Pensions, 2014). Yet disabled people are bearing the brunt of more than a third of all benefit cuts. To begin with, under the 2010–15 coalition government, disabled people saw their incomes reduced. Further cuts under the new Conservative government are now planned. The Independent Living Fund, which had been so important for so many people in enabling them to live a fuller and more independent life, has been withdrawn altogether. Another important source of income for many disabled people, the Disability Living Allowance, is now also under threat and more and more disabled people risk being sanctioned as they are compelled to look for work that too often seems not to be there. The withdrawal of mobility allowances also means that more disabled people are becoming socially isolated with the subsequent risks of depression, purposelessness and mental ill health. Rumours are also circulating in the public domain that carers' allowances might be cut or subject to tighter eligibility criteria.

The impact of poverty and food poverty upon families is causing concern to many social workers. The numbers of children living in poverty are rising dramatically under the austerity agenda – Save the Children estimated in 2012 that there are 3.5 million children living in poverty in the UK, and that this is likely to soar by 400,000 in the following few years (Whitham, 2012). 'In work' poverty is growing and policies such as the withdrawal of tax credits for lower income families means that many families will be put under significant stress and will be forced to use foodbanks. Lower incomes mean that many families will suffer in terms of diet and health. The Marmot Review (2010) has stressed how this can in turn perpetuate the so-called cycle of deprivation with poorer families suffering increased levels of suicide and perinatal deaths.

Save the Children (Whitham, 2012) has suggested that about one third of people in the UK now experience income poverty and that 5 million children in the UK could be living in poverty by 2020. An estimated 13.5 million people are already 'income poor', which means that their income is 60 per cent below that of median income after their housing costs are paid. Average household debt is also rising. Financial pressures can impact on familial relationships adversely and whilst causal relationships can be difficult to pin down most people would recognise the stresses that not having enough money can put upon family life. In the meantime, government rhetoric tends to promote a discourse of 'shirkers and workers' despite evidence that many children who suffer the effects of poverty are from families where one or more parents are in work. In terms of child protection services, whilst the emphasis is upon early intervention, reductions in support services mean that social workers are increasingly being forced to adopt more authoritarian approaches that fail to even recognise the impact that poverty has upon families (Featherstone et al., 2013). Funding for addressing issues of domestic violence is also being stretched to the limit and social workers report more difficulties in finding safe spaces for women and children who are in abusive relationships.

Allan (2015) has highlighted that referrals to mental health services have increased by almost 20 per cent in the space of just five years, and has argued that this is largely due to the impact of the austerity agenda. A newly formed group called Psychologists against Austerity has argued that the result of the poverty that has been caused by the policies of austerity has been an increase in people feeling humiliation and shame (both trebling the chances of a person being treated for depression), isolation and loneliness, fear and mistrust, instability and insecurity and feelings of being trapped and powerless (McGrath et al., n.d.).

As Knapp (2012) has highlighted, the links between financial problems and mental illness are very much appreciated by people working within the mental health field. People who have had mental health problems often find it harder to secure meaningful work. Unemployment itself also increases the chances of mental health problems such as a loss of self-worth and identity. Reduced income and not being able to pay bills can also result in some people borrowing money to pay off debts and sometimes people turn to credit companies and loan sharks who charge very high rates of interest. This in turn becomes an added source of stress.

Mental health problems can result in reduced social interaction and a poorer sense of overall wellbeing – these are problems common to many people with mental health issues. These are compounded by increasingly tight regulations around 'actively looking for work' and even tougher sanctions and withholding of income if people are judged not to comply. The popular press has reported on cases of suicides where people have been labelled as 'incompliant' and have lost their income. Church Action on Poverty has drawn attention to how many people, including people who have mental health problems, are going hungry and are having to resort to foodbanks. Church Action on Poverty has also highlighted the pressures being put upon staff in employment centres to sanction claimants in order to meet government-imposed targets (Perry et al., 2015).

ACTIVITY 8.2

How might social workers raise awareness of the adverse effects of austerity in their workplace and in the wider community?

What barriers and obstacles might social workers face in resisting the austerity agenda?

How should social work seek to provide hope?

The social work response – how can we move forward?

This chapter has tried to argue that the austerity agenda is posing increasing risks for the wellbeing of service users and that attacks on welfare provision have resulted in the deterioration of the quality of services and this is making people more vulnerable. How then should social work respond to protect the rights and interests of the people it serves?

It is important to recognise that there are no simple solutions in terms of how social work responds to the issues raised. Governments clearly claim to have a mandate and whilst they have political power this does not mean they cannot be challenged. Fortunately there are values and principles that can guide social work in its response. The need for social work to emphasise human rights and equality and to challenge injustice is paramount. As a profession, social work is about 'speaking truth to power'. This involves resisting policies that degrade, cause harm and put people at risk, and speaking up on their behalf. As a profession, social work has a duty to high-light risks people face as a result of policies and to highlight the structural causes that make people vulnerable. Poverty and hardship that result from austerity and the stereotyping and labelling of people who are disadvantaged need to be challenged.

For individual social workers this might seem overwhelming within their own settings and social workers are often acutely aware of how vulnerable they feel in the face of managerialist approaches. This is why collective action and solidarity are crucial and why social workers also need to make connections with other organisations and professionals as well as service user and carer groups. Fortunately, social work is not starting from scratch. Social work bodies such as the Social Work Action Network already have a proud record of standing up for the rights and dignity of service users. Belonging to member organisations such as SWAN can help reduce the sense of pow-erlessness and isolation that social workers can feel, and workers can feed in their concerns, alongside helping other social workers to formulate appropriate actions (see www.socialworkfuture.org/). Trade unions have also striven to challenge the worst impacts of the austerity agenda and deserve active support.

Lessons can be drawn from other countries which have experienced the austerity agenda. Internationally social workers are continuing to try to defend the rights and interests of the people they work alongside. Social workers in the UK need to listen to and learn from the experiences of social workers in these countries, strengthen links and learn lessons from them. Responses require social workers to have courage, to be politicised, to challenge in a range of ways and to be creative in their responses. This further requires not only being satisfied with the status quo but also imagining alter-natives and model examples of good practice. Experience tells us that responses must be in partnership with service users and carers, other professionals and 'all people of goodwill'. As a profession, social work has to be about reading the signs of the times and bringing people hope.

It is vitally important that social work as a profession, and social workers individu-ally, have a high level of political awareness and appreciate that the austerity agenda is not inevitable but is a political choice. Individual social workers can challenge assumptions and dominant discourses about the inevitability of cuts in their every-day language and conversations. It is important to challenge discourses that seek to locate issues around risk and vulnerability that individuals face solely within the life circumstances of that individual. In practical terms a level of structural and criti-cal analysis is required that can and should inform social work assessments and care plans. Social workers need to work in person-centred ways but also need to recog-nise that people need good and well-funded universal services and that people are interdependent as well as independent actors.

Social work as a profession must also work with other public sector staff in resisting cuts and highlighting the harm that cuts may cause. It is important that the voices of service users and carers are not lost. Social workers can forge links with service user and carer campaigning groups that continue to exist, and find space to be involved in the promotion and creation of new groups. Campaigns against the withdrawal of state support services and resources should be supported by the profession at all levels.

Prevention of risks before they arise is the ideal. Social work needs to continually stress that individual people do not exist in isolation and that human beings need support systems. Some of these are provided informally – friends, families and neighbours – but these need the support of universal services. Safeguarding also needs to be located within the context of community and communities need a level of government resource and support if they are to thrive. Cases of hate crime show that communities sometimes need to be challenged, citizens need to be educated and a level of statutory services is needed to protect the most vulnerable whilst also recognising that all people have strengths.

Whilst it is important not to underestimate the barriers that face the profession and its ability to safeguard the people it serves, there are also some signs that in spite of adversities social work can still be creative in its approaches.

Community work and community-based social work

Community work might well offer some hope to social workers within the current climate. This approach was once considered valuable and was used by social workers in that it recognised that people often share common interests and benefit from common services. This way of working seems to be being rediscovered. Community work (which incorporates both the idea of working with geographical communities as well as communities of interests – which includes older people, families and people with disabilities) starts with the premise that people need to be facilitated and enabled to identify issues that are important to them. There is an argument to suggest that there is scope for social work to be imaginative in using this approach and to gain insight into community organising approaches around self-interest. This could well be effective in responding to the challenges that austerity brings, in safeguarding interests and rights, and in promoting the needs of service users.

People – service users and families – often do want to participate and influence services. Social workers can use organisational and networking skills to bring groups of service users and families together, to enable them to share experiences, to help identify issues and areas of self-interest, to analyse responses to issues, to identify resources and help develop appropriate responses and services. Social workers, using knowledge and skills around community development and community organising, can adopt strengths-based and asset-based approaches to working with groups. This means that social workers can be involved in the creation of 'spaces' where people would no longer solely be seen in the context of their vulnerabilities but also in the context of their strengths and assets and as members of neighbourhoods. Some good examples of this type of working already exist and have led to projects such as credit unions, day clubs, good neighbour schemes, mental health support services and childcare.

Listening skills, skills in strengthening and fostering community networks and skills in fostering and promoting local leadership are skills that social workers have or can develop. To be effective, adequate funding and resources for such community oriented approaches will be required. Social workers also need to be aware not to fall into the trap of assuming that all state services are paternalistic, or to use a discourse that implies people need to become 'less dependent' on state services. All human beings have dependencies but that does not mean that service users and carers cannot also have their independence promoted whilst having their needs met. Best practice examples exist where service users and carers are actively involved in the planning and running of services. Social workers as ever will need to be sensitive to political agendas and it will be important to ensure that voluntary effort and effective community work is not used as an excuse to argue that other services are unnecessary.

As Holman (2013) has argued, support services for families played a valuable role in social work in the 1970s and these need to be reinstated and extended. Social work teams are best placed in the communities that they serve where social workers can build positive and enduring relationships with the local people and community groups that they seek to serve. Talent, gifts, skills and resources exist in all communities and social workers can work in partnership with local people in tapping into these. By being closer to these communities, social workers can also be more aware of and attentive to the risks that people within these communities face from other individuals, groups and wider social, economic, political and other forces. Social workers can also identify alongside local people those issues that pertain to local communities and help people work towards solutions, some of which can best be tackled at a local level.

Social work needs to be a profession that fosters hope and social workers need to fully embrace the notion that they can make a difference in terms of influencing policy developments and in being the innovators of new ways of working. Social workers can both challenge and be creative, they can imagine alternatives and they do have a role in protecting existing services and articulating their need to be there. The question for our time is whether social work can rise to the challenge.

FURTHER READING

Ferguson, I and Woodward, R (2009) *Radical Social Work in Practice*. Bristol: Policy Press.

Henley, J (2015) Life at the sharp end: five families hit by five years of austerity. *The Guardian*, 27 April. Available at: www.theguardian.com/uk-news/2015/apr/27/life-at-the-sharp-end-five-families-hit-by-five-years-of-austerity (accessed 30 October 2015).

Jordan, B and Drakeford, M (2012) *Social Work and Social Policy Under Austerity*. Basingstoke: Palgrave Macmillan.

Ledwith, M (2011) *Community Development: A Critical Approach*. Bristol: Policy Press.

McNicoll, A (2013) A survival guide to practising ethical social work in a time of austerity. *Community Care*, 20 June. Available at: www.communitycare.co.uk/blogs/social-work-blog/2013/06/a-survival-guide-to-practising-ethical-social-work-in-a-time-of-austerity/ (accessed 30 October 2015).

Popple, K (2015) *Analysing Community Work: Theory and Practice*. Oxford: Oxford University Press.

Turbitt, C (2014) *Doing Radical Social Work*. Basingstoke: Palgrave Macmillan.

Conclusion

In this book we have considered the range of factors which impact on working with children and adults at risk and have explored emerging themes in safeguarding across the lifespan. Comparison of different sectors of safeguarding activity has allowed reflection on how discourse in specific fields can impact on responses, such as different approaches between elder abuse and domestic abuse services. While highlighting contrasts, the aim has also been to extract common themes in terms of understandings, priorities and approaches to safeguarding. Whatever context practitioners are based in they are likely to work with service users, families and carers of all ages. Having an understanding of key knowledge in relation to abuse and approaches to safeguarding that permeates work with people at risk whatever their life stage is essential. The core principle of effective collaborative working in safeguarding has been raised throughout the book. Effective collaborative working across disciplines and agencies requires practitioners to approach their work using a wider lens in terms of assessing, intervening and evaluating their work with people at risk.

The lifespan approach to safeguarding used here aims to counteract the narrowness of thinking which can come from practice systems which compartmentalise people and reflect organisational priorities rather than the real lives of people. Safeguarding adults and children should not be two separate entities. There are differences in legal frameworks, especially in relation to adults' rights to make what may be deemed unwise choices, but even in this there are grey areas where adults may be subject to undue influence or coercion and decisions cannot be taken simply at face value. Concepts of where childhood ends and adulthood begins change over time and between cultures. Children do not suddenly become adults, there is always a gradual process of maturation and work with young people should reflect their individual developmental needs and take account of the increased role of autonomy. However, the duties associated with protecting children are often seen as more important than promoting rights to autonomy. The tension between duty to protect and respect for autonomy becomes most acute when society perceives that a child or vulnerable adult maybe at risk. Supported decision making is a key task in working with adults and young people at risk. Enforced protectionist approaches are disempowering for anyone with the capacity to understand and be involved in aspects of their planning for safety. It could be suggested that at times society's duty to protect has been counterproductive to the development of individual rights and autonomy.

The relatively recent emergence and development of societal responses to abuse and neglect has been considered in Chapter 1 along with the impact of previous approaches on current practice. Chapter 2 has reviewed evidence around the nature and prevalence of abuse and drawn parallels across the lifespan in terms of ways of understanding abuse and wider factors impacting on this. Policy and legislation for safeguarding children and adults has been discussed in Chapter 3. Legal measures to protect individuals from abuse are a vital tool in any society which values the welfare of citizens, whether they are children or adults. Chapter 4 has considered a range of factors which can increase the likelihood of abuse of individuals across the lifespan in family and domestic settings. Key themes emerged in terms of defining and looking at the potential underlying causes of abuse. While abuse at any age can be seen to be closely linked to power and control in specific relationships, it is also very much connected to the position of individuals in wider society which was explored further in Chapter 5. People who are looked after in residential settings are often the most at risk members of society and safeguarding people in care settings has been considered in Chapter 6. The impact of isolating environments and the need for more open cultures of care have been considered here along with themes around improved regulation and training. Chapter 7 has reviewed skills for safeguarding and decision making around risk and common themes in this across the lifespan. The priorities for safeguarding have been considered in Chapter 8, particularly in relation to the prevailing financial climate and the impacts of this on wider social care and welfare.

While social workers often take a lead role in protecting children and adults, it is essential that wider agencies and practitioners see their own central roles in safeguarding. The skills and knowledge that social workers have can be used to support wider acquisition of skills for safeguarding. Expanding knowledge and approaches around exploitation, grooming, trafficking, hate crime and domestic violence are a challenge to practitioners to work across boundaries and they require coherent responses and the sharing of good practice between disciplines. This theme of raising awareness runs throughout the book. Individuals need to have the knowledge they require to help them protect themselves. Communities need to understand abuse and how to share their concerns with statutory agencies. The role of the independent sector in care and support continues to increase and this has to be accompanied by a good understanding of safeguarding.

Although there has been an attempt to identify common themes across safeguarding, the dangers of over-generalisation or assumptions about needs and experiences are fully acknowledged here. Factors such as age, ethnicity, disability and socio-economic status intersect to create different dynamics of oppression for different people. The historical aspects of oppression are also crucial in defining the present lived experiences of different groups. The diversity of experience also means that individuals do not fit into neat categories in terms of presenting issues – so, making blanket assumptions about the needs of someone with a learning disability, for instance, does not take into account that they may also have a mental health issue or problematic substance use which can entirely change the needs and desired outcomes of the individual. Serious case reviews have highlighted that organisational attempts to try to create artificial categories around needs have often resulted in people being obscured from service supports completely, with sometimes fatal consequences.

While it is central to look at the uniqueness of the individual it is also essential to consider the role of wider forces in shaping needs and solutions to these. The social and political climate at the time of writing directly impacts on safeguarding and has been a theme throughout the book. The concept of profit making within the context of care provision has become prevalent although it still does not sit comfortably for many people involved and can obscure the needs of individuals and lead to abuse and neglect. An overriding focus on financial targets has also had a negative impact on state-provided health and care systems. The funding crisis in local authorities and health and welfare systems is a core challenge to effective safeguarding and to the wider context of supporting individuals with health and care needs. Disadvantaged groups and communities are those most affected by financial cuts. Maintaining recreation centres or cancer care tends to harness public support more than services to people at risk.

The overhaul of legislation and policy across the lifespan in recent decades has been a response to emerging evidence of the requirement for more effective and person-alised responses to need. It has also been in line with political rhetoric which shifts responsibility for risk onto individuals, families and communities. Choice and auton-omy are entirely valid principles and are central in maintaining human rights. It is, however, difficult to achieve these aims in the context of diminishing opportunities for choice and reductions or removal of funding to support community initiatives. Enhancing community involvement in safeguarding also relies on the notion that communities are able and willing to achieve this. Given the current financial climate many individuals and families are struggling to meet their own needs, let alone other peoples. The evidence from child sexual exploitation or hate crime and inherent insti-tutional discrimination within many systems, such as criminal justice or healthcare, also highlights the fact that society is not necessarily nurturing and there is much work to do to improve social responses to those at risk.

Despite this challenging social and political context, emerging evidence from research has led to new approaches. Initiatives like *Making Safeguarding Personal* (MSP) have provided an invaluable opportunity for significant change and creative thinking in safe-guarding. The challenge it presents to process-driven practice is in itself a milestone in driving forward change. The use of evidenced-based approaches and the focus on outcomes is pivotal in rethinking work with people at risk. MSP also acknowledges the key notion of this book that effective approaches to safeguarding can be shared and adapted to practice across the lifespan. This has been clearly evidenced through initia-tives such as attachment-based work in care settings, the principles of Signs of Safety®, *Think Family* and group conferencing. The changing environment presents a great opportunity to rethink and develop practice and ensuring that children and adults at risk are given their rightful place at the centre of all safeguarding work is central to this. Involving individuals, families and wider support networks in planning for safety is cru-cial in safeguarding but also in all aspects of care and support, including wider contexts such as service regulation, design and improvements. In covering themes which involve abuse and neglect, there is a danger of obscuring the positive central role that families and care workers play in the lives of children and adults at risk. It is a good opportunity in concluding the book to acknowledge the excellent care and support provided to indi-viduals across the lifespan in so many different contexts.

Many of the themes in this book are not new. Dialogue around the need for effective inter-agency working and the value of preventative approaches has been present for many years. There are also excellent examples of innovative and progressive practice within a range of safeguarding and wider contexts. For instance, in relation to community involvement and preventative work, initiatives such as the Safe Places schemes and Dementia Friends have very successfully engaged the wider public in supporting individuals. Groups such as Mencap and local People's Parliaments have given people forums to campaign for their rights alongside a range of advocacy movements. Similarly in Scotland the Children's Parliament was established to provide children and young people with the opportunity to voice their opinions and thoughts, ensuring that their views were heard and represented within a wider political arena. A National Voice (ANV) has been set up as an independent body which supports the rights of young people who are in care. Time to Change campaigns have raised awareness of the discrimination and marginalisation of people with mental health problems. These wider developments have a central role in creating a society where all individuals are listened to and valued. This is the foundation of a proactive and preventative approach to safeguarding but also fundamentally about changing society to be a more inclusive place for everyone.

In the current environment where there are debates about the separation of training for adults' and children's social work, it seems that to view them as entirely separate entities does them a disservice. It is counter intuitive to the *Think Family* approach which has been espoused here. It also negates the fact that social work is a highly skilled role which requires not just assimilation of information but interpretation, and a key part of this is transferable skills. Practice with people at risk is not simply technical or mechanical. It requires a high level of skill and application of key knowledge and evidence to interpret information and work with people in ways which create real and positive change.

Safeguarding is a central theme within social work practice and all social workers should be facilitated to identify and respond effectively to people of any age who are at risk. The aim here has been to use the similarities in safeguarding across the lifespan to develop wider understandings of abuse and approaches to planning for safety. A large proportion of the knowledge and skills required to do this are relevant to both children and adults. The support and protection needs of individuals at any age and stage of development are also inextricably linked with people around them and need to be viewed in the context of wider systems. A key theme throughout the book has been the need for partnership working which encompasses service users, families, agencies, health and care practitioners and wider society. This is central to effective safeguarding across the lifespan and requires continued work to develop awareness and ownership.

Appendix 1

Professional Capabilities Framework

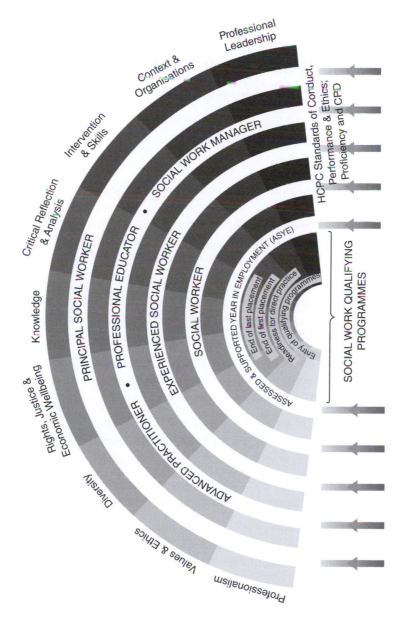

Professional Capabilities Framework diagram reproduced with permission of The College of Social Work.

Appendix 2
Subject benchmark for social work

5 Subject knowledge, understanding and skills
Subject knowledge and understanding

5.1 During their degree studies in social work, honours graduates should acquire, critically evaluate, apply and integrate knowledge and understanding in the following five core areas of study.

5.1.1 **Social work services, service users and carers**, which include:

- the social processes (associated with, for example, poverty, migration, unemployment, poor health, disablement, lack of education and other sources of disadvantage) that lead to marginalisation, isolation and exclusion, and their impact on the demand for social work services

- explanations of the links between definitional processes contributing to social differences (for example, social class, gender, ethnic differences, age, sexuality and religious belief) to the problems of inequality and differential need faced by service users

- the nature of social work services in a diverse society (with particular reference to concepts such as prejudice, interpersonal, institutional and structural discrimination, empowerment and anti-discriminatory practices)

- the nature and validity of different definitions of, and explanations for, the characteristics and circumstances of service users and the services required by them, drawing on knowledge from research, practice experience, and from service users and carers

- the focus on outcomes, such as promoting the well-being of young people and their families, and promoting dignity, choice and independence for adults receiving services

- the relationship between agency policies, legal requirements and professional boundaries in shaping the nature of services provided in interdisciplinary contexts and the issues associated with working across professional boundaries and within different disciplinary groups.

5.1.2 **The service delivery context**, which includes:

- the location of contemporary social work within historical, comparative and global perspectives, including European and international contexts

- the changing demography and cultures of communities in which social workers will be practising

- the complex relationships between public, social and political philosophies, policies and priorities and the organisation and practice of social work, including the contested nature of these

- the issues and trends in modern public and social policy and their relationship to contemporary practice and service delivery in social work

- the significance of legislative and legal frameworks and service delivery standards (including the nature of legal authority, the application of legislation in practice, statutory accountability and tensions between statute, policy and practice)

- the current range and appropriateness of statutory, voluntary and private agencies providing community-based, day-care, residential and other services and the organisational systems inherent within these

- the significance of interrelationships with other related services, including housing, health, income maintenance and criminal justice (where not an integral social service)

- the contribution of different approaches to management, leadership and quality in public and independent human services

- the development of personalised services, individual budgets and direct payments

- the implications of modern information and communications technology (ICT) for both the provision and receipt of services.

5.1.3 **Values and ethics**, which include:

- the nature, historical evolution and application of social work values

- the moral concepts of rights, responsibility, freedom, authority and power inherent in the practice of social workers as moral and statutory agents

- the complex relationships between justice, care and control in social welfare and the practical and ethical implications of these, including roles as statutory agents and in upholding the law in respect of discrimination

- aspects of philosophical ethics relevant to the understanding and resolution of value dilemmas and conflicts in both interpersonal and professional contexts

- the conceptual links between codes defining ethical practice, the regulation of professional conduct and the management of potential conflicts generated by the codes held by different professional groups.

5.1.4 **Social work theory**, which includes:

- research-based concepts and critical explanations from social work theory and other disciplines that contribute to the knowledge base of social work, including their distinctive epistemological status and application to practice

187

- the relevance of sociological perspectives to understanding societal and structural influences on human behaviour at individual, group and community levels

- the relevance of psychological, physical and physiological perspectives to understanding personal and social development and functioning

- social science theories explaining group and organisational behaviour, adaptation and change

- models and methods of assessment, including factors underpinning the selection and testing of relevant information, the nature of professional judgement and the processes of risk assessment and decision-making

- approaches and methods of intervention in a range of settings, including factors guiding the choice and evaluation of these

- user-led perspectives

- knowledge and critical appraisal of relevant social research and evaluation methodologies, and the evidence base for social work.

5.1.5 **The nature of social work practice**, which includes:

- the characteristics of practice in a range of community-based and organisational settings within statutory, voluntary and private sectors, and the factors influencing changes and developments in practice within these contexts

- the nature and characteristics of skills associated with effective practice, both direct and indirect, with a range of service-users and in a variety of settings

- the processes that facilitate and support service user choice and independence

- the factors and processes that facilitate effective interdisciplinary, interprofessional and interagency collaboration and partnership

- the place of theoretical perspectives and evidence from international research in assessment and decision-making processes in social work practice

- the integration of theoretical perspectives and evidence from international research into the design and implementation of effective social work intervention, with a wide range of service users, carers and others

- the processes of reflection and evaluation, including familiarity with the range of approaches for evaluating service and welfare outcomes, and their significance for the development of practice and the practitioner.

Subject-specific skills and other skills

5.2 As an applied subject at honours degree level, social work necessarily involves the development of skills that may be of value in many situations (for example, analytical thinking, building relationships, working as a member of an organisation, intervention, evaluation and reflection). Some of these skills are specific to social work but many are also widely transferable. What helps to define the specific nature of these skills in a social work context are:

- the context in which they are applied and assessed (eg, communication skills in practice with people with sensory impairments or assessment skills in an interprofessional setting)

- the relative weighting given to such skills within social work practice (eg, the central importance of problem-solving skills within complex human situations)

- the specific purpose of skill development (eg, the acquisition of research skills in order to build a repertoire of research-based practice)

- a requirement to integrate a range of skills (ie, not simply to demonstrate these in an isolated and incremental manner).

5.3 All social work honours graduates should show the ability to reflect on and learn from the exercise of their skills. They should understand the significance of the concepts of continuing professional development and lifelong learning, and accept responsibility for their own continuing development.

5.4 Social work honours graduates should acquire and integrate skills in the following five core areas.

Problem-solving skills

5.5 These are sub-divided into four areas.

5.5.1 **Managing problem-solving activities:** honours graduates in social work should be able to plan problem-solving activities, ie to:

- think logically, systematically, critically and reflectively

- apply ethical principles and practices critically in planning problem-solving activities

- plan a sequence of actions to achieve specified objectives, making use of research, theory and other forms of evidence

- manage processes of change, drawing on research, theory and other forms of evidence.

5.5.2 **Gathering information:** honours graduates in social work should be able to:

- gather information from a wide range of sources and by a variety of methods, for a range of purposes. These methods should include electronic searches, reviews of relevant literature, policy and procedures, face-to-face interviews, written and telephone contact with individuals and groups

- take into account differences of viewpoint in gathering information and critically assess the reliability and relevance of the information gathered

- assimilate and disseminate relevant information in reports and case records.

5.5.3 **Analysis and synthesis:** honours graduates in social work should be able to analyse and synthesise knowledge gathered for problem-solving purposes, ie to:

- assess human situations, taking into account a variety of factors (including the views of participants, theoretical concepts, research evidence, legislation and organisational policies and procedures)

- analyse information gathered, weighing competing evidence and modifying their view-point in light of new information, then relate this information to a particular task, situation or problem

- consider specific factors relevant to social work practice (such as risk, rights, cultural differences and linguistic sensitivities, responsibilities to protect vulnerable individuals and legal obligations)

- assess the merits of contrasting theories, explanations, research, policies and procedures

- synthesise knowledge and sustain reasoned argument

- employ a critical understanding of human agency at the macro (societal), mezzo (organisational and community) and micro (inter and intrapersonal) levels

- critically analyse and take account of the impact of inequality and discrimination in work with people in particular contexts and problem situations.

5.5.4 **Intervention and evaluation:** honours graduates in social work should be able to use their knowledge of a range of interventions and evaluation processes selectively to:

- build and sustain purposeful relationships with people and organisations in community-based, and interprofessional contexts

- make decisions, set goals and construct specific plans to achieve these, taking into account relevant factors including ethical guidelines

- negotiate goals and plans with others, analysing and addressing in a creative manner human, organisational and structural impediments to change

- implement plans through a variety of systematic processes that include working in partnership

- undertake practice in a manner that promotes the well-being and protects the safety of all parties

- engage effectively in conflict resolution

- support service users to take decisions and access services, with the social worker as navigator, advocate and supporter

- manage the complex dynamics of dependency and, in some settings, provide direct care and personal support in everyday living situations

- meet deadlines and comply with external definitions of a task

- plan, implement and critically review processes and outcomes

- bring work to an effective conclusion, taking into account the implications for all involved

- monitor situations, review processes and evaluate outcomes

- use and evaluate methods of intervention critically and reflectively.

Communication skills

5.6 Honours graduates in social work should be able to communicate clearly, accurately and precisely (in an appropriate medium) with individuals and groups in a range of formal and informal situations, ie to:

- make effective contact with individuals and organisations for a range of objectives, by verbal, paper-based and electronic means

- clarify and negotiate the purpose of such contacts and the boundaries of their involvement

- listen actively to others, engage appropriately with the life experiences of service users, understand accurately their viewpoint and overcome personal prejudices to respond appropriately to a range of complex personal and interpersonal situations

- use both verbal and non-verbal cues to guide interpretation

- identify and use opportunities for purposeful and supportive communication with service users within their everyday living situations

- follow and develop an argument and evaluate the viewpoints of, and evidence presented by, others

- write accurately and clearly in styles adapted to the audience, purpose and context of the communication

- use advocacy skills to promote others' rights, interests and needs

- present conclusions verbally and on paper, in a structured form, appropriate to the audience for which these have been prepared

- make effective preparation for, and lead meetings in a productive way

- communicate effectively across potential barriers resulting from differences (for example, in culture, language and age).

Bibliography

Action on Elder Abuse (2006) *Adult Protection Data Collection and Reporting Requirements. Conclusions and Recommendations from a Two Year Study into Adult Protection Recording Systems in England, Funded by the Department of Health*. London: Action on Elder Abuse. Available at: www.elderabuse. org.uk/Documents/AEA%20documents/AEA%20Report%20-%20Data%20Monitoring%20-%20DH%20 Monitoring%20Project.pdf (accessed 1 November 2015).

Advisory Council on the Misuse of Drugs (ACMD) (2003) *Hidden Harm: Responding to the Needs of Children of Problem Drug Users*. Available at: www.gov.uk/government/uploads/system/uploads/ attachment_data/file/120620/hidden-harm-full.pdf (accessed 31 October 2015).

Age Concern (2006) *Hungry to be Heard: The Scandal of Malnourished Older People in Hospital*. London: Age Concern England.

Age UK (2014a) *Care Matters 2014*. London: Age UK. Available at: www.ageuk.org.uk/Documents/ EN-GB/Campaigns/CIC/Care_in_Crisis_report_2014.pdf?epslanguage=en-GB?dtrk%3Dtrue (accessed 31 October 2015).

Age UK (2014b) *Agenda for Later Life 2014: Public Policy for Later Life*. Available at: www.ageuk.org.uk/ Documents/EN-GB/For-professionals/Policy/ID202014_agenda_for_later_life_report_2014.pdf?dtrk=true (accessed 26 November 2015).

Age UK London (2010) *Still Hungry to Be Heard. London: Age UK*. Available at: www.ageuk.org.uk/ brandpartnerglobal/londonvpp/documents/still_hungry_to_be_heard_report.pdf (accessed 27 November 2015).

Aldgate, J and Stratham, J (2001) *The Children Act Now: Messages from Research*. London: The Stationery Office.

Allan, C (2015) Only less austerity will improve our mental health. *The Guardian*, 19 August. Available at: www.theguardian.com/society/2015/may/05/austerity-mental-distress-parties-fund-mental-health (accessed 26 November 2015).

Allen, G (2011) *Early Intervention: The Next Steps*. London: Cabinet Office.

Alzheimer's Society (n.d.) *Short Changed - Protecting People with Dementia from Financial Abuse - Executive Summary*. Available at: www.alzheimers.org.uk/site/scripts/download_info. php?downloadID=742 (accessed 28 October 2015).

Alzheimer's Society (2014) *Factsheet: Deprivation of Liberty Safeguards (DoLS)*. Available at: www. alzheimers.org.uk/site/scripts/documents_info.php?documentID=1327 (accessed 31 October 2015).

Association of Directors of Adult Social Services (ADASS) and Local Government Association (LGA) (2013) *Safeguarding Adults: Advice and Guidance to Directors of Adult Social Services*. London: ADASS and LGA.

Association of Directors of Adult Social Services (ADASS), The Children's Society and Association of Directors of Children's Services (ADCS) (2012) *Working Together To Support Young Carers – A Template for a Local Memorandum of Understanding between Statutory Directors for Children's Services and Adult Social Services*. London: ADASS/ADCS.

Association of Directors of Social Services (ADSS) (2005) *Safeguarding Adults: A National Framework of Standards for Good Practice and Outcomes in Adult Protection Work*. London: ADSS.

Aveyard, H (2015) *A Beginner's Guide to Critical Thinking and Writing in Health and Social Care*, 2nd edn. Maidenhead: Open University Press.

Bandura, A, Ross, D and Ross, SA (1961) Transmission of aggression through the imitation of aggressive models. *Journal of Abnormal and Social Psychology*, 63: 575–82.

Barnardo's (2012) *Cutting them Free*. Available at: www.barnardos.org.uk/cuttingthemfree.pdf (accessed 27 November 2015).

Barnardo's (2014) *Report of the Parliamentary Inquiry into the Effectiveness of Legislation for Tackling Child Sexual Exploitation and Trafficking within the UK*. London: Barnardo's. Available at: www.barnardos.org.uk/cse_parliamentary_inquiry_report.pdf (accessed 28 October 2015).

Barrett, D (2015) British parents should be banned from smacking, United Nations report says. *Telegraph*, 23 July. Available at: www.telegraph.co.uk/news/uknews/law-and-order/11758403/British-parents-should-be-banned-from-smacking-United-Nations-report-says.html (accessed 20 November 2015).

Barry, M (2007) *Effective Approaches to Risk Assessment in Social Work: An International Literature Review*. Available at: www.scotland.gov.uk/Resource/Doc/194419/0052192.pdf (accessed 31 October 2015.

Barter, C, McCarry, M, Berridge, D and Evans, K (2009) *Partner Exploitation and Violence in Teenage Intimate Relationships*. London: NSPCC/Bristol University.

Bartlett, P (2014) Reforming the Deprivation of Liberty Safeguards (DOLS): What is it exactly that we want? *European Journal of Current Legal Issues*, 20 (3). Available at: webjcli.org/article/view/355/465 (accessed 31 October 2015).

BASW England (2015) *BASW Response to DfE Consultation on Working Together to Safeguard Children: Revisions*. Birmingham: BASW. Available at: cdn.basw.co.uk/upload/basw_115513-5.pdf (accessed 23 November 2015).

Batty, D (2003) Catalogue of cruelty. *The Guardian*, 27 January. Available at: www.theguardian.com/society/2003/jan/27/childrensservices.childprotection (accessed 1 November 2015).

BBC News (1999) Elderly patients punched and abused. 22 January. Available at: news.bbc.co.uk/1/hi/health/260422.stm

BBC News (2013) Orchid View Inquest: Home riddled by 'institutional abuse'. 18 October. Available at: www.bbc.co.uk/news/uk-england-sussex-24579496 (accessed 30 October 2015).

BBC News (2014) Hundreds of 'missing' children at risk in Greater Manchester. 29 October. Available at: www.bbc.co.uk/news/uk-england-manchester-29814588 (accessed 29 October 2015).

BBC News (2015a) Anti-slavery powers come into force in England and Wales. 31 July. Available at: www.bbc.co.uk/news/uk-33728684

BBC News (2015b) 1,400 child abuse suspects identified. 20 May. Available at: www.bbc.co.uk/news/uk-32812449 (accessed 29 October 2015).

BBC News (2015c) Historical child abuse: Key investigations. 17 August. Available at: www.bbc.co.uk/news/uk-28194271 (accessed 30 October 2015).

BBC News (2015d) Tax credits: Lords vote to delay controversial cuts. 26 October. Available at: www.bbc.co.uk/news/uk-politics-34631156 (accessed 23 November 2015).

Beckett, C (2010) *Child Protection*, 2nd edn. London: Sage Publications.

Bee, M (2015) If nurses or care workers can be jailed for wilful neglect, then why not social workers? *Community Care*, 14 October. Available at: www.communitycare.co.uk/2015/10/14/if-nurses-or-care-workers-can-be-jailed-for-wilful-neglect-then-why-not-social-workers/ (accessed 27 November 2015).

Bee, P, Berzins, K, Calam, R, Pryjmachuk, S and Abel, KM (2013) Defining quality of life in the children of parents with severe mental illness: A preliminary stakeholder-led model. *PLoS ONE,* 8 (9): e73739. doi:10.1371/journal.pone.0073739.

Berelowitz, S, Clifton, J, Firimin, C, Gulyurtlu, S and Edwards, G (2013) *'If only someone had listened': Office of the Children's Commissioner's Inquiry into Child Sexual Exploitation in Gangs and Groups. Final Report*. London: Office of the Children's Commissioner.

Bibby, A and Becker, S (2000) *Young Carers in their own Words*. London: Turnaround Publisher Services.

Biehal, N, Cusworth, L, Wade, J and Clarke, S (2014) *Keeping Children Safe: Allegations Concerning the Abuse or Neglect of Children in Care*. London: NSPCC.

Bigby, C and Frawley, P (2010) *Social Work Practice and Intellectual Disability*. Basingstoke: Palgrave Macmillan.

Biggs, S (1996) A family concern: Elder abuse in British social policy. *Critical Social Policy*, 16 (2): 63–88.

Blakemore, K and Warwick-Booth, L (2013) *Social Policy: An Introduction*, 4th edn. Maidenhead: Open University Press

Bowes, A, Avan, G and Macintosh, S (2011) *Dignity and Respect in Residential Care: Issues for Black and Minority Ethnic Groups*. Report to the Department of Health. London: Department of Health.

Bowlby, J (1951) *Maternal Care and Mental Health*. Geneva: WHO.

Brammer, A (2014) *Safeguarding Adults*. Basingstoke: Palgrave Macmillan.

Brandon, M, Bailey, S, Belderson, P, Gardner, R, Sidebotham, P, Dodsworth, J, Warren, C and Black, J (2009) *Understanding Serious Case Reviews and their Impact: A Biennial Analysis of Serious Case Reviews 2005-07*. London: Department for Children, Schools and Families.

Brandon, M, Bailey, S and Belderson, P (2010) *Building on the Learning from Serious Case Reviews: A two-year analysis of child protection database notifications 2007–2009*. Research Report. London: Department for Education.

Brandon, M, Sidebotham, P, Bailey, S, Belderson, P, Hawley, C, Ellis, C and Megson, M. (2012) *New Learning from Serious Case Reviews: A Two Year Report for 2009-2011*. Available at: www.gov.uk/government/uploads/system/uploads/attachment_data/file/184053/DFE-RR226_Report.pdf (accessed 31 October 2015).

Brandon, M, Bailey, S, Belderson, P and Larsson, B (2013) *Neglect and Serious Case Reviews*. London: NSPCC.

Braye, S, Orr, D and Preston-Shoot, M (2011) *Self-neglect and Adult Safeguarding: Findings from Research: Final Report to the Department of Health*. London: SCIE.

Braye, S, Orr, D and Preston-Shoot, M (2014) *Self-neglect Policy and Practice: Building an Evidence Base for Adult Social Care*. SCIE Report 69. Available at: www.scie.org.uk/publications/reports/report69.asp (accessed 31 October 2015).

Brayne, H and Carr, H (2013) *Law for Social Workers*, 12th edn. Oxford: Oxford University Press.

Brindle, D (2015) Social care is on the cusp of a crisis. *The Guardian*, 14 October. Available at: www.theguardian.com/social-care-network/2015/oct/14/social-care-cusp-crisis (accessed 31 October 2015).

Brintnall-Peterson, M (2012) *Caregiving is Different for Everyone*. Extension Family Caregiving Community of Practice, University of Wisconsin, Madison, WI. Available at: www.extension.org/pages/9355/caregiving-is-different-for-everyone#.UvG1V3lRf1o (accessed 25 November 2015).

Bronfenbrenner, U (1979) *The Ecology of Human Development: Experiments by Nature and Design*. Cambridge, MA: Harvard University.

Brown, H, Kingston, P and Wilson, B (1999) Adult protection: An overview of research and policy. *The Journal of Adult Protection*, 1 (1): 6–16.

Brown, R and Ward, H (2013) *Decision Making Within a Child's Timeframe: An Overview of Current Research Evidence for Family Justice Professionals Concerning Child Development and the Impact of Maltreatment*. London: Childhood Wellbeing Research Centre, Working Paper No. 16.

Bunn, A (2013) *Signs of Safety® in England: An NSPCC Commissioned Report on the Signs of Safety Model in Child Protection*. London: NSPCC.

Butler, G (2011) Domestic violence: understanding connections. In T Scragg and A Mantell (eds), *Safeguarding Adults in Social Work*, 2nd edn. Exeter: Learning Matters.

Cabinet Office (2015) *Tackling Child Sexual Exploitation*. London: Cabinet Office. Available at: www.gov.uk/government/uploads/system/uploads/attachment_data/file/408604/2903652_RotherhamResponse_acc2.pdf (accessed 28 October 2015).

Care Quality Commission (CQC) (n.d.) *Safeguarding Adults: Roles and Responsibilities in Health and Care Services*. Available at: www.cqc.org.uk/sites/default/files/20140416_safeguarding_adults_-_roles_and_responsibilities_-_revised_draf....pdf (accessed 31 October 2015).

Care Quality Commission (CQC) (2015a) *Regulation 20: Duty of Candour Information for all Providers: NHS Bodies, Adult Social Care, Primary Medical and Dental Care, and Independent Healthcare*. Available at: www.cqc.org.uk/sites/default/files/20150327_duty_of_candour_guidance_final.pdf (accessed 1 November 2015).

Care Quality Commission (CQC) (2015b) *Annual Report and Accounts 2014–15*. Available at: www.cqc.org.uk/sites/default/files/20150721_annual-report-accounts-2014-15-final.pdf (accessed 1 November 2015).

Care Quality Commission (2015c) *The Fundamental Standards*. Available at: www.cqc.org.uk/content/fundamental-standards (accessed 1 November 2015).

Casey, L. (2015) *Report of Inspection of Rotherham Metropolitan Borough Council*. London: Department for Communities and Local Government.

Chand, A (2014) [open discussion session] TCSW Regional Conference, December 2014.

Chase, E, Simon, A and Jackson, S (eds) (2006) *In Care and After: A Positive Perspective*. London: Routledge.

Child Exploitation and Online Protection Centre (CEOP) (2011) *Out of Mind, Out of Sight. Breaking Down the Barriers to Understanding Child Sexual Exploitation*. London: CEOP.

Children's Commissioner (2012) *Silent Voices: Supporting Children and Young People Affected by Parental Alcohol Misuse*. London: Community Research Company.

Children's Society (2014) *Response to Government's Announcement on its Modern Slavery Strategy*. London: The Children's Society. Available at: childrenssociety.org.uk/news-and-blogs/press-releases/response-to-government-announcement-on-its-modern-slavery-strategy (accessed 27 November 2015).

Chow, C and Tiwari, A (2014) Experience of family caregivers of community-dwelling stroke survivors and risk of elder abuse: A qualitative study. *The Journal of Adult Protection*, 16 (5): 276–93.

Cleaver, H, Nicholson, D, Tarr, S and Cleaver, D (2007) *Child Protection, Domestic Violence and Parental Substance Misuse: Family Experiences and Effective Practice*. London: Jessica Kingsley Publishers.

Cleaver, H, Unell, I and Aldgate, J (2011) *Children's Needs – Parenting Capacity. Child Abuse: Parental Mental Illness, Learning Disability, Substance Misuse, and Domestic Violence*, 2nd edn. London: The Stationery Office.

Coffey, A (2014) *Real Voices: Child Sexual Exploitation in Greater Manchester*. An independent report by Ann Coffey, MP. Available from: www.gmpcc.org.uk/wp-content/uploads/2014/02/81461-Coffey-Report_v5_WEB-single-pages.pdf (accessed 28 October 2015).

Colton, M (2002) Factors associated with abuse in residential child care institutions. *Children and Society*, 16: 33–44.

Comic Relief (2007) *UK Study of Abuse and Neglect of Older People: Prevalence Survey Report*. London: Comic Relief and the Department of Health

Compton, SA, Flanagan, P and Gregg, W (1997) Elder abuse in people with dementia in Northern Ireland: Prevalence and predictors in cases referred to a psychiatry of old age service. *International Journal of Geriatric Psychiatry*, 12 (6): 632–5.

Cooklin, A (2014) *Parental Mental Illness: The Impact on Children and Adolescents: Information for Parents, Carers and Anyone who Works with Young People*. Available at: www.rcpsych.ac.uk/healthadvice/parentsandyouthinfo/parentscarers/parentalmentalillness.aspx (accessed 31 October 2015).

Cooper, C (2015) Care of elderly in state of 'calamitous decline' amid £1bn of austerity cuts. *The Independent*, 21 January. Available at: www.independent.co.uk/life-style/health-and-families/health-news/care-for-elderly-in-state-of-calamitous-decline-amid-1bn-of-austerity-cuts-9991321.html (accessed 26 November 2015).

Cooper, C, Selwood, A, and Livingston, G (2008) The prevalence of elder abuse and neglect: A systematic review. *Age and Ageing*, 37 (2): 151–60.

Co-ordinated Action Against Domestic Abuse (CAADA) (2010) *Saving Lives, Saving Money: MARACs and High Risk Domestic Abuse*. Available from: www.caada.org.uk/sites/default/files/resources/Saving_lives_saving_money_FINAL_REFERENCED_VERSION.pdf (accessed 27 November 2015).

Co-ordinated Action Against Domestic Abuse (CAADA) (2012) *In Plain Sight: Effective Help for Children Exposed to Domestic Abuse*. Available at: www.caada.org.uk/sites/default/files/resources/Final%20policy%20report%20In%20plain%20sight%20-%20effective%20help%20for%20children%20exposed%20to%20domestic%20abuse.pdf (accessed 31 October 2015).

Corby, B (2006) *Child Abuse: Towards a Knowledge Base*, 3rd edn. Maidenhead: Open University Press.

Corby, B, Shemmings, D and Wilkins, D (2012) *Child Abuse: An Evidence Base For Confident Practice*, 4th edn. Maidenhead: Open University Press.

Coventry Local Safeguarding Children Board (2013) *Final Overview Report of Serious Case Review re Daniel Pelka*. Available at: www.coventry.gov.uk/downloads/file/17081/daniel_pelka_-_serious_case_review_overview_report (accessed 31 October 2015).

Council of Europe (2005) *Convention on Action against Trafficking in Human Beings*. Strasbourg: Council of Europe. Available at: www.coe.int/t/dghl/monitoring/trafficking/default_en.asp (accessed 28 October 2015).

Crawford, K and Walker, J (2014) *Social Work and Human Development*, 3rd edn. London: Sage Publications.

Culpitt, I (1999) *Social Policy and Risk*. London: Sage Publications.

Cunningham, J and Cunningham, S (2014) *Sociology and Social Work*, 2nd edn. London: Sage/Learning Matters.

Dalzell, R and Sawyer, E (2007) *Putting Analysis into Assessment*. London: National Children's Bureau.

Daniel, B, Wassell, S and Gilligan, R (2010) *Child Development for Child Care and Protection Workers*, 2nd edn. London: Jessica Kingsley Publishers.

Dar, A (2013) *Domestic Violence Statistics*. London: House of Commons Library. Available at: www.parliament.**uk**/briefing-papers/SN00950.pdf (accessed 25 November 2015).

Davidson, J (2010) Residential care for children and young people: Priority areas for change. *Child Abuse Review*, 19: 405–22.

Davies, C and Ward, H (2012) *Safeguarding Children across Services: Messages from Research*. London: Jessica Kingsley Publishers.

Davies, L and Duckett, N (2008) *Proactive Child Protection*. Exeter: Learning Matters.

Davies, L, Kline, R, Douieb, B and Goodman, K (2013) *Working Together Revision Documents are not Fit for Purpose. A Critical Focus on Two Documents: 'Working Together to Safeguard Children' and 'Managing Individual Cases'*. graphic-room.com/lizdavies/wpcontent/uploads/2012/11/REVISION_OF_WORKING_TOGETHER_RESPONSE_TO_CONSULTATION.pdf (accessed 30 October 2015).

De Donder, L, Lang, G, Luoma, M-L, Penhale, B, Ferreira Alves, J, Tamutiene, I, Santos, A J, Koivusilta, M, Enzenhofer, E, Perttu, S, Savola, T and Verté, D (2011) Perpetrators of abuse against older women: A multi-national study in Europe. *The Journal of Adult Protection*, 13 (6): 302–14.

Department for Children, Schools and Families (DCSF) (2003) *Every Child Matters*. London: DCSF.

Department for Children, Schools and Families (DCSF) (2008) *Information Sharing: Guidance for Practitioners and Managers*. London: DCSF.

Department for Children, Schools and Families (DCSF) and Home Office (2009) *Safeguarding Children and Young People from Sexual Exploitation: Supplementary Guidance to Working Together to Safeguard Children*. London: DCSF.

Department for Communities and Local Government (DCLG) (2012) *The Troubled Families Programme: Financial Framework*. London: DCLG. Available at: www.gov.uk/government/publications/the-troubled-families-programme-financial-framework (accessed 25 November 2015).

Department for Constitutional Affairs (2007) *Mental Capacity Act 2005 Code of Practice*. London: The Stationery Office.

Department for Education (2014a) *Care of Unaccompanied and Trafficked Children: Statutory Guidance for Local Authorities on the Care of Unaccompanied Asylum Seeking and trafficked Children*. London: DfE. Available at: www.gov.uk/government/uploads/system/uploads/attachment_data/file/330787/Care_of_unaccompanied_and_trafficked_children.pdf (accessed 28 October 2015).

Department for Education (2014b) *Children in Care: Research Priorities and Questions.* London: DfE. Available at: www.gov.uk/government/uploads/system/uploads/attachment_data/file/292032/Children_in_Care_Research_priorites_and_questions_FINAL_v1_1.pdf (accessed 29 October 2015).

Department for Education (2014c) *Statistical First Release: Characteristics of Children in Need in England, 2013–14*. London: DfE. Available at: www.gov.uk/government/uploads/system/uploads/attachment_data/file/367877/SFR43_2014_Main_Text.pdf (accessed 23 November 2015).

Department for Education (2015a) *Statistics: Looked-after Children*. London: DfE. Available at: www.gov.uk/government/collections/statistics-looked-after-children.

Department for Education (2015b) *Children Looked After in England (Including Adoption and Care Leavers) Year Ending 31 March 2015*. Available at: www.gov.uk/government/uploads/system/uploads/attachment_data/file/464756/SFR34_2015_Text.pdf (accessed 1 November 2015).

Department for Education (2015c) *Characteristics of Children in Need in England, 2014 to 2015*. Available at: www.gov.uk/government/uploads/system/uploads/attachment_data/file/469737/SFR41-2015_Text.pdf (accessed 23 November 2015).

Department for Education and Skills (2006) *Care Matters: Transforming the Lives of Children and Young People in Care*. London: DfES. Available at: www.education.gov.uk/consultations/downloadableDocs/6781-DfES-CM%20Summary.pdf (accessed 29 October 2015).

Department of Health (1993) *No Longer Afraid*. London: Department of Health.

Department of Health (1998) *Quality Protects: Framework for Action*. Available at: webarchive.nationalarchives.gov.uk/20130107105354/www.dh.gov.uk/prod_consum_dh/groups/dh_digitalassets/@dh/@en/documents/digitalasset/dh_4013760.pdf (accessed 29 October 2015).

Department of Health (2000) *No Secrets: Guidance on Developing and Implementing Multi-agency Policies and Procedures to Protect Vulnerable Adults from Abuse*. London: Department of Health.

Department of Health (2002) *Women's Mental Health: Into the Mainstream*. Available at: webarchive.nationalarchives.gov.uk/+/www.dh.gov.uk/en/Consultations/Closedconsultations/DH_4075478 (accessed 25 November 2015).

Department of Health (2009) *Safeguarding Adults: Report on the Consultation of the Review of No Secrets*. London: Department of Health.

Department of Health (2010) *A Vision for Adult Social Care: Capable Communities and Active Citizens*. London: Department of Health.

Department of Health (2011) *Statement of Government Policy on Adult Safeguarding*. London: Department of Health.

Department of Health (2012) *Transforming Care: A National Response to Winterbourne View Hospital. Final Report*. London: Department of Health.

Department of Health (2013) *The Fifth Year of the Independent Mental Capacity Advocacy (IMCA) Service – 2011 /2012*. London: Department of Health. Available at: www.gov.uk/government/uploads/ system/uploads/attachment_data/file/158009/Independent-Mental-Capacity-Service-_-fifth-annual-report. pdf (accessed 24 November 2015).

Department of Health (2014) *Care and Support: Statutory Guidance Issued under the Care Act 2014*. London: Department of Health. Available at: www.gov.uk/government/uploads/system/uploads/ attachment_data/file/366104/43380_23902777_Care_Act_Book.pdf (accessed 27 October 2015).

Department of Health (2015) *Factsheet 7: The Care Bill – Protecting Adults from Abuse or Neglect*. London: Department of Health. Available at: www.gov.uk/government/uploads/system/uploads/attachment_data/ file/198104/9520-2900986-TSO-Factsheet07-ACCESSIBLE.pdf (accessed 1 November 2015).

Disability Rights Commission (2006) *Equal Treatment: Closing the Gap. A Formal Investigation into Physical Health Inequalities Experienced by People with Learning Disabilities and/or Mental Health Problems*. Manchester: DRC.

Dominelli, L (2004) *Social Work: Theory and Practice for a Changing Profession*. Cambridge: Polity Press.

Donnelly, L (2015) Revealed: More than 500,000 home care visits last less than five minutes. *The Telegraph*, 15 February. Available at: www.telegraph.co.uk/news/health/news/11302534/Revealed-more-than-500000-home-care-visits-last-less-than-five-minutes.html (accessed 26 October 2015).

Donovan, T. (2015) Inspection data reports decline in quality of children's services and homes. *Community Care*, 13 August. Available at: www.communitycare.co.uk/2015/08/13/inspection-data-reports-decline-quality-childrens-services-homes/ (accessed 30 October 2015).

Doyle, L (2014) *28 Days Later: Experiences of New Refugees in the UK*. London: Refugee Council.

Dugan, E (2013) Domestic violence: 'As a man it's very difficult to say I've been beaten up'. *The Independent*, 14 April. Available from: www.independent.co.uk/life-style/health-and-families/health-news/domestic-violence-as-a-man-its-very-difficult-to-say-ive-been-beaten-up-8572143.html (accessed 26 October 2015).

Easton, M (2015) Have we changed our mind about asylum? Available at: www.bbc.co.uk/news/ uk-34176851 (accessed 28 October 2015).

Emerson, E, Hatton, C, Robertson, J, Baines, S, Christie, A and Glover, G (2012) *People with Learning Disabilities in England*. Cambridge: The Learning Disabilities Observatory, Public Health England.

Equality and Human Rights Commission (EHRC) (2011) *Close To Home: An Inquiry into Older People and Human Rights in Home Care*. Available at: www.equalityhumanrights.com/publication/close-home-inquiry-older-people-and-human-rights-home-care (accessed 27 November 2015).

Essex Autonomy Project (2011) *Vulnerable Adults and the Inherent Jurisdiction of the High Court*. Available at: autonomy.essex.ac.uk/vulnerable-adults-and-the-inherent-jurisdiction-of-the-high-court (accessed 31 October 2015).

Family and Childcare Trust (2013) *Families in the Age of Austerity – the Impact of Revenue Spending Cuts on Children's Services*. Available from: www.familyandchildcaretrust.org/families-age-austerity (accessed 24 October 2014).

Featherstone, B, Morris, K and White, S (2013) A marriage made in hell: Early intervention meets child protection. *British Journal of Social Work*, 44 (7): 1735–49.

Ferguson, I (2009) Another social work is possible! Reclaiming the radical tradition. In V Leskosek (ed.) *Theories and Methods of Social Work*. Ljubljana: University of Ljubljana.

Ferguson, I and Woodward, R (2009) *Radical Social Work in Practice*. Bristol: Policy Press.

Finkelhor, D (1984) *Child Sexual Abuse: New Theory and Research*. New York: Free Press.

Flynn, M (2007) *The Murder of Steven Hoskin: A Serious Case Review*. Executive Summary. Truro: Cornwall Adult Protection Committee.

Flynn, M (2011) *The Murder of Adult A (Michael Gilbert) A Serious Case Review*. Luton Safeguarding Vulnerable Adults Board. Available at: www.luton.gov.uk/Health_and_social_care/Lists/LutonDocuments/PDF/Community%20Care/Protecting%20Vulnerable%20Adults/Adult%20A%20Exec%20Summary.pdf (accessed 31 October 2014).

Flynn, M and Citarella, V (2012) *Winterbourne View Hospital: A Serious Case Review. Executive Summary*. South Gloucestershire Safeguarding Adults Board. Available at: www.hosted.southglos.gov.uk/wv/report.pdf (accessed 30 October 2015).

Forrester, D and Harwin, J (2011) *Parents Who Misuse Drugs and Alcohol: Effective Interventions in Social Work and Social Protection*. Chichester: Wiley.

Francis, R (2013) *Report of the Mid Staffordshire NHS Foundation Trust Public Inquiry Executive Summary*. London: The Stationery Office.

Francis, R (2015) *Freedom to Speak Up. An Independent Review into Creating an Open and Honest Reporting Culture in the NHS*. Available at: www.webarchive.nationalarchives.gov.uk/20150218150343/www.freedomtospeakup.org.uk/wp-content/uploads/2014/07/F2SU_web.pdf (accessed 30 October 2015).

Franklin, A, Raws, P, Smeaton, E (2015) *Unprotected, Overprotected: Meeting the Needs of Young People with Learning Disabilities who Experience, or are at Risk of Sexual Exploitation*. London: Barnardo's.

Frizzell, E. (2009) *Independent Inquiry into Abuse at Kerelaw Residential School and Secure Unit*. Edinburgh: The Scottish Government. Available at: www.gov.scot/Resource/Doc/271997/0081066.pdf (accessed 29 October 2015).

Fyson, R (2009) Independence and learning disabilities: Why we must also recognise vulnerability. *Journal of Integrated Care*, 17 (1): 3–8.

Galilee, J (2005) *Literature Review on Media Representations of Social Work and Social Workers* (21st Century Social Work, Social Work Scotland). Edinburgh: Scottish Executive.

Gallagher, J (2015) Learning disability care hospital beds reduced. BBC News, 30 October. Available at: www.bbc.co.uk/news/health-34667806 (accessed 27 November 2015).

Galpin, D (2014) Reading between the lines: The role of discourse in shaping responses to safeguarding older people. *The Journal of Adult Protection*, 16 (6): 399–410.

Gambrill, E (2006) *Social Work Practice: A Critical Thinkers Guide*. New York: Oxford University Press.

Gilligan, R (2009) *Promoting Resilience*. London: BAAF.

Gisby, J and Butler, G (2012) Skills in safeguarding older people. In B Hall and T Scragg (eds) *Social Work with Older People: Approaches to Person-centred Practice*. Maidenhead: Open University Press.

Goble, C (2011) Developing user-focused communication skills. In A Mantell and T Scragg (eds) *Safeguarding Adults in Social Work*, 2nd edn. Exeter: Learning Matters.

Goffman, E (1961) *Asylums*. Harmondsworth: Penguin

Gohir, S. (2013) *'Unheard Voices': The Sexual Exploitation of Asian Girls and Women*. Birmingham: Muslim Women's Network. Available at: www.mwnuk.co.uk/go_files/resources/UnheardVoices.pdf (accessed 28 October 2015).

Golightly, M (2014) *Social Work and Mental Health*, 5th edn. London: Sage Publications.

Green, S E (2007) 'We're tired, not sad': Benefits and burdens of mothering a child with a disability. *Social Science and Medicine*, 64: 150–63.

Green, SL (2013) 'An unnoticing environment': Deficiencies and remedies – services for adults with learning disabilities, *Journal of Adult Protection* 15 (4): 192–202.

Hague, G and Bridge, S (2008) Inching forward on domestic violence: The 'co-ordinated community response' and putting it in practice in Cheshire. *Journal of Gender Studies*, 17 (3): 185–99.

Hague, G, Thiara, R and Mullender, A (2011) Disabled women and domestic violence: Making the links – a national UK study. *Psychiatry, Psychology and Law*, 18 (1): 117–36.

Hampshire Safeguarding Adults Board (2015) *Learning from Experience Database – Serious Case Reviews: Margaret Panting*. Available at: www.hampshiresab.org.uk/learning-from-experience-database/serious-case-reviews/margaret-panting-sheffield/ (accessed 19 November 2015).

Hanley, J and Marsland, D (2014) Unhappy anniversary? *The Journal of Adult Protection*, 16 (2): 104–12.

Hansard (1989) *HC Deb 26 October 1989*, vol. 158, col. 1075.

Harbottle, C, Jones, M and Thompson, L (2014) From reactionary to activist: A model that works. *The Journal of Adult Protection*, 16 (2): 113–19.

Haringey Local Safeguarding Children Board (2009) *Serious Case Review: Baby Peter*. London: Haringey LSCB. Available at: www.haringeylscb.org/sites/haringeylscb/files/executive_summary_peter_final.pdf (accessed 31 October 2015).

Harne, L and Radford, J (2008) *Tackling Domestic Violence: Theories, Policies and Practice*. Maidenhead: Open University Press.

Hasted, C (2012) How family group conferences have the power to change lives. *The Guardian,* 10 October. Available at: www.theguardian.com/social-care-network/2012/oct/10/family-group-conferences-change-lives (accessed 26 October 2015).

Health and Social Care Information Centre (HSCIC) (2014) *Safeguarding Adults Return Annual Report, England 2013–14. Experimental Statistics*. Leeds: HSCIC. Available at: www.hscic.gov.uk/catalogue/PUB15671/sar-1314-rep.pdf (accessed 26 October 2015).

Health and Social Care Information Centre (HSCIC) (2015) *Mental Capacity Act (2005) Deprivation of Liberty Safeguards (England) Annual Report, 2014–15*. Available at: www.hscic.gov.uk/catalogue/PUB18577/dols-eng-1415-rep.pdf (accessed 1 November 2015).

Hendrick, H (2003) *Child Welfare, Historical Dimensions, Contemporary Practice*. Bristol: Policy Press.

Henley, J (2015) Life at the sharp end: Five families hit by five years of austerity. *The Guardian,* 27 April. Available at: www.theguardian.com/uk-news/2015/apr/27/life-at-the-sharp-end-five-families-hit-by-five-years-of-austerity (accessed 1 November 2015).

Heslop, P, Blair, P, Fleming, P, Hoghton, M, Marriott, A, and Russ, L (2013) *Confidential Inquiry into Premature Deaths of People with Learning Disabilities (CIPOLD) Final Report*. Bristol: Norah Fry Research Centre. Available at: www.bristol.ac.uk/media-library/sites/cipold/migrated/documents/fullfinalreport.pdf (accessed 1 November 2015).

Heslop, P, Blair, P, Fleming, P, Hoghton, M, Marriott, A and Russ, L (2014) Poor adherence to the mental capacity act and premature death. *The Journal of Adult Protection*, 16 (6): 367–76.

HM Government (1998) *The Government's Response to the Children's Safeguards Review*. London: The Stationery Office. Available at: www.gov.uk/government/uploads/system/uploads/attachment_data/file/265484/4105.pdf (accessed 29 October 2015).

HM Government (2006) *Working Together to Safeguard Children: A Guide to Inter-agency Working to Safeguard and Promote the Welfare of Children*. London: The Stationery Office.

HM Government (2009) *Safeguarding Children and Young People from Sexual Exploitation Supplementary Guidance to Working Together to Safeguard Children*. London: The Stationery Office.

HM Government (2011) *No Health without Mental Health.* London: Department of Health.

HM Government (2013) *Working Together to Safeguard Children: A Guide to Inter-agency Working to Safeguard and Promote the Welfare of Children*. London: The Stationery Office.

HM Government (2014) *Modern Slavery Strategy*. Available at: www.gov.uk/government/uploads/system/uploads/attachment_data/file/383764/Modern_Slavery_Strategy_FINAL_DEC2015.pdf (accessed 23 November 2015).

HM Government (2015a) *Working Together to Safeguard Children: A Guide to Inter-agency Working to Safeguard and Promote the Welfare of Children*. London: The Stationery Office. Available at: www.workingtogetheronline.co.uk/ (accessed 28 October 2015).

HM Government (2015b) *What to Do if You are Worried that a Child is Being Abused: Advice for Practitioners*. London: The Stationery Office.

Holland, S (2011) *Child and Family Assessment in Social Work Practice*, 2nd edn. London: Sage Publications.

Holman, B (2013) The case for community social work is continuing. *The Guardian*, 16 October. Available at: www.theguardian.com/society/2013/oct/16/social-work-preventive-community (accessed 26 November 2015).

Home Office (2010a) *Crime in England and Wales 2009/10*. London: The Stationery Office.

Home Office (2010b) *Drug Strategy 2010. Reducing Demand, Restricting Supply, Building Recovery: Supporting People to Live a Drug Free Life*. London: The Stationery Office.

Home Office (2011) *Domestic Violence Protection Orders*. London: The Stationery Office. Available at: www.gov.uk/government/publications/domestic-violence-protection-orders (accessed 1 August 2014).

Home Office (2012) *The Government's Alcohol Strategy: Response from Alcohol Research UK*. London: The Stationery Office.

Home Office (2013a) *Multi-agency Working and Information Sharing Project: Early Findings*. Available at: www.gov.uk/government/uploads/system/uploads/attachment_data/file/225012/MASH_Product.pdf (accessed 31 October 2015).

Home Office (2013b) *Domestic Violence and Abuse Guidance*, updated 25 November 2013. Available at www.gov.uk/domestic-violence-and-abuse (accessed 31 October 2015).

Home Office (2013c) *Circular: New Government Domestic Violence and Abuse Definition*. Home Office circular 003/2013. London: Home Office.

Hoong Sin, C, Hedges, A and Cook, C (2011) Adult protection and effective action in tackling violence and hostility against disabled people: Some tensions and challenges. *The Journal of Adult Protection*, 13 (2): 63–74.

Horwath, J (2007) *Child Neglect: Identification and Assessment*. Basingstoke: Palgrave Macmillan.

Hothersall, S and Maas-Lowit, M (2010) *Need, Risk and Protection in Social Work Practice*. Exeter: Learning Matters.

House of Commons Committee of Public Accounts (2015) *Care Services for People with Learning Disabilities and Challenging Behaviour*. London: The Stationery Office. Available at: www.publications.parliament.uk/pa/cm201415/cmselect/cmpubacc/973/973.pdf (accessed 30 October 2015).

House of Commons Health Committee (2003) *The Victoria Climbié Inquiry Report. Sixth Report of Session 2002–03. Report, and formal minutes together with oral evidence*. London: The Stationery Office. Available at: www.publications.parliament.uk/pa/cm200203/cmselect/cmhealth/570/570.pdf (accessed 19 October 2015).

House of Commons Health Committee (2004) *Elder Abuse: Second Report of Session 2003-04*. Volume 1. London: The Stationery Office. Available at: www.publications.parliament.uk/pa/cm200304/cmselect/cmhealth/111/111.pdf (accessed 19 November 2015).

House of Lords Select Committee on the Mental Capacity Act 2005 (2014) *Mental Capacity Act 2005: Post-legislative Scrutiny*. London: The Stationery Office. Available at: www.publications.parliament.uk/pa/ld201314/ldselect/ldmentalcap/139/139.pdf (accessed 30 October 2015).

Howe, D (2011) *Attachment across the Life Course. A Brief Introduction.* Basingstoke: Palgrave Macmillan.

Humphreys, C and Stanley, N (eds) (2015) *Domestic Violence and Protecting Children: New Thinking and Approaches.* London: Jessica Kingsley Publishers.

Independent Inquiry into Child Sexual Abuse (IICSA) (n.d.) *Investigating the Extent to which Institutions have Failed to Protect Children from Sexual Abuse.* Available at: www.iicsa.org.uk/ (accessed 29 October 2015).

Ingleby, E (2010) *Applied Psychology for Social Work*, 2nd edn. Exeter: Learning Matters.

Jago, S, Arocha, L, Brodie, I, Melrose, M, Pearce, J and Warrington, C (2011) *What's Going On to Safeguard Children and Young People from Sexual Exploitation? How Local Partnerships Respond to Child Sexual Exploitation.* Luton: University of Bedfordshire. Available at: www.beds.ac.uk/__data/assets/pdf_file/0004/121873/wgoreport2011-121011.pdf (accessed 31 October 2015).

Jay, A (2014) *Independent Inquiry into Child Sexual Exploitation in Rotherham 1997–2013.* Rotherham. Available at: www.rotherham.gov.uk/downloads/file/1407/independent_inquiry_cse_in_rotherham (accessed 31 October 2015).

Johannesen, M and LoGuidice, D (2013) Elder abuse: A systematic review of risk factors in community-dwelling elders. *Age and Ageing*, 42 (3): 292–8.

Jones, R (2015) Plans to privatise child protection are moving at pace. *The Guardian*, 12 January. Available at: www.theguardian.com/social-care-network/2015/jan/12/child-protection-privatisation-ray-jones (accessed 26 November 2015).

Jordan, B and Drakeford, M (2012) *Social Work and Social Policy under Austerity.* Basingstoke: Palgrave Macmillan.

Jütte, S, Bentley, H, Tallis, D, Mayes, J, Jetha, N, O'Hagan, O, Brookes, H and McConnell, N (2105) *How Safe are our Children?* London: NSPCC.

Keilty, J and Connelly, G (2001) Making a statement: An exploratory study of barriers facing women with an intellectual disability when making a statement about sexual assault to police. *Disability & Society*, 16 (2), 273–91.

Kelly, F (2010) Abusive interactions: Research in locked wards for people with dementia. *Social Policy and Society*, 9 (1), April: 267–78.

Kempe, CH, Silverman, FN, Steele, BF, Droegemueller, W and Silver, HK (1962) The Battered-Child Syndrome. *Journal of the American Medical Association,* 181 (1): 17–24.

Kempe, R and Kempe, C (1978) *Child Abuse.* London: Fontana.

Kendrick, A (ed.) (2007) *Residential Child Care: Prospects and Challenges.* London: Jessica Kingsley Publishers.

Keogh, B (2013) *Review into the Quality of Care and Treatment Provided by 14 Hospital Trusts in England: Overview Report.* Available at: www.nhs.uk/nhsengland/bruce-keogh-review/documents/outcomes/keogh-review-final-report.pdf (accessed 29 October 2015).

Khan, S (2015) The jihadi girls who went to Syria weren't just radicalised by Isis — they were groomed. *The Independent,* 25 February. Available at: www.independent.co.uk/voices/comment/the-jihadi-girls-who-went-to-syria-werent-just-radicalised-by-isis-they-were-groomed-10069109.html (accessed 28 October 2015.

Kharicha, K, Levin, E, Illiffe, S and Davey, B (2004) Social work, general practice and evidence-based policy in the collaborative care of older people. *Health and Social Care in the Community,* 12 (2): 134–41.

Kingston, P (2015) Scams can have a devastating impact on older people's health. *The Guardian*, 8 September. Available at: www.theguardian.com/society/2015/sep/08/scams-on-older-people-affect-mental-health (accessed 28 October 2015).

Knapp, M (2012) Mental health in an age of austerity. *Evidence Based Mental Health*, 15: 54–5.

Knott, C and Scragg, T (2013) *Reflective Practice in Social Work,* 3rd edn. London: Sage.

Kroll, B and Taylor, A (2008) *Interventions for Children and Families where there is Parental Drug Misuse*. London: Department of Health

Laing, L, Humphreys, C and Cavanagh, K (2013) *Social Work and Domestic Violence: Developing Critical and Reflective Practice*. London: Sage.

Laming, H (2003) *The Victoria Climbié Inquiry: Report of an Inquiry by Lord Laming*. London: The Stationery Office. Available from: www.gov.uk/government/publications/the-victoria-climbie-inquiry-report-of-an-inquiry-by-lord-laming (accessed 24 October 2015).

Laming, H (2009) *The Protection of Children in England: A Progress Report*. London: The Stationery Office.

Landman, R (2014) 'A counterfeit friendship': Mate crime and people with learning disabilities. *The Journal of Adult Protection*, 16 (6): 355–66.

Law Commission (n.d.) *Mental Capacity and Deprivation of Liberty*. Available at: www.lawcom.gov.uk/project/mental-capacity-and-deprivation-of-liberty/ (accessed 30 October 2015).

Lawson, J, Lewis, S and Williams, C (2014) *Making Safeguarding Personal: Guide 2014*. London: Local Government Association.

Lay, M and Papadopoulos, I (2009) Sexual maltreatment of unaccompanied asylum-seeking minors from the Horn of Africa: A mixed method study focusing on vulnerability and prevention. *Child Abuse & Neglect*, 33 (10): 728–38.

Ledwith, M (2011) *Community Development: A Critical Approach*. Bristol: Policy Press.

Lennard, C (2015) Deprivation of Liberty Safeguards (DoLS) – where do we go from here? *The Journal of Adult Protection*,17 (1): 41–50.

Levy, A and Kahan, B (1991) *The Pindown Experience and the Protection of Children*. Stafford: Staffordshire County Council.

Local Government Association (LGA) (2013) *Making Safeguarding Personal: Executive Summary*. London: Local Government Association.

Local Government Association (LGA) (2015) *Making Safeguarding Personal: A Toolkit of Responses*, 4th edn. London: Local Government Association. Available at: www.local.gov.uk/documents/10180/6869714/Making+safeguarding+personal_a+toolkit+for+responses_4th+Edition+2015.pdf (accessed 1 November 2015).

Local Government Association/ADASS (2014) *Making Safeguarding Personal 2013/14 Summary of findings*. Available at: www.local.gov.uk/documents/10180/11779/Making+Safeguarding+Personal+2013-14+-+Executive+Summary/e147ddbe-ef16-403d-8218-add332f846a4 (accessed 24 November 2015).

Local Government Association/ADASS (2015) *Adult Safeguarding and Domestic Abuse: A Guide to Support Practitioners and Managers*. London: Local Government Association. Available at: www.local.gov.uk/publications/-/journal_content/56/10180/3973717/PUBLICATION#sthash.TGS1DVgU.dpuf (accessed 31 October 2015).

Lombard, D (2010) Young carers of parents with mental health issues. *Community Care*, 1834 (1): 32.

Maguire, A, Hughes, C, Cardwell, C and O'Reilly, D (2013) Psychotropic medications and the transition into care: A national data linkage study. *Journal of the American Geriatrics Society*, 61 (2): 215–21.

Maikovich-Fong, AK and Jaffee, S (2010) Sex differences in childhood sexual abuse characteristics and victims' emotional and behavioural problems: Findings from a national sample of youth. *Child Abuse and Neglect*, 34 (6): 429–37.

Mandelstam, M (2014) Wilful neglect and health care. *The Journal of Adult Protection*, 16 (6): 342–54.

Manning, V, Best, DW, Faulkner, N and Thitherington, E (2009) New estimates of the number of children living with substance misusing parents: Results from UK national household surveys. *BMC Public Health*, 9 (1): 377.

Manthorpe, J, Samsi, K and Rapaport, J (2012) Responding to the financial abuse of people with dementia: A qualitative study of safeguarding experiences in England. *International Psychogeriatrics*, 24 (9): 1454–64.

Manthorpe, J, Samsi, K and Rapaport, J (2013) 'Capacity is key': Investigating new legal provisions in England and Wales for adult safeguarding. *Journal of Elder Abuse and Neglect*, 25 (4): 355–73.

Manthorpe, J, Stevens, M, Samsi, K, Aspinal, F, Woolham, J, Hussein, S, Ismail, M and Baxter, K (2015) Did anyone notice the transformation of adult social care? An analysis of Safeguarding Adult Board Annual Reports. *The Journal of Adult Protection*, 17 (1): 19–30.

Marmot, M (2010) *Fair Society, Healthy Lives*. The Marmot Review. London: UCL Institute of Health Equity. Available at: www.instituteofhealthequity.org/projects/fair-society-healthy-lives-the-marmot-review (accessed 31 October 2015).

Marsland, D, Oakes, P and White, C (2007) Abuse in care? The identification of early indicators of the abuse of people with learning disabilities in residential settings. *The Journal of Adult Protection*, 9 (4): 6–20.

Marsland, D, Oakes, P and White, C (2015) Abuse in care? A research project to identify early indicators of concern in residential and nursing homes for older people. *The Journal of Adult Protection*, 17 (2): 111–25.

Maslow, A (1970) *Motivation and Personality*. New York: Harper Collins.

May-Chahal, C and Antrobus, R (2012) Engaging community support in safeguarding adults from self-neglect. *British Journal of Social Work*, 42 (8): 1478–94.

McConnell, N and Taylor, J (2014) Evaluating programmes for violent fathers: Challenges and ethical review. *Child Abuse Review*, DOI: 10.1002/car.2342.

McDonald, L and Thomas, C (2013) Elder abuse through a life course lens. *International Psychogeriatrics*, 25 (8): 1235–43.

McGarry, J (2008) Older women and domestic violence: Defining the concept and raising awareness in practice. *Nursing Older People*, 20 (6): 10–11.

McGarry, J and Simpson, C (2011) Domestic abuse and older women: Exploring the opportunities for service development and care delivery. *The Journal of Adult Protection*, 13 (6): 294–301.

McGarry, J, Simpson, C and Hinsliff-Smith, K (2014) An exploration of service responses to domestic abuse among older people: Findings from one region of the UK. *The Journal of Adult Protection*, 16 (4): 202–12.

McGrath, L, Griffin, V and Mundy, E (n.d.) *The Psychological Impact of Austerity A Briefing Paper*. Psychologists against Austerity. Available at: www.psychagainstausterity.files.wordpress.com/2015/03/paa-briefing-paper.pdf (accessed 31 October 2015).

McLeod, A (2012) What research findings tell social workers about family support, in M Davies (ed.) *Social Work with Children and Families*. Basingstoke: Palgrave Macmillan.

McNicholl, A (2013) A survival guide to practising ethical social work in a time of austerity. *Community Care*, 20 June. Available at: www.communitycare.co.uk/blogs/social-work-blog/2013/06/a-survival-guide-to-practising-ethical-social-work-in-a-time-of-austerity/ (accessed 31 October 2015).

McNicholl, A (2015) Deprivation of Liberty: Law Commission eyes 'simpler' system to protect rights. *Community Care*, 22 April. Available at: www.communitycare.co.uk/2015/04/22/deprivation-liberty-commission-eyes-simpler-system-protect-rights/ (accessed 1 November 2015).

Melrose, M and Pearce, J (2013) *Critical Perspectives on Child Sexual Exploitation and Related Trafficking*. Basingstoke: Palgrave Macmillan.

Mencap (2007) *Death by Indifference: Following up the Treat Me Right! Report*. London: Mencap. Available at: www.mencap.org.uk/sites/default/files/documents/2008-03/DBIreport.pdf (accessed 31 October 2015).

Mencap (2015) *Police Forces Commit to End Disability Hate Crime*. Available at: www.mencap.org.uk/get-involved/campaigns/successes/police-forces-commit-end-disability-hate-crime (accessed 20 February 2015).

Mental Health Foundation (2012) *Mental Capacity and The Mental Capacity Act 2005: A Literature Review*. Available at: www.mentalhealth.org.uk/content/assets/PDF/publications/mca-lit-review.pdf?view=Standard (accessed 1 November 2015).

Mental Health Foundation (2015) *Mental Health Statistics*. Available at: www.mentalhealth.org.uk/help-information/mental-health-statistics (accessed 1 November 2015).

Miller, D and Brown, J (2014) *'We have the Right to be Safe': Protecting Disabled Children from Abuse*. London: NSPCC.

Mind (2015) *Advocacy in Mental Health*. Available at: www.mind.org.uk/information-support/guides-to-support-and-services/advocacy/# (accessed 14 October 2014).

Modern Slavery (2015) *Slavery Types and Who is Affected*. Available at: www.modernslavery.co.uk/who.html# (accessed 8 January 2015).

Moon, J (2008) *Critical Thinking: An Exploration of Theory and Practice*. Abingdon: Routledge.

Moss, P and Petrie, P (2002) *From Children's Services to Children's Spaces*. London: HMSO.

Mullender, A (2004) *Tackling Domestic Violence: Providing Support for Children who have Witnessed Domestic Violence*. London: Home Office.

Munro, E (2008) *Effective Child Protection*, 2nd edn. London: Sage Publications.

Munro, E (2011) *The Munro Review of Child Protection: Final Report: A Child-centred System*. London: Department for Education.

National Assembly for Wales (2000) *In Safe Hands: Implementing Adult Protection Procedures in Wales*. Cardiff: National Assembly for Wales.

National Audit Office (NAO) (2015) *Capacity and Capability to Regulate the Quality and Safety of Health and Adult Social Care*. Report by the Comptroller and Auditor General. Available at: www.nao.org.uk/wp-content/uploads/2015/07/Capacity-and-capability-to-regulate-the-quality-and-safety-of-health-and-adult-social-care-Summary.pdf (accessed 31 October 2015).

National Crime Agency (2013a) *CEOP Thematic Assessment. The Foundations of Abuse: A Thematic Assessment of the Risk of Child Sexual Abuse by Adults in Institutions*. London: The Stationery Office.

National Crime Agency (2013b) *Operation Pallial: The Investigation of Recent Allegations of Historic Abuse in the Care System in North Wales*. Available at: www.nationalcrimeagency.gov.uk/publications/43-operation-pallial-report-eng/file (accessed 1 November 2015).

Naughton, C, Drennan, J, Lyons, I, Lafferty, A, Treacy, M, Phelan, A, O'Loughlin, A and Delaney, L (2012) Elder abuse and neglect in Ireland: Results from a National Prevalence Survey. *Age and Ageing*, 41: 98–103.

NHS Choices (2013) Worry over antipsychotic drugs in care homes. Available at: www.nhs.uk/news/2013/02February/Pages/Antipsychotic-drugs-care-homes.aspx (accessed 27 November 2015).

Nolte, L (2013) Becoming visible. In R Loshak (ed.) *Out of the Mainstream: Helping the Children of Parents with a Mental Illness*. Hove, East Sussex: Routledge.

NSPCC (2009a) *The Definitions and Signs of Child Abuse: Child Protection Fact sheet*. London: NSPCC.

NSPCC (2009b) *Family Group Conferences in Child Protection: An NSPCC Fact sheet*. London: NSPCC.

NSPCC (2013) *Domestic Abuse: Learning from Case Reviews*. Available at: www.nspcc.org.uk/preventing-abuse/child-protection-system/case-reviews/learning/domestic-abuse (accessed 25 November 2015).

NSPCC (2014a) *'We Have the Right to be Safe': Protecting Disabled Children from Abuse*. London: NSPCC.

NSPCC (2014b) *Serious Case Review No. 2014/C5019*. Available at: www.westsussexscb.org.uk/wp-content/uploads/Unnamed-LSCB-Child-D.pdf (accessed 31 October 2015).

NSPCC (2014c) *Child Killings in England and Wales: Explaining the Statistics*. Available at: www.nspcc.org.uk/globalassets/documents/information-service/factsheet-child-killings-england-wales-homicide-statistics.pdf (accessed 23 November 2015).

NSPCC (2015) *Child Abuse and Neglect.* Available at: www.nspcc.org.uk/preventing-abuse/child-abuse-and-neglect/ (accessed 27 November 2015).

NWG Network (2014) *Summary of Recommendations: A Summary of all recommendations from a Range of Reports, Inquiries, Serious Case Reviews and Research.* Derby: NWG.

O'Driscoll, D (2013) Happy anniversary? *Learning Disability Practice,* 16 (9): 11.

Office for Disability Issues and Department for Work and Pensions (2014) *Disability Facts and Figures.* Available at: www.gov.uk/government/statistics/disability-facts-and-figures (accessed 26 November 2015).

Office for National Statistics (ONS) (2014) *Chapter 4: Violent Crime and Sexual Offences – Intimate Personal Violence and Serious Sexual Assault.* Available at: www.ons.gov.uk/ons/dcp171776_352362.pdf (accessed 26 October 2015)

Ofsted (2011) *Ages of Concern: Learning Lessons from Serious Case Reviews: A Thematic Report of Ofsted's Evaluation of Serious Case Reviews from 1 April 2007 t0 31 March 2011.* London: Ofsted.

Ofsted (2013a) *What About the Children?* Manchester: Ofsted.

Ofsted (2013b) *Missing Children.* Available at: www.gov.uk/government/publications/missing-children (accessed 29 October 2015).

Ofsted (2014) *The Sexual Exploitation of Children: It Couldn't Happen Here, Could It?* Manchester: Ofsted.

Ofsted (2015) *Social Care Annual Report 2013–14.* Manchester: Ofsted. Available at: www.gov.uk/government/publications/ofsted-social-care-annual-report-201314 (accessed 30 October 2015).

O'Hagan, K (2006) *Identifying Emotional and Psychological Abuse: A Guide for Childcare Professionals.* New York: Open University Press.

Oliver, M (1996) *Understanding Disability: From Theory to Practice.* Basingstoke: Macmillan.

O'Sullivan, T (2011) *Decision Making in Social Work.* Basingstoke: Palgrave Macmillan.

Parrott, L, Jacobs, G and Roberts, D (2008) *SCIE Research Briefing 23: Stress and Resilience Factors in Parents with Mental Health Problems and their Children.* London: Social Care Institute for Excellence, pp. 1–9.

Parson, K (2015) Care Act right to advocacy being undermined by chaotic commissioning and lack of resources. *Community Care,* 3 August. Available at: www.communitycare.co.uk/2015/08/03/care-act-right-advocacy-undermined-chaotic-commissioning-lack-resources/ (accessed 30 October 2015).

Parton, N (2014) *The Politics of Child Protection.* Basingstoke: Palgrave Macmillan.

Pearce, J (2009) *Young People and Sexual Exploitation.* Abingdon: Routledge.

Pearce, J and Jago, S (2008) *Gathering Evidence of the Sexual Exploitation of Children and Young People: A Scoping Exercise.* Bedford: University of Bedfordshire.

Pemberton, C (2013) Social care must 'fundamentally rethink' the way children are protected, says Minister. *Community Care,* 18 October. Available at: www.communitycare.co.uk/2013/10/18/childrens-social-care-must-fundamentally-rethink-way-children-are-protected-says-minister/ (accessed 27 October 2015).

Perry, J, Purcell, L and Cooper, N (2015) *Restoring Faith in the Safety Net.* Church Action on Poverty. Available at: www.church-poverty.org.uk/safetynet/report/safetynetreport (accessed 31 October 2015).

Petrie, P and Simon, A (2006) Residential care: Lessons from Europe, in E Chase, A Simon and S Jackson (eds) *In Care and After: A Positive Perspective.* London: Routledge.

Pettitt, B, Greenhead, S, Khalifeh, K, Drennan, V, Hart, T, Hogg, J, Borschmann, R, Mamo, E and Mora, P (2013) *At Risk, Yet Dismissed: The Criminal Victimisation of People with Mental Health Problems.* London: Victim Support/Mind. Available at: www.mind.org.uk/media/187663/At-risk-yet-dismissed-report_FINAL_EMBARGOED.pdf (accessed 31 October 2015).

Popple, K (2015) *Analysing Community Work: Theory and Practice.* Oxford: Oxford University Press.

Pritchard, J (2007) *Working with Adult Abuse: A Training Manual for People Working with Vulnerable Adults.* London: Jessica Kingsley Publishers.

Puffett, N (2015) Massive rise in number of children in care under coalition. *Children and Young People Now*, 23 June. Available at: www.cypnow.co.uk/cyp/news/1152176/massive-rise-in-number-of-children-in-care-under-coalition#sthash.uNbHu7bW.dpuf (accessed 19 November 2015)

Quarmby, K (2011) *Scapegoat: How We are Failing Disabled People.* London: Portobello Press.

Radford, L, Corral, S, Bradley, C, Fisher, H, Bassett, C, Howat, N and Collishaw, S (2011) *Child Abuse and Neglect in the UK Today*. London: NSPCC.

Redley, M, Jennings, S Holland, A and Clare, I (2015) Making adult safeguarding personal. *The Journal of Adult Protection*, 17 (3): 195–204.

Refugee Council (n.d.) *The Facts About Asylum*. Available at: www.refugeecouncil.org.uk/policy_research/the_truth_about_asylum/facts_about_asylum_-_page_1 (accessed 28 October 2015).

Robbins, R, McLaughlin, H, Banks, C, Bellamy, C and Thackray, D (2014) Domestic violence and multi-agency risk assessment conferences (MARACs): A scoping review. *The Journal of Adult Protection*, 16 (6): 389–98.

Royal College of Psychiatrists (2014) *Parental Mental Illness: The Impact on Children and Adolescents: Information for Parents, Carers and Anyone who Works with Young People*. London. Royal College of Psychiatrists.

Ruck Keene, A and FitzGerald, G (2014) *Briefing Paper on the Need for a New Power of Entry.* Action on Elder Abuse. Available at: www.elderabuse.org.uk/Documents/AEA%20documents/AEA%20Powers%20of%20Entry%20-%20analysis%20of%20the%20Law.pdf (accessed 31 October 2015).

Sales, R (2002) The deserving and the undeserving? Refugees, asylum seekers and welfare in Britain. *Critical Social Policy*, 22 (3): 456–78.

Samsi, K, Manthorpe, M and Chandaria,K (2014) Risks of financial abuse of older people with dementia: Findings from a survey of UK voluntary sector dementia community services staff. *The Journal of Adult Protection*, 16 (3): 180–92.

Samuel, M (2013) The depressing failure of some social workers to follow the Mental Capacity Act, *Community Care*, 4 October. Available at: www.communitycare.co.uk/blogs/adult-care-blog/2013/10/the-depressing-failure-of-some-social-workers-to-follow-the-mental-capacity-act/#sthash.nPwc50WW.dpuf (accessed 31 October 2105).

Samuel, M (2014) Social care lawyer rejects government claim that existing safeguarding powers are sufficient to protect adults from abuse. *Community Care*, 25 February. Available at: www.communitycare.co.uk/2014/02/25/social-care-lawyer-rejects-government-claim-existing-safeguarding-powers-sufficient-protect-adults-abuse/ (accessed 1 November 2015).

Schofield, G and Beek, M (2006) *Attachment Handbook*. London: BAAF.

Schwehr, B (2014a) What the Care Act 2014 will mean for safeguarding – a legal view. *Community Care*, 3 March. Available at: www.communitycare.co.uk/2014/03/03/care-act-2014-will-mean-safeguarding-legal-view/ (accessed 1 November 2015).

Schwehr, B (2014b) Why the Care Act 2014 guidance on safeguarding short-changes social workers. *Community Care*, 21 July. Available at www.communitycare.co.uk/2014/07/21/care-act-2014-guidance-safeguarding-short-changes-social-workers/ (accessed 1 November 2015).

SCIE (2009) *Think Child, Think Parent, Think Family: A Guide to Parental Mental Health and Child Welfare*. London: SCIE.

SCIE (2012) *Safeguarding Adults: Mediation and Family Group Conferences*. Available at: www.scie.org.uk/publications/mediation/ (accessed 27 November 2015).

SCIE (2013) *Maximising the Potential of Reablement*. SCIE Guide 49. Available at: www.scie.org.uk/publications/guides/guide49/index.asp (accessed 31 October 2015).

SCIE (2014) *Gaining Access to an Adult Suspected to be at Risk of Neglect or Abuse: A Guide for Social Workers and their Managers in England.* Available at: www.scie.org.uk/care-act-2014/safeguarding-adults/adult-suspected-at-risk-of-neglect-abuse/ (accessed 31 October 2015).

SCIE (2015a) *At a Glance 69: Adult Safeguarding – Types and Indicators of Abuse.* Available at: www.scie.org.uk/publications/ataglance/69-adults-safeguarding-types-and-indicators-of-abuse.asp (accessed 1 November 2015).

SCIE (2015b) *Adult Safeguarding: Sharing Information.* Available at: www.scie.org.uk/care-act-2014/safeguarding-adults/sharing-information/ (accessed 1 November 2015).

SCIE (2015c) *Adult Safeguarding: Practice Questions.* Available at: www.scie.org.uk/care-act-2014/safeguarding-adults/adult-safeguarding-practice-questions/files/adult-safeguarding-practice-questions.pdf (accessed 1 November 2015).

SCIE (2015d) *Report 47: User Involvement in Adult Safeguarding.* Available at: www.scie.org.uk/publications/reports/report47/safeguardingadults.asp (accessed 19 November 2015).

Scope (2009) *A Long Road to Travel: The Impact of the Mental Capacity Act on Adults with Complex Needs in Residential Settings.* Available at: www.scie.org.uk/publications/mca/files/longroadtotravel.pdf (accessed 23 November 2015).

Scottish Government (2015) *Getting it Right for Every Child.* Available at: www.gov.scot/Topics/People/Young-People/gettingitright (accessed 1 November 2015).

Scragg, T and Mantell, A (2011) *Safeguarding Adults in Social Work,* 2nd edn. Exeter: Learning Matters.

Sempik, J and Becker, S (2014) *Young Adult Carers and Employment.* London: Carers Trust.

Shakespeare, T (2014) *Disability Rights and Wrongs Revisited*, 2nd edn. Abingdon: Routledge.

Sherry, M (2010) *Disability Hate Crimes: Does Anyone Really Hate Disabled People?* Farnham: Ashgate.

Silverman, B (2014) *Modern Slavery: An Application of Multiple Systems Estimation.* Available at: www.gov.uk/government/uploads/system/uploads/attachment_data/file/386841/Modern_Slavery_an_application_of_MSE_revised.pdf (accessed 23 November 2015).

Sin, CH, Hedges, A, Cook, C, Mguni, N and Comber, N (2009) *Research Report: 21 Disabled People's Experiences of Targeted Violence and Hostility.* Equality and Human Rights Commission. Available at: www.opm.co.uk/wp-content/uploads/2014/01/Disabled-people-experiences-of-violence-1.pdf (accessed 23 November 2015).

Skrivankova, K (2014) *Forced Labour in the United Kingdom*. York: Joseph Rowntree Foundation.

Slack, K and Webber, M (2007). Do we care? Adult and mental health professionals' attitudes towards supporting service users' children. *Child and Family Social Work*, 13 (1): 72–8.

Smethurst, C (2012) Contextualising the experience of older people. In B Hall and T Scragg (eds) *Social Work with Older People: Approaches to Person-centred Practice.* Maidenhead: Open University Press.

Smith, A (2014) 'There were hundreds of us crying out for help': The afterlife of the whistleblower. *The Guardian*, 22 November. Available at: www.theguardian.com/society/2014/nov/22/there-were-hundreds-of-us-crying-out-for-help-afterlife-of-whistleblower (accessed 27 November 2015).

Smith, J (2002) *The Shipman Enquiry. First Report.* Available at: webarchive.nationalarchives.gov.uk/20090808154959/www.the-shipman-inquiry.org.uk/firstreport.asp (accessed 19 November 2015).

Southend Safeguarding Adults Board (2011) *Mr and Mrs A (Mary Russell) Serious Case Review. Executive Summary.* Southend: Southend SAB.

Staffordshire and Stoke-on-Trent Safeguarding Children Boards (2013) *Lessons to be Learned Briefing No.16: In Respect of the Death of Daniel Pelka, Coventry, 2013.* Available at: www.staffordbc.gov.uk/live/Documents/PolicyAndImprovement/Serious—Case-Review—Daniel-Pelka.pdf (accessed 19 November 2015).

Standing, M (2011) *Clinical Judgement and Decision Making for Nursing Students.* Exeter: Learning Matters.

Stanley, N (2011) *Children Experiencing Domestic Violence: A Research Review*. Dartington: Research in Practice.

Stanley, N, and Cox, P (2009) *Parental Mental Health and Child Welfare: Reviews of Policy and Professional Education*. London: SCIE. Available at: www.scie.org.uk/publications/guides/guide30/files/FullResearchReview.pdf?res=true (Accessed 26 October 2015).

Stanley, N, Miller, P and Richardson Foster, H (2012) Engaging with children's and parents' perspectives on domestic violence. *Child and Family Social Work*, 17 (2), 192–201.

Stanley, T. (n.d.) *An Introduction to Signs of Safety and Wellbeing: A Solution, Safety and Wellbeing Oriented Approach To Adult Social Care*. Available at: www.towerhamlets.gov.uk/idoc.ashx?docid=1c67b232-1fec-47e0... (Accessed 26 October 2015).

Stein, M (2012) *Young People Leaving Care: Supporting Pathways to Adulthood*. London: Jessica Kingsley Publishers.

Stein, M and Munro, ER (eds) (2008) *Young People's Transitions from Care to Adulthood*. London: Jessica Kingsley Publishers.

Stevenson, L (2013) Social workers to face five years in prison for failing to protect children from sexual abuse, warns Cameron. *Community Care*, 3 March. Available at: www.communitycare.co.uk/2015/03/03/social-workers-face-five-years-prison-failing-protect-children-sexual-abuse-warns-cameron/ (accessed 31 October 2015).

Stevenson, L (2014) 'Social workers will not be sorry to see Gove go': Reaction to cabinet reshuffle. *Community Care*, 16 July. Available at: www.communitycare.co.uk/2014/07/16/adoption-frontline-outsourcing-michael-goves-legacy-childrens-social-care/ (accessed 23 November 2015).

Stewart, A and Atkinson, J (2012) Citizenship and adult protection in the UK: An exploration of the conceptual links. *The Journal of Adult Protection*, 14 (4): 163–75.

Stothart, C (2014) Government to outlaw wilful neglect and ill-treatment of adults in social care. *Community Care*, 11 June. Available at: www.communitycare.co.uk/2014/06/11/government-outlaw-wilful-neglect-ill-treatment-adults-social-care/ (accessed 30 October 2015).

Sullivan, P and Knutson, J (2000) Maltreatment and disabilities: A population-based epidemiological study. *Child Abuse and Neglect*, 24 (10): 1257–73.

Taylor, B (2013) *Professional Decision Making and Risk in Social Work*. London: Sage/Learning Matters.

Taylor, B J (2012) Models for professional judgement in social work. *European Journal of Social Work*, 15 (4): 546–62.

Thackeray, L and Eatough, V (2015) 'Well the future, that is difficult': A hermeneutic phenomenological analysis exploring the maternal experience of parenting a young adult with a developmental disability. *Journal of Applied Research in Intellectual Disabilities*, 28: 265–75.

Thompson, N (2012) *Anti-Discriminatory Practice*, 5th edn. Basingstoke: Palgrave Macmillan.

Thompson, N (2015) *Understanding Social Work: Preparing for Practice*, 4th edn. Basingstoke: Palgrave Macmillan.

Townsend, P (1962) *The Last Refuge*. London: Routledge & Kegan Paul.

Trevithick, P (2008) Revisiting the Knowledge Base of Social Work: A Framework for Practice. *British Journal of Social Work (2008)* 38, 1212–37 doi:10.1093/bjsw/bcm026 Advance Access publication May 24, 2007.

Turbitt, C (2014) *Doing Radical Social Work*. Basingstoke: Palgrave Macmillan.

Turnell, A and Edwards, S (1998) Aspiring to partnership: The Signs of Safety approach to child protection casework. *Child Abuse Review*, 6: 179–90.

Turner, D (2012) 'Fraudulent' disability in historical perspective. *History and Policy*, 1 February. Available at: www.historyandpolicy.org/policy-papers/papers/fraudulent-disability-in-historical-perspective (accessed 19 November 2015).

UKQCS (2014) *Well-being in Wales*. Available at www.ukqcs.co.uk/well-wales/ (accessed 31 October 2015).

UNHCR Global Trends (2013) *War's Human Cost*. Available at: www.unhcr.org/5399a14f9.html (accessed 27 November 2014).

United Nations (1989) *Convention on the Rights of the Child*. Geneva: United Nations Office of the High Commissioner for Children's Rights. Available at: www.ohchr.org/en/professionalinterest/pages/crc.aspx (accessed 28 October 2015).

United Nations (2006) *United Nations Convention on the Rights of Persons with Disabilities*. Geneva: United Nations.

United Nations (2007) *Convention on the Rights of Persons with Disabilities*. Resolution Adopted by the General Assembly (A61/611). Geneva: United Nations. Available at: www.un.org/disabilities/default. asp?id=61 (accessed 1 November 2015).

Utting, W (1997) *People Like Us: The Report on the Review of Safeguards for Children Living Away from Home*. London: The Stationery Office.

Walker, J and Crawford, K (2014) *Social Work and Human Development*. London: Sage.

Walter-Brice, A, Cox, R, Priest, H and Thompson, F (2012) What do women with learning disabilities say about their experiences of domestic abuse within the context of their intimate partner relationships? *Disability and Society*, 27 (4): 503–17.

Ward, H and Davies, C (2011) *Safeguarding Children across Services: Messages from Research*. London: Jessica Kingsley Publishers.

Ward, T, Polachek, DLL and Beech, AR (2006) *Theories of Sexual Offending*. Chichester: Wiley.

Warwickshire Safeguarding Adults Partnership (2010) *Serious Case Review: The Murder of Gemma Hayter*. Available at: www.apps.warwickshire.gov.uk/api/documents/WCCC-779-97 (accessed 23 November 2015).

Waterhouse, R (2000) *Lost in Care: Report of the Tribunal of Inquiry into the Abuse of Children in Care in the Former County Council Areas of Gwynedd and Clwyd Since 1974*. London: The Stationery Office.

Webb, S (2002) Evidence-based practice and decision making analysis in social work: An implementation model. *Journal of Social Work*, 2 (1): 45–63.

Wendt, S, Bagshaw, D, Zannettino, L and Adams, V (2013) Financial abuse of older people: A case study. *International Social Work*, doi: 10.1177/0020872813477882

West Sussex Adult Safeguarding Board (2014) *Orchid View: Serious Case Review*. Available at: www. hampshiresab.org.uk/wp-content/uploads/June-2014-Orchid-View-Serious-Case-Review-Report.pdf (accessed 30 October 2015).

White, R, Carr, AP and Lowe, N (2008) *The Children Act in Practice*, 4th edn. London: LexisNexis Butterworth.

Whitham, G (2012) *Ending Child Poverty: The Importance of Income in Measuring and Tackling Child Poverty*. London: Save the Children.

Wilkins, D and Boahen, G (2013) *Critical Analysis Skills for Social Workers*. Maidenhead: Open University Press.

Women's Aid (2015) *Topic: Statistics*. Available from: www.womensaid.org.uk/domestic_violence_topic. asp?section=0001000100220036sionTitle=statistics (accessed 28 October 2015).

Woodhouse, J (2015) *The Voluntary Sector and the Big Society*. House of Commons Briefing Paper Number 5883, 13 August 2015. London: House of Commons.

World Health Organisation (WHO) (2015) *Child Maltreatment*. Available at: www.who.int/topics/child_abuse/en/ (accessed 24 November 2015).

Statutes

Available at: www.legislation.gov.uk

Adoption and Children Act 2002

Adult Support and Protection (Scotland) Act 2007

Care Act 2014

Care Standards Act 2000

Children Act 1989

Children Act 2004

Children and Families Act 2014

Children and Young People (Scotland) Act 2014

Children (Scotland) Act 1995

Children's Hearing (Scotland) Act 2011

Crime and Security Act 2010

Criminal Justice and Courts Act 2015

Criminal Justice (Scotland) Act 2003

Domestic Violence, Crime and Victims Act 2004

Domestic Violence, Crime and Victims (Amendment) Act 2012

Employment Rights Act 1996

Female Genital Mutilation Act 2003

Health and Social Care Act 2008

Health and Social Care Act 2012

Human Rights Act 1998

Local Authority Social Services Act 1970

Mental Capacity Act 2005

Mental Health Act 1983

Mental Health Act 2007

Modern Slavery Act 2015

NHS and Community Care Act 1990

Police and Criminal Evidence Act 1984

Public Interest Disclosure Act 1998

Sexual Offences Act 2003

Social Services and Well-Being (Wales) Act 2014

Index